LEGENDARY LOCALS OF PRINCETON NEW JERSEY

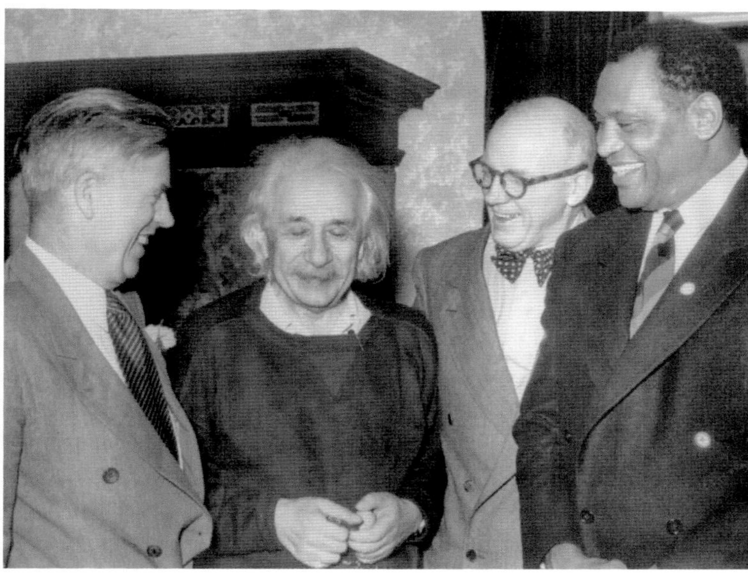

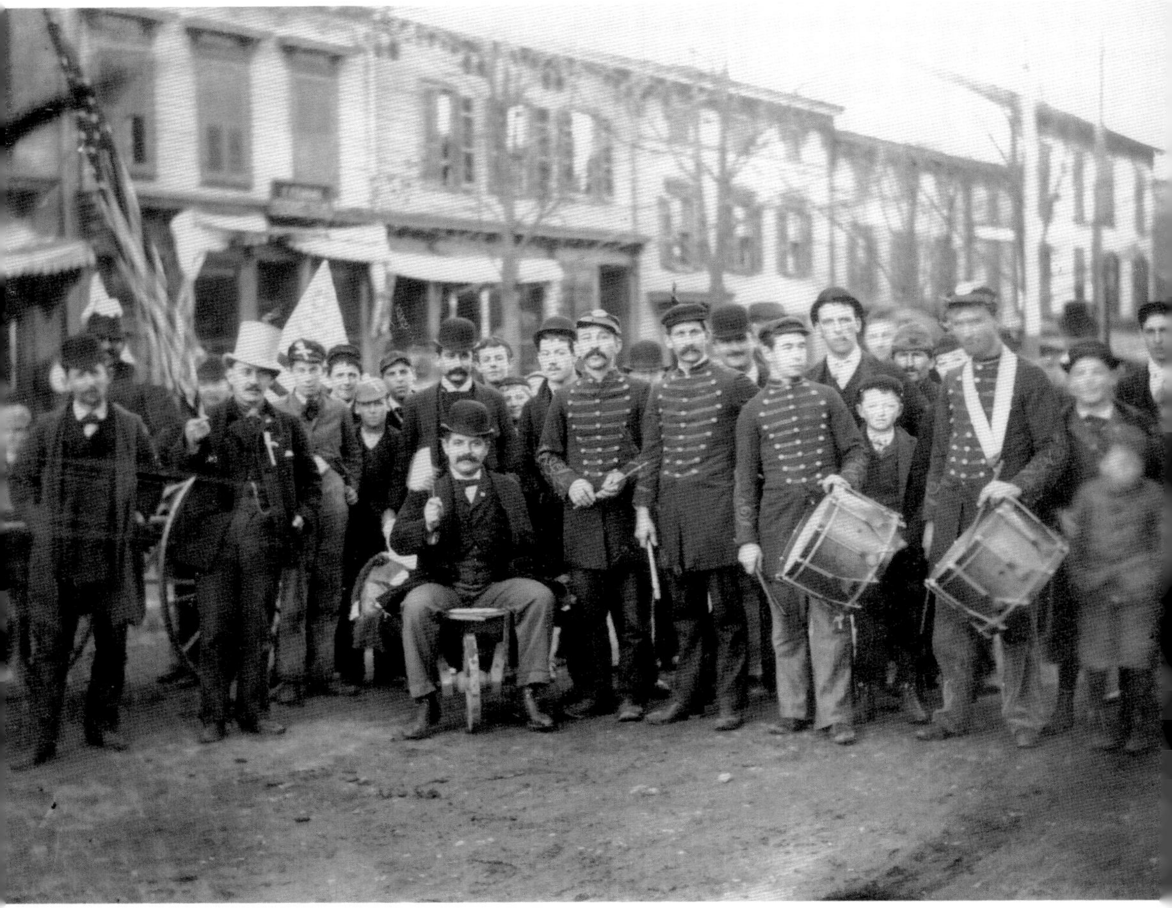

The Jugtown Band
Arriving from their homes in the neighborhood of Nassau and Harrison Streets to assemble in the center of town, the Jugtown Band was featured at many local parades in the early 20th century. (Historical Society of Princeton.)

Page 1: Einstein and Robeson
Albert Einstein (second from left) and Paul Robeson (far right)—perhaps the most legendary of all Princeton locals—are joined on September 21, 1947, by former US vice president Henry Wallace (far left) and Lewis L. Wallace of Princeton University. Renowned physicist Einstein met Robeson at a 1935 Princeton concert given by the great African American performer. Both were strong activists for human rights and, later, cochaired the American Crusade to End Lynching. (Corbis.)

LEGENDARY LOCALS

OF

PRINCETON

NEW JERSEY

RICHARD D. SMITH

LEGENDARY LOCALS

ISBN 978-1-4671-0049-6

Legendary Locals is an imprint of Arcadia Publishing
Charleston, South Carolina

Printed in the United States of America

Library of Congress Control Number: 2012944456

For all general information, please contact Arcadia Publishing:
Telephone 843-853-2070
Fax 843-853-0044
E-mail sales@arcadiapublishing.com
For customer service and orders:
Toll-Free 1-888-313-2665

Visit us on the Internet at www.arcadiapublishing.com

Dedication

This book is dedicated with gratitude to Elric Endersby, Constance M. Greiff, Wanda S. Gunning, Shirley A. Satterfield, and Jean Stratton. The trail you've blazed in chronicling Princeton history has become the King's Highway upon which I have journeyed.

On the Front Cover: Clockwise from top left:
Albert Einstein, humanitarian and Nobel Prize–winning physicist (Courtesy of Corbis; page 38), Francis Callery, Princeton-area aviation pioneer (Courtesy of PHP; page 36), Barbara Sigmund, Princeton Borough mayor, with colleague Thomas Poole (Courtesy of PP/HSP; page 119), students at the Evelyn College women's school (Courtesy of HSP; page 37), Peter Benchley, *Jaws* author and ocean conservationist (Courtesy of Scott Stallard; page 54), Christopher Reeve, actor, director, and medical research advocate (Courtesy of Hultan-Deutsch Collection/Corbis; page 68), Gallup Poll opinion research executives (Courtesy of Corbis; page 35), Paul Robeson, actor, singer, and civil rights activist (Courtesy of Corbis; page 28), George Washington, local resident during Congress's 1783 stay in Princeton (Courtesy of Corbis; page 15).

On the Back Cover: From left to right:
Jimmy Johnson, vendor and escapee from slavery (Courtesy of HSP; page 75), Phyllis Britcher, owner of the Stuff N' Nonsense toy shop (Courtesy of PHP; page 79).

CONTENTS

ACKNOWLEDGMENTS

This book was done in partnership with the Historical Society of Princeton (HSP). Profuse thanks to HSP director Erin Dougherty and her cheerful, effective staff, including Eileen Morales, Jennifer Floyd, and Stephanie Schwartz, for help with archival research and image scanning, and Eve Mandel for general support and encouragement.

In the HSP collection are the archives of the Princeton History Project, directed by Ric Endersby in the 1970s and 1980s, and a complete run of its wonderful publication, the *Princeton Recollector.* Without them, I simply could not have done this book. Independent scholar Wanda Gunning, who has literally forgotten more about Princeton history than I will ever know, was especially helpful. Shirley Satterfield was the ultimate source of most information about the vital African American community. Jean Stratton's personality profiles in the *Town Topics* newspaper were invaluable resources. Jenni Griffin at Princeton High School and the staff of numerous interviewees were tremendously responsive to my inquiries. Thanks go to Victor Davis for Einstein's telescope and Teri Noel Towe for Library Place liaison.

Valuable published resources were *Literary Landmarks of Princeton* (1968) by Alfred L. Bush; *Princeton: On the Streets Where We Live* (1990) by Jeanne Silvester and Randy Hobler; *Bricks and Mortals: The Story of Princeton's 20th Century Recognition Walk* (2001) by the Spirit of Princeton Committee, with great thanks going to Herb Hobler for this and other material; Jean Stratton's store and business guide *Pleasure and Treasures of Princeton*, which is in its 15th year at the time of this writing; and the catalog of a landmark Historical Society of Princeton exhibit, *Old Traditions, New Beginnings: Two Hundred Fifty Years of Princeton Jewish History* (2002) by editor Alice M. Greenwald. Princeton Cemetery superintendent Douglas G. Sutphen directed me to the resting places of many notables.

Affectionate thanks go to my mother, Mae W. Smith (formerly of nearby Montgomery Township), and many friends who shared the process. Of course, I also deeply thank the interviewees, not only for telling their stories but also for frequently recommending other worthy persons.

Last but decidedly not least, I would like to thank the people at Arcadia Publishing, especially Erin Vosgien, senior acquisitions editor, for her professionalism and saintly patience during what became an arduous process; Arcadia's superb graphics and layout artists; and publisher Kris McDonagh for the opportunity to write about the remarkable—and truly legendary—people who have defined Princeton.

Photograph credits are abbreviated as follows: the collection at the Historical Society of Princeton (HSP); the *Princeton Recollector* (PR); Princeton History Project archives at Historical Society of Princeton (PHP); *Princeton Packet* Collection at Historical Society of Princeton (PP/HPS); Corbis Photo Service (Corbis); and images loaned by individuals (credited by name).

INTRODUCTION

On name recognition alone, Princeton is one of the most famous towns in America. There are some 20 places in the United States and Canada named "Princeton," but mention of the name brings immediate and widespread association with one in particular—the New Jersey community that is also home to a world-famous university.

Another basic level of familiarity will bring associations with the colonial era, with George Washington and the War for Independence, with Albert Einstein, and with a largely wealthy and cultured community.

Although broadly accurate, such impressions are the stuff of legend. And as with all legends, there are halos of great lore and horns of persistent myth. Ultimately, Princeton is a rather modest locale, with the combined populations of downtown and surrounding rural areas being approximately 28,500 persons, a trifle compared to the nearly 8.5 million people in greater New York to its northeast and 1.5 million in greater Philadelphia to its southwest.

Located almost directly mid-center of what became the state of New Jersey, the area was originally, if sparsely and seasonally, populated by Native Americans. Once Whites established a settlement in the late 17th and early 18th centuries, Princeton became an important stop on the main travel route through the colonies, especially during the journey between New York and Philadelphia. Its fortunes grew further in 1756 with the relocation here of the College of New Jersey—the future Princeton University. Like the rest of the state, it was a true "crossroads of the American Revolution," with George Washington securing an additional crucial triumph here after his victories at Trenton.

As Princeton University went from strength to strength in the 19th century, it became a destination for visiting lecturers, particularly in literature and the humanities, and for other famous and affluent persons pleased to settle in the lovely community. The arts began to flourish in town, first as a function of university activities but later with independent music, theater, and lecture events. The municipal divisions between the Borough of Princeton (basically the downtown) and surrounding, largely rural Princeton Township became more pronounced in the late 19th and early 20th centuries. After decades of debate, this distinction was ended in 2012 when voters approved a referendum for consolidation.

During the 1930s and through World War II, Princeton became a haven for European scientific and other intellectual émigrés. The presence of Princeton University had already provided a climate and synergy for the establishment of other local institutions of higher learning and research. This trend continued during the postwar boom of the 1950s and prosperity of the 1960s. It enjoyed renewed life in the 1980s and 1990s as an entrepreneurial boom boosted the development of what is now widely referred to as the "Princeton business corridor."

Is it any wonder then that Princeton—synonymous with history, higher learning, and wealth—is a truly legendary place? And is it surprising that the community itself would have so many legendary locals?

But Princeton's significance has created a certain contradictory and confusing lore, which, at times, affects perceptions of both the town and its locals.

The introductory statement "I'm from Princeton" can be an effective door opener if addressed to someone with a favorable impression of the town as a center of profound learning and high accomplishment. But it is an equally effective—and final—door closer if uttered to anyone who associates Princeton with unrelieved elitism and stubborn snobbery.

Neither extreme stereotype serves Princeton, especially not its inhabitants. Yes, like many other American towns, it was once beset by rigid class distinctions and even racism. To its genuine credit, Princeton is now a multicultural community, with an increased awareness of the special contributions made by residents of widely varied ethnic heritages, educational experiences, and incomes. Dwelling in town does not automatically confer a professorial appointment on the campus across the street nor does it mean a local person is an elitist.

So it is my great pleasure as the author of *Legendary Locals of Princeton* to present not only nationally and internationally famous Princeton residents—persons whose names have become household words, pioneers in the historic panorama, giants in research, and immortals in the pantheons of literature and the performing arts—but also humbler folk. These have been as beloved locally as the great names are venerated at large. They are teachers and storekeepers, public servants and private-sector entrepreneurs, and activists and advocates, all community characters who have in one way or another defined Princeton. The Christmas movie classic *It's a Wonderful Life*, for all its unremitting sentimentality, espouses a central truth: any town would be different if certain pivotal lives had not been lived within it.

And so it is here. In *Legendary Locals of Princeton*, you will revisit—or perhaps encounter for the first time—not only notables whose thoughts and deeds changed the world but also common people whose personalities and daily presence defined their community.

But if there is misapprehension about Princeton—Is it an intellectual and cultural enclave? Country town? A garden state of mind within the Garden State?—there is misunderstanding about the community itself.

When we speak of Princeton, just what are we talking about? The historic downtown borough? Or the scenic surrounding township? Are the town and the internationally famous research university that bears its name so closely entwined as to be nearly synonymous? And what of the research/business/entrepreneurial/educational corridor that widely self-identifies as "Princeton" regardless of being officially situated in both Princeton and several neighboring municipalities?

This, then, has been the great challenge in assembling *Legendary Locals of Princeton*. Any of the above-cited locales are, in my considered opinion, quite worthy—historically, culturally, and economically—of being called "Princeton." But in the interests of the publisher-mandated 128-page brevity, some restrictions were observed of necessity.

So, here at the outset, I must beg the reader's patience, understanding, and, perhaps, forgiveness.

I have been forced to limit most of the subjects of *Legendary Locals of Princeton* to local residents not (with a very few exceptions) faculty and/or scientists at Princeton University, the Institute for Advanced Study, or the RCA/Sarnoff labs. There are numerous worthy legends of local research at these famed institutions. The author has already featured many renowned researchers in his other Arcadia Publishing books, such as *Princeton University* (2005). Alexander B. Magoun has highlighted some in his excellent *David Sarnoff Research Center: RCA Labs to Sarnoff Corporation* (2003), and Linda G. Arntzenius did similarly superb work in her Images of America: *Institute for Advanced Study* (2011).

A certain amount of overlap is unavoidable, but the crucial criterion for *Legendary Locals of Princeton* has been significant local residency. Each featured person has to have been more predominately a Princeton resident than a Princeton professor. The few exceptions will further explain: Woodrow Wilson was an undergraduate, a professor, and, finally, president at Princeton University, but he maintained a legal residence in town while serving as governor of New Jersey and president of the United States, returning here to vote; Pulitzer Prize–winning author John McPhee has taught for many years in the university writing program but was locally born and has nurtured his Princeton and New Jersey roots.

Another challenge—and, for the author, a more worrisome one—is that Princeton has been home to scores of humble but memorable residents, like teachers, coaches, business owners, and other local figures, whose inclusion should be a given in a book of this type. Indeed, I have been constantly mindful of not just who to include but who simply should not be left out.

Like a coach with an especially "deep bench," the problem has not been finding players but deciding who to put on the field. So, my apologies in advance for many worthy subjects not represented in this volume due to strict space limitations. And because this is a thoroughly illustrated work, the availability of superior images was a necessity. If a high-quality picture was not available (and, in far too many cases, no image at all was discovered), the person could not be allocated his/her own page but typically was featured for special mention in a chapter introduction.

The next vital question is, simply, "Why Princeton?" Why has this community had such an abundance of notables? And why is there no end in sight? And there are many answers and factors.

We start considering these in Chapter One, "Early History, Early Legends." This is not a definitive history of Princeton from precolonial times through the Civil War era nor is it intended to be. But here, you will find a representative spectrum of people; through their backgrounds and lives will shine the tones of their times.

Several persons featured in Chapter Two, "On the National and World Stages," could easily have been selections for other chapters. Most notable of these is the astonishingly accomplished Paul Robeson, arguably one of the most broadly talented of human beings. He was a collegiate athlete, a scholar who earned a law degree, a much-admired concert vocalist, an acclaimed stage and screen actor, and an outspoken activist for civil and human rights. Princeton-born Robeson could have been in the chapters on history or the performing arts. But so international was his stardom and the political issues in which he became embroiled that he truly strode across the world stage.

Chapter Three, "Finding the Way and the Why," is representative of the challenges mentioned earlier about assembling a book of this type. Surveying all the legendary researchers of Princeton would be like surveying all the wines of the Napa Valley. The potentially (and happily) endless task is, again, relieved by referring the reader to the previous Arcadia Publishing books about Princeton University, the Institute for Advanced Study, and RCA Sarnoff Laboratories. *Legendary Locals of Princeton* provides a condensed and eclectic collection of researchers in diverse fields.

Of course, the chapter is dominated by Albert Einstein, who, admittedly, has graced many previous Arcadia pages. But it just would not be Princeton nor legendary without Einstein. And included here is an extraordinarily touching and little-known episode from the twilight year of this great scientist's life, illustrated with a rarely seen photograph. This simple anecdote illuminates his humble thoughtfulness and how he inspired others. It eloquently bespeaks to why Albert Einstein was as locally beloved as he was internationally venerated.

By contrast, trying to survey all the legendary authors, educators, and journalists of Princeton in Chapter Four, "Telling the Story," would not be like surveying all the wines of the Napa Valley—it would be like surveying all the wines of France. Again, I heartily recommend other Arcadia books. And again, what is presented here emphasizes variety. The strong connection of some major literary lights to the town of Princeton may come as a surprise. If the reader exclaims, "Did they really live here in Princeton?," then the author—who made identical exclamations during his research—will be pleased.

The breadth of performing and graphic artists who have been attracted to Princeton as a place to live and create is well known. Chapter Five, "Creative Legends," reveals a rather astonishing number of now-famous actors and musicians who spent a formative youth here. Not surprisingly, several of these future stars gravitated to each other when they were high school students, striking their first creative chords together. Surprisingly, Princeton, for all its fame, has never received its due in popular music history as a cradle of such talent. Although cities are clearly conducive to channeling performers together, the critical wisdom may not accept that a country town could do the same.

Nearly every settlement has commerce and trade. But as detailed in Chapter Six, "The Entrepreneurial Spirit," there is something outstanding about the legends of local businesses, both great and small. Historically, Princeton's situation along the busy King's Highway ensured the success of commerce. Princeton Borough's centrality in relation to surrounding Princeton Township made downtown the destination where farmers and estate managers would purchase needed goods and access shipping to the state and nation at large. Historic buildings, once constructed, may stand on their own for centuries as monuments to their builders or most famous inhabitants. But memorable businesses stand thanks to the life and vision of a founder and, typically, the ongoing dedication of his or her successors. Modest but successful ventures are special joys because they become identified with one memorable person—the independent beautician who was as skilled as a chemist as she was a stylist, the kindly toy store proprietress, and the crusty but large-hearted general store maven. It is of no small significance that so many Princeton entrepreneurial spirits were also genuinely public spirited. Valued as convenient local sources of quality goods or services, they have also been treasured as good neighbors, who have often gone the extra distance in giving back in thoughtful and dedicated community service.

Princeton has been frequently described as "a garden," "garden-like," or "parklike." One cannot have roses without thorns, and large trees possess some particularly shady branches. Such will be revealed in Chapter Seven, "Mystery, Myth, and Controversy." Let it be stressed—inclusion in this chapter does not constitute guilt nor infer any high crimes or even low misdemeanors! Several subjects are persons of notoriety, but they should not be labeled as "notorious." A few were simply caught up in controversy. A few are victims of historical myth and distortion.

Some community leaders, especially businesspersons, have expressed their devotion to Princeton and their fellow residents in brick, stone, and steel. Chapter Eight, "Community Mainstays," also celebrates those whose goodwill came in deeds. It is noteworthy, for example, that the elected officials sampled here came from both sides of the political aisle; they earned respect from colleagues, constituents, and even rivals. They were in the truest sense public servants. If a few individuals may not be Princeton household names themselves, they represent local institutions central to Princeton's quality of life, like the police departments, rescue and fire squads, and hospital.

And so, here are Princeton personalities worthy of entering local lore, yet many led humble lives by the standards of fame and fortune. Discovering or rediscovering them has been delightful for the author. May it also be for you. Their stories are occasionally amusing and frequently moving. And they firmly and forever rebut the stereotype of a Princeton populated by wealthy elitists. Princeton is flavorful because, mixed with the spice of its rich and famous, it has always had the salt of the earth.

CHAPTER ONE

Early History, Early Legends

The history of Princeton is completely intertwined with the history of America, back to the region's first inhabitants.

Centuries ago, the Leni Lenape, of the greater indigenous group now referred to as the Delaware Nation, blazed a walking path that followed a well-drained, easily defended ridge line running from the Raritan River (near what is now New Brunswick) to the Delaware River (at modern-day Trenton). Today, if one drives between these two cities on Routes 27 and 206, he or she basically follows the route of what is now called the Upper Assunpink Trail (a Lower Assunpink Trail, also beginning and ending at the major waterways, curved some miles to the south). And the section of the original Upper Assunpink Trail going through Princeton became the town's main thoroughfare, Nassau Street.

With the coming of the Europeans, this trail was widened into a horse and wagon road. In colonial times, it became an important segment of the Post Road (mail carriage route) and was later formalized as part of the King's Highway between New York and Philadelphia. (In 1913, this route assumed new historical importance as a section of the Lincoln Highway, the first continuous motor vehicle road between New York and California.) Princeton's location along a prime transportation artery significantly factored in the relocation here in 1756 of the College of New Jersey, which had been founded in Elizabeth, 10 years earlier. (The school officially took the name Princeton University during its sesquicentennial in 1896; for convenience, it will be generally cited as such here, even for the pre-1896 period.)

Also, because the town of Princeton grew along the sides of a well-traveled road, its street layout is much different from towns and cities that sprung up around harbors, fortifications, or county courthouses.

In addition to existing pathways, the Europeans followed other Native American establishments. The first local settlement was not on the site of today's town. Rather, it was a few miles to the west where today's Route 206 crosses the Stony Brook. Evidence has been found in this area of seasonal Leni Lenape encampments. Even if the whites did not purposely build near native sites, the locality was congenial, being temperate and fertile, with fish and game for food and waterpower for mills. The little settlement was known, even into the 20th century, as "Stony Brook."

The settlers were members of the Society of Friends (Quakers), who, in July 1696, had purchased tracts from their friend and coworshipper William Penn, the prominent regional landowner and encourager of peaceable settlements after whom Pennsylvania ("Penn's forest land") was named. The family names of this first group, including those of Benjamin Clarke, Benjamin Fitz Randolph, John Horner, William Olden, Richard Stockton, and Joseph Worth, have entered into Princeton lore in many street and place names.

Indeed, the first college building ("hall") constructed in Princeton in 1756 and the main street of town were both named "Nassau" in honor of William III of England, who was also Prince of Nassau-Orange and had lifted religious sanctions against the Society of Friends.

The relative absence of outright conflict between the early white settlers and the Leni Lenapes in precolonial Nova Caesaria (also known as "New Jersey") did not make the Indians' subsequent history happier. By the 19th century, few of the Delawares, including the Lenapes, remained, many having been forcibly repatriated to Oklahoma and other Western territories. The names of most great leaders of the Delaware Nation—surely legendary in oral traditions—have sadly gone unpreserved. But we remember their peoples.

Today's town, situated on a rise above Stony Brook to the west and the Millstone River to the south, can be traced to the most legendary local family of 18th and early-19th century Princeton, the Stocktons. Founder Richard Stockton acquired a large tract from Penn for £900; it was on this land that the Stockton family estate of "Morven" and most of the surrounding village were soon established. As the senior Stockton began to resell land, homes were built, and shops and inns sprang up to serve travelers on the busy thoroughfare of the Post Road/King's Highway.

English Anglicans, Scottish Presbyterians, and Dutch Reformed Church members soon followed the English/Pennsylvanian Quakers. The Princeton community grew in tandem with America, the nation. Immigrants from the Old World or from the new country's increasingly crowded cities made their mark on the largely unwritten pages of what was, to them, a new territory—creating new lore and new legends in the New World.

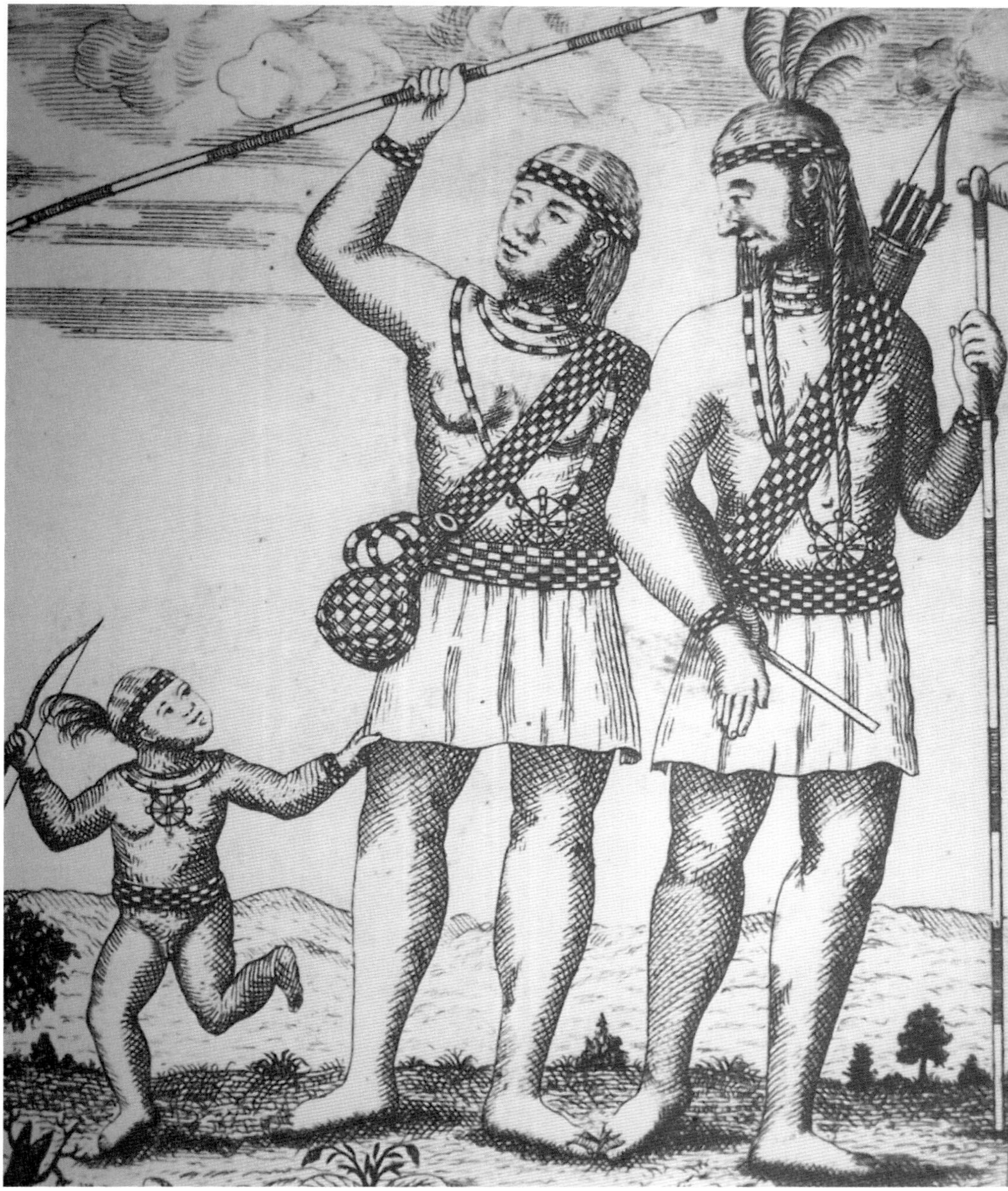

The Leni Lenape
A subgroup of the Delaware Nation, these Native Americans were the original settlers of Princeton, living seasonally along the Stony Brook. It was this section, a few miles west of today's downtown, that saw the first white settlement. Peter Lindstrom, an engineer from Stockholm, Sweden, created this engraving of a Leni Lenape family around 1654. The Native Americans depicted were from the lower Delaware Valley, probably near Philadelphia, but would have been very similar to those living in what is today Princeton. Though the image is a bit romanticized, it still contains a certain degree of accuracy, and it shows that, at least early on, European visitors to the Mid-Atlantic looked upon indigenous peoples with great measures of curiosity and respect. (Peter Lindstrom, *Philadelphia: Portrait of an American City.*)

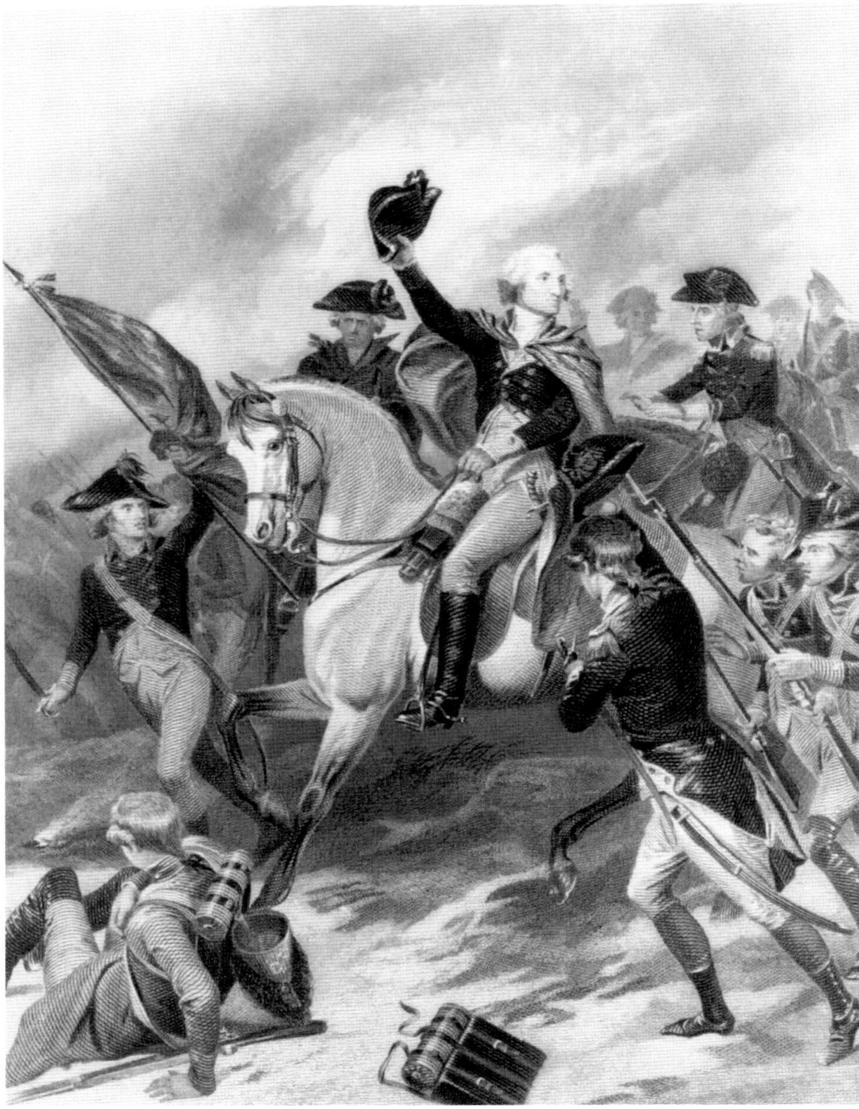

George Washington (1732–1799)
Washington's crucial January 3, 1777, victory at Princeton continued the momentum of the American cause after his decisive crossing of the Delaware River and two victories at Trenton (the famous event on Christmas Day 1776 and the second engagement on January 2, 1777, lesser known but of great import). Princeton was arguably the true turning point in the War for Independence because it was the third time in 10 days that the Continentals had bested, or at least thwarted, seasoned British troops. The location of the Battle of Princeton, recent research has indicated, was more extensive than long thought; it is now the site of a state park, featuring the still-extant Thomas Clark House and an oak that is likely a genetic descendant of the tree under which Washington's esteemed officer Gen. Hugh Mercer (the namesake of Mercer County) was fatally bayoneted. After successfully subduing the remaining garrison in the college's Nassau Hall, Washington and his troops escaped north to Kingston, up the King's Highway, and from there to a safe wintering in the hills above Somerville, ready to start the struggle for independence anew. (Corbis.)

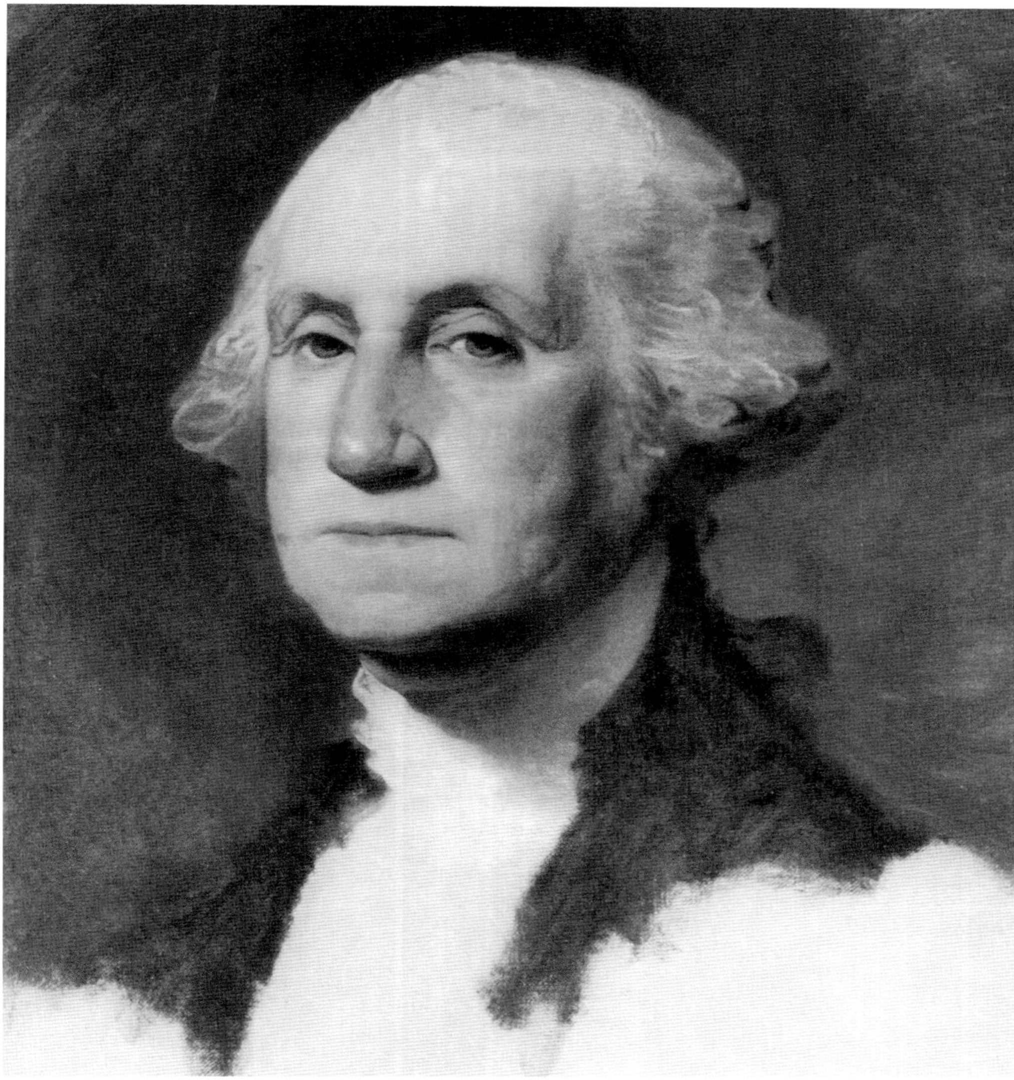

Washington at the Berrien Family Estate
Washington would be back in the Princeton environs as a temporary local resident. He resided at the nearby Berrien family estate of Rockingham for several months in 1783 when Congress met at Nassau Hall and the town was thus the de facto capital of the new United States. (The fledgling government had left Philadelphia hurriedly when unpaid soldiers of the 1st Pennsylvania Line openly threatened mutiny.) Owner John Berrien, a successful landowner and New Jersey Supreme Court justice, had drowned in the nearby Millstone River under mysterious circumstances. Although foul play was not suspected, it is unclear whether it was an accident or whether Berrien had taken his own life during a period of depression. Margaret Berrien rented the home to Washington while she lived in Princeton. Here, he sat for portraits, composed his farewell to the Army, received old friends and comrades, did an experiment demonstrating that swamp gas causes mysterious river lights, and, quietly but gratefully, celebrated his unlikely victory. After three moves in the 20th century to accommodate a growing traprock quarry, a restored Rockingham now stands open to the public near Kingston, only a short distance from its original location. (Corbis.)

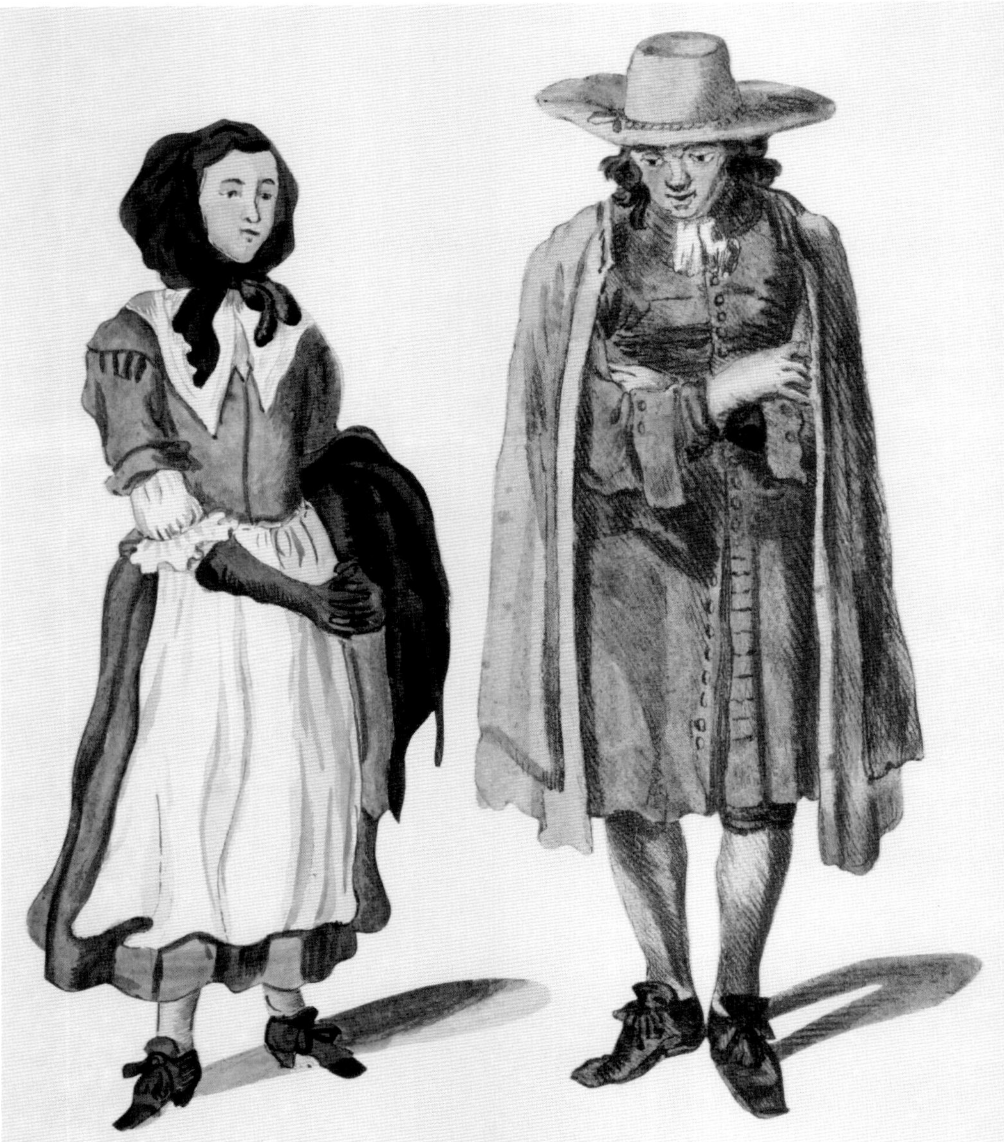

The Quakers
Members of the Society of Friends were among the first white settlers who farmed and lived between the original Stony Brook settlement in the small river valley and the village of Prince Town that grew on either side of the King's Highway stagecoach road. It was in the fields and orchards of Thomas and Benjamin Clarke that British and Continental troops clashed at the Battle of Princeton. Their grandfather Benjamin Clarke II was one of the first settlers at Stony Brook in 1696 (in 1709, Clarke and nine fellow Quakers established a meetinghouse and adjacent cemetery for the Society of Friends). Although this engraving is not specifically of the Clarkes, it is probably quite representative of how 18th-century Princeton members of the Society of Friends looked. (Corbis.)

Annis Boudinot Stockton (1736–1801)

Richard Stockton Sr. (1730–1781) was a signer of the Declaration of Independence and the master of Morven, the family's beloved mansion and estate (later owned by such local notables as Paul Tulane, page 99, and Gen. Robert Wood Johnson Jr., page 106, and today a carefully restored museum open to the public). The senior Stockton married Annis Boudinot, a sister of Elias Boudinot, president of the Continental Congress in the time before independence. Annis was an able manager of their estate during his frequent travels and was an accomplished poet. In keeping with the symbolic system used in much 18th-century portraiture, she here holds a sprig of rosemary, a sign of poetic inspiration. Some of her poems were dedicated to George Washington, an honored guest at Morven dinners whom she greatly admired. After Richard's death, she was courted by the elderly widower John Witherspoon, the fourth president of the College of New Jersey (Princeton University) but gently declined his suit. (Princeton University Library, the Boudinot Collection.)

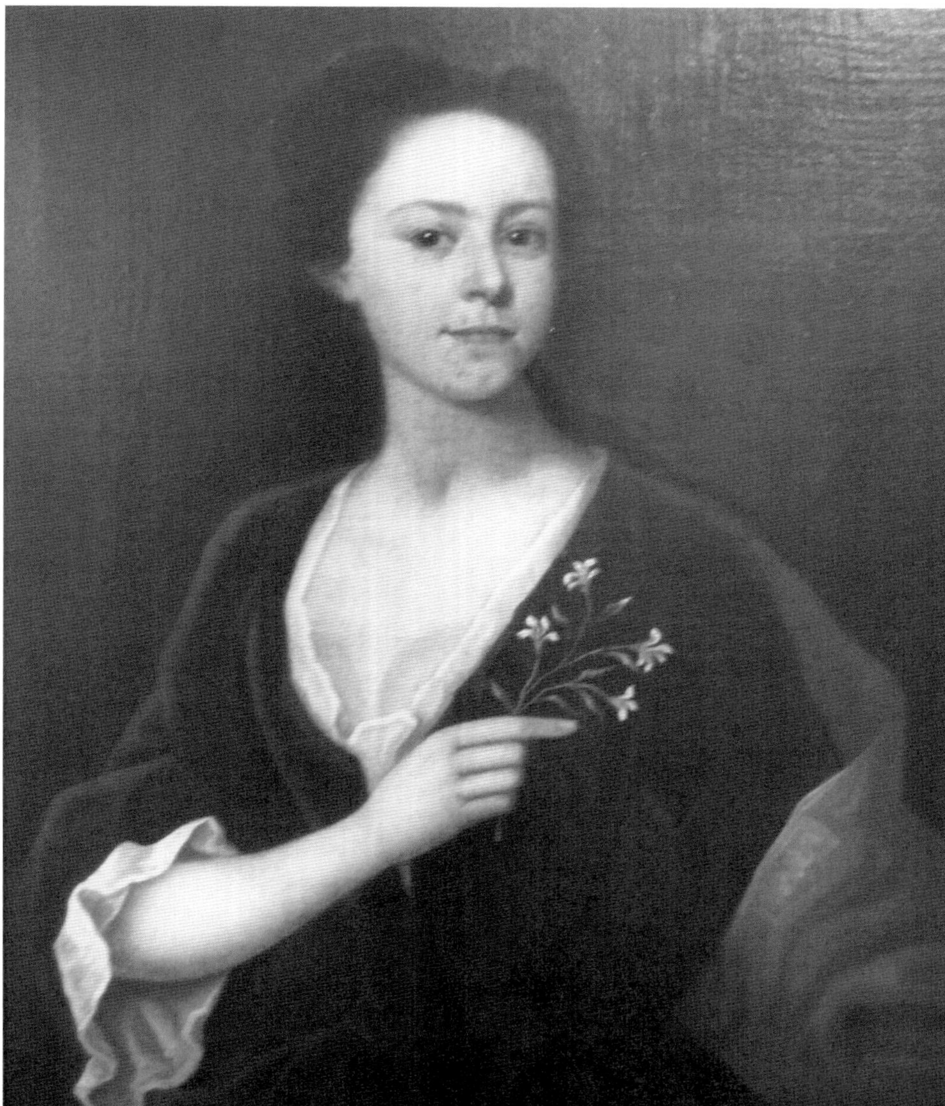

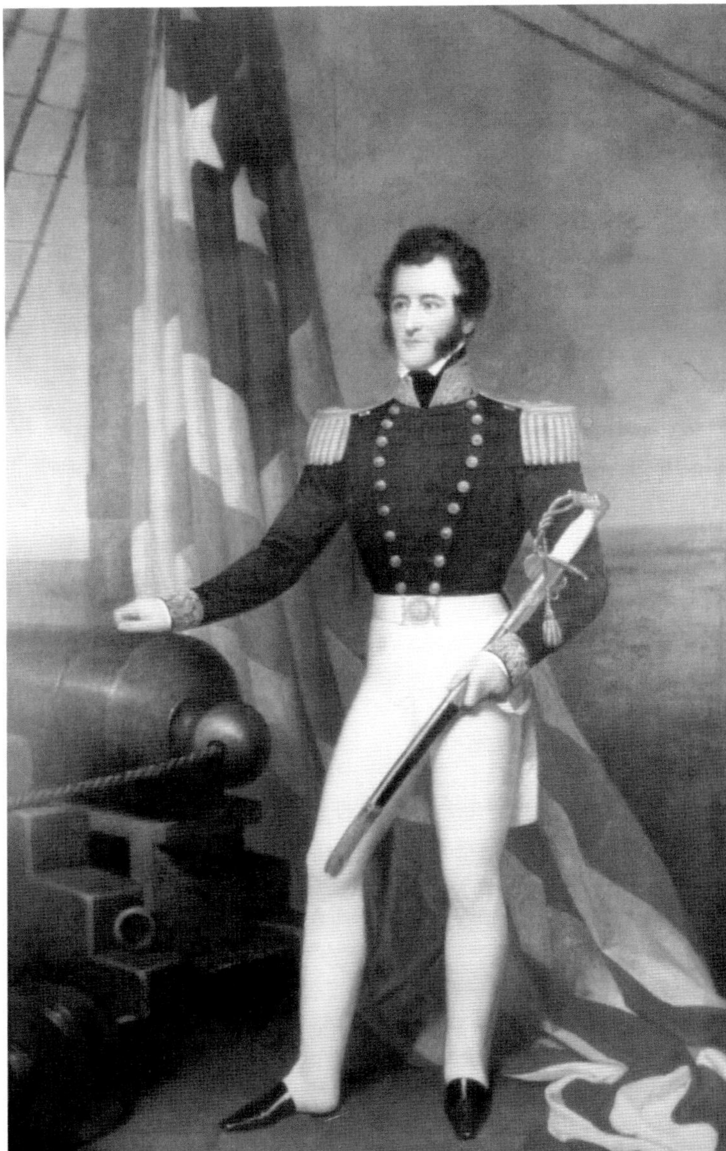

Robert Field Stockton (1795–1866)

As a naval officer, this son of Richard Stockton Jr., fought both slave traders and pirates. Commodore Stockton's accomplishments, like many of his family's, were achieved in both business and politics. He was instrumental in America's acquiring of the California Territory during the Mexican-American War and founding a government there. He also served as a US senator from New Jersey from 1851 to 1853. Like many abolitionists of his era, he favored repatriating freed slaves to Africa; for this purpose, he was a founder of the American Colonization Society and helped organize the West African nation of Liberia. He was also a successful investor in two of the most important and profitable shipping and transportation entities of mid-19th-century New Jersey, the Delaware & Raritan Canal (of which he became president) and the Camden & Amboy Railroad, both of which served the centrally situated community of Princeton. (HSP.)

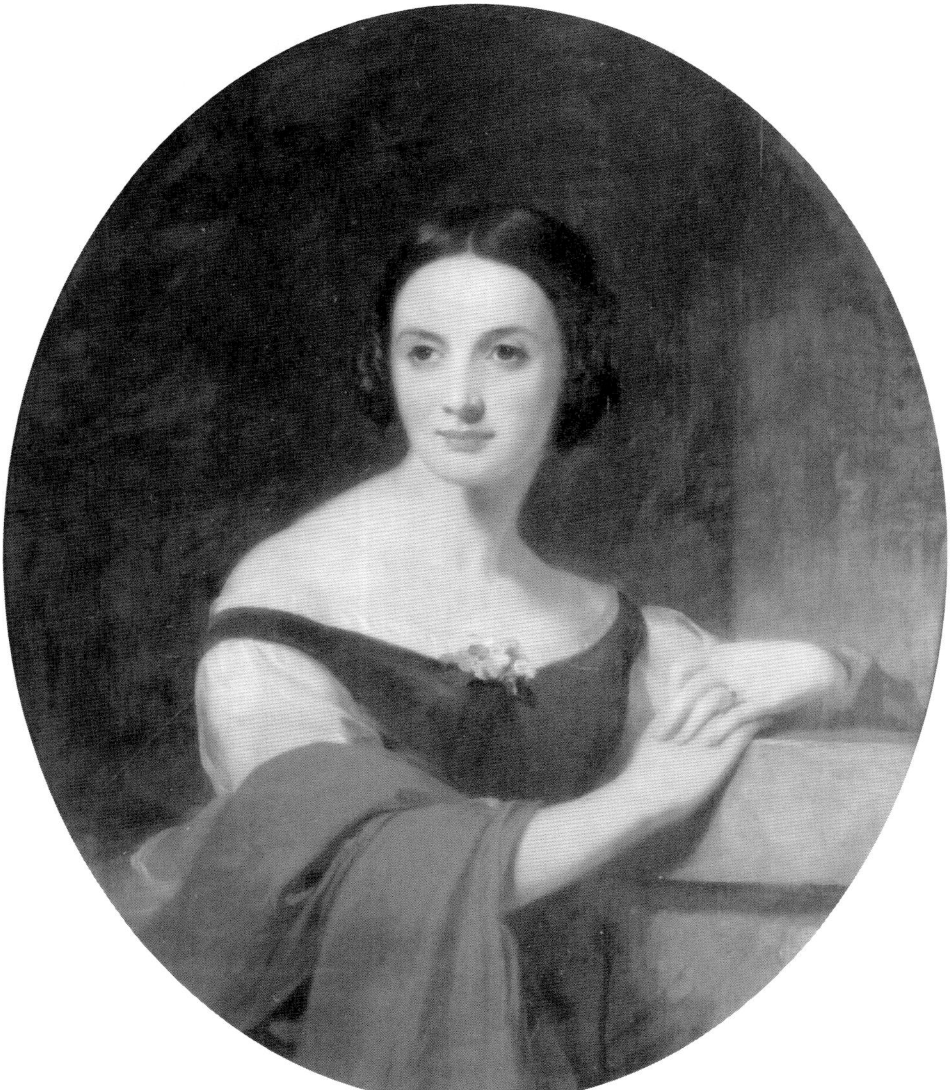

Sara Marks Stockton (1828–1887)
Originally from New Orleans, Sara Marks met John Potter Stockton while attending school in Philadelphia. They married in May 1845, causing a scandal in Princeton because Sara was Jewish, and John was Protestant. A scion of the prominent and historic local family, the groom was assured of future social and life success, eventually becoming a US senator and state attorney general. A year after their wedding, Sara Stockton was baptized as an Episcopalian at Trinity Church. This portrait of 19-year-old Sara was created in October 1847 by artist Thomas Sully (1783–1872). Despite being widely acknowledged for her intelligence as well as her beauty, she was made aware of being a Jew by birth even if now a Christian convert. (Shortly before his death in 1850 at her home, her father, English-born Albert J. "Roley" Marks, also converted.) Her diaries, kept between 1848 and 1854, give valuable information about life at Morven, but, she also occasionally laments being neglected by her in-laws and other leading Princetonians who evidently believed John had married beneath him. (Anne and Robert Stockton.)

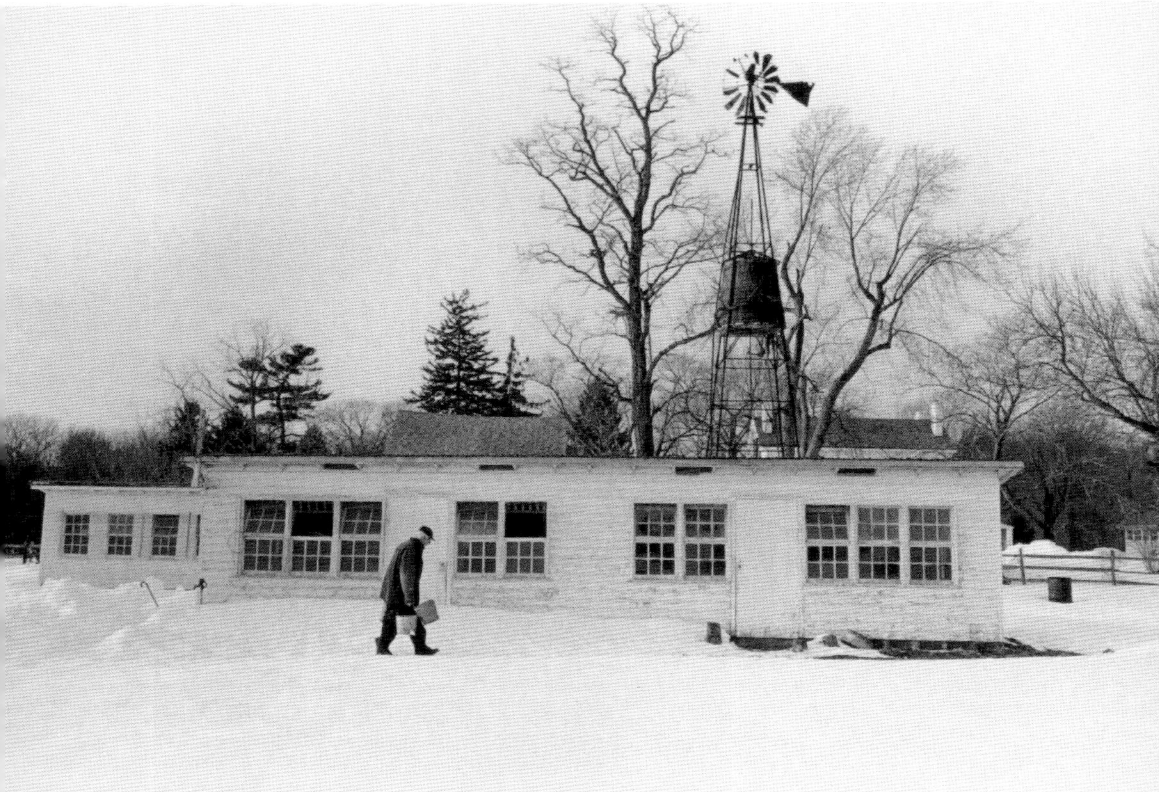

Updike Family and Farm (ABOVE AND OPPOSITE PAGE)
Established by deed to Benjamin Clark in 1721 on the "Quaker Road" (the route by which George Washington would lead his Army by night before the Battle of Princeton), this was a working farm until 2002, bucking the trend for surrounding land to be converted into sod fields. It was acquired by the Historical Society of Princeton and has been renovated for special shows, educational programs, receptions, and (soon) the society's offices and archives. (Bainbridge House, the current HSP headquarters, will continue to serve the community as an expanded exhibit gallery.) The Updike family had owned the 160-acre tract property after 1890. A century later, in 1990, photographer Michael Johnson frequently visited the remaining central six-acre farm, whose outlying property had been preserved from development under a permanent conservation easement. In his own act of preservation, he lovingly documented the daily routine of the final years of its last residents, his great-uncle Stanley Updike and great-aunt Sarah Updike. (All, courtesy of *The Windmill Turns Slowly on the Updike Farm*, Michael Johnson.)

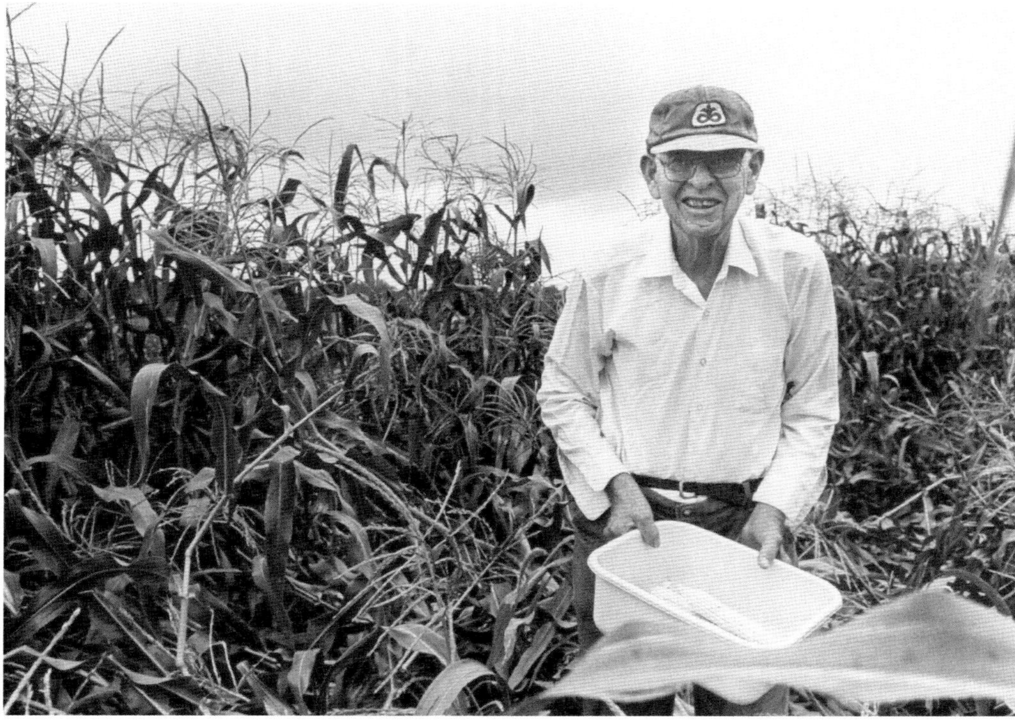

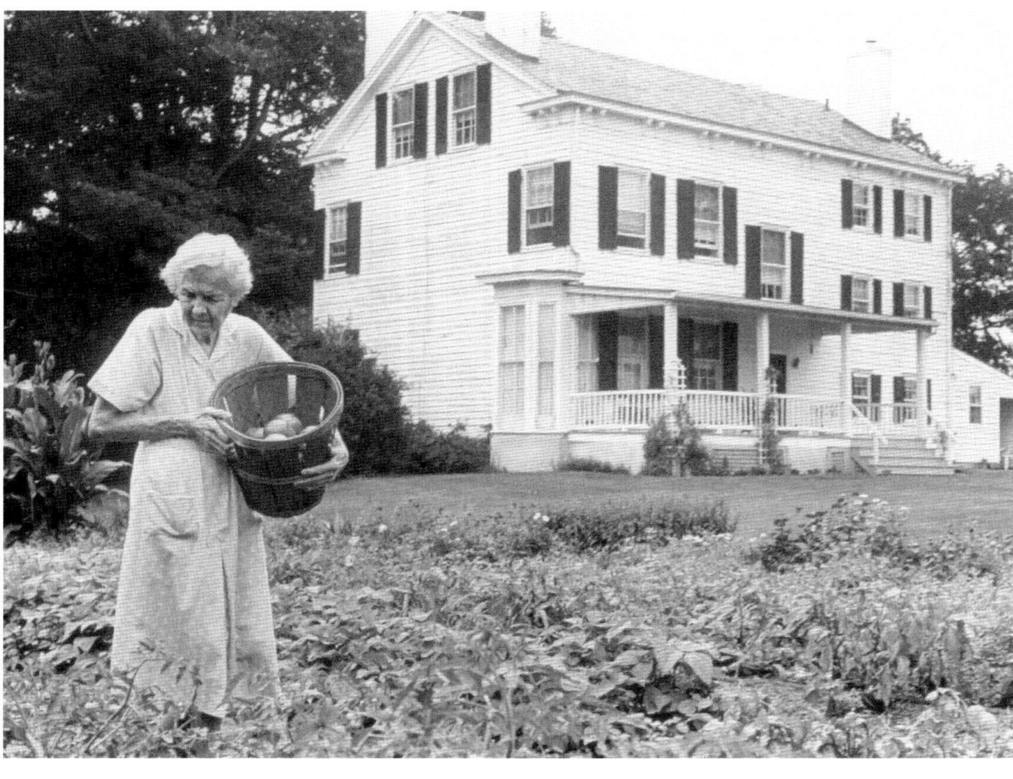

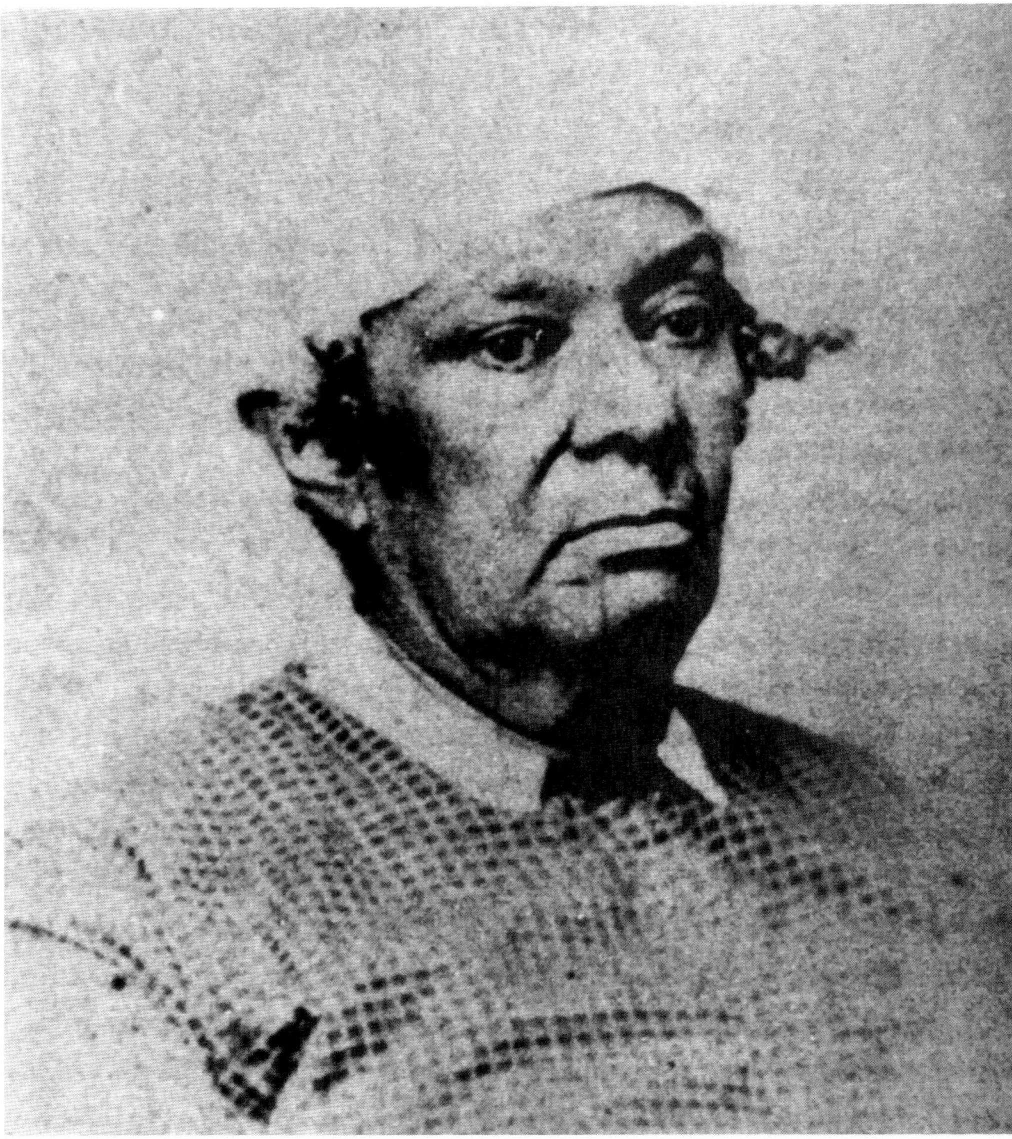

Betsey Stockton (178?–1865)
Born in slavery to the Elizabeth Stockton Green family, Betsey was freed in 1817. She continued to work for the Greens as a paid servant and became a devout member of the local Presbyterian church. Showing a zeal for education as well as religion, she was allowed to use the family's library and was mentored by Elizabeth's father, prominent scholar and future College of New Jersey president Rev. Ashbel Green. Her dream of becoming a missionary was realized in November 1822 when she sailed with Rev. and Mrs. Charles S. Stewart to the Sandwich Islands (present day Hawaii). She started the first school for non-royal islanders, teaching English, Latin, algebra, and history. Green published her accounts in his *Christian Advocate* magazine. Betsey Stockton later returned to Princeton where she founded the pioneering Witherspoon Street Colored School. Greatly esteemed by the white clergymen and educators with whom she worked, she was buried in the Stewart family's plot in Cooperstown, New York. (Mission Houses Museum.)

CHAPTER TWO

On the National and World Stages

Princeton's roles in the events of the War for Independence and the founding of America raised the curtain for it to play a prominent role in the nation's history. And of course, where there are great centers of learning, there will be great thinkers and leaders

By the late 1800s, the town of Princeton had become attractive for writers, wealthy businesspersons, and retired public figures. During the 1896 celebrations of the sesquicentennial of the College of New Jersey, a great boost came when it was announced that the school, now with an established and blossoming graduate program, would henceforth be known as "Princeton University."

Princeton's climate was temperate; its location, almost exactly halfway between New York and Philadelphia and, by extension, between Boston and Washington, DC, ideal; its links for transportation and shipping handy; its institutions reliable; and society highly respectable. And so, the prominent and powerful came. (So did émigrés seeking respite in Princeton. And serving them in business, education, government, and the arts arose a surprising and delightful population of equally legendary locals.)

Interestingly, the construction in the 1800s of hotels with "modern" amenities helped make Princeton an attractive and viable year-round address for the wealthy and prominent. Today, central heating and hot water are taken for granted; but at one time, it was extremely expensive to install and operate these utilities year-round in an entire mansion. When the Princeton Inn, University Hotel, and similar businesses were established, the wealthy could close up their estates in late autumn and comfortably winter at a hotel.

Additional living options for those well educated but of modest means were also vital in establishing Princeton as a world center. As the university greatly expanded in the 1870s and 1880s (thanks to energetic university president James McCosh), suitable housing for new professors and research staff was, for a time, in critically short supply. (In his correspondence, Prof. Joseph Henry, the pioneer of telegraphy and future secretary of the Smithsonian Institution, frequently discusses his efforts to secure living quarters for colleagues.) The development of homes along University Place and apartments on Bank Street in downtown greatly eased this shortage, as did Mose Taylor Pyne's development of "White City" on Princeton's eastern side (see page 106).

Amusements and recreational opportunities expanded. There had been horserace tracks locally for many years. There was one on Stockton family land below Morven in the 1890s, and this sport was likely contested back to colonial times. But the nine-hole golf course constructed in the late 19th century on Bayard Lane across from the Stanworth estate, which has been supplanted by the present-day Springdale Golf Club, was the harbinger of Princeton as a place of genteel enjoyments. Another notable—if sometimes misunderstood and underappreciated—boost to the local quality of life was the creation of Carnegie Lake in 1906. Scottish-born steel magnate and philanthropist Andrew Carnegie was persuaded to fund the acquisition and clearing of land along the Millstone River and its damming at the eastern end to create what was initially referred to as "Loch Carnegie." Its purpose was not, as is often assumed, solely to provide a world-class rowing venue for the Princeton University crew team; the project was specifically planned to remove significant acreage from future development and provide a bucolic setting for the recreation of future generations of university and town persons. Thus, Carnegie Lake was a true "green way," a century ahead of its time and another draw for national and world-famous leaders, writers, businesspersons, and others to become part of the community.

Some legendary locals moved to Princeton after achieving power or to be sheltered from the misuse of it. Many of the Princeton residents entered fully onto the world stage by virtue of their talents, aspiration, belief, sense of duty, or, in some cases, a potent combination of many of these.

The dawning of the era of Princeton as an address of cache in its own right, apart from the university likely came with the arrival of former US president Grover Cleveland to spend his retirement here (see page 26). In addition to his attraction by the festivities surrounding the university's 150th anniversary and the urging of his friend Dean West, Cleveland was encouraged to settle here by another good friend, Henry Van Dyck. The scion of an Old Dutch American family, Van Dyck was a clergyman and an author and poet of note who lived on Avalon Place, at the site of what is now the Princeton YM/YWCA, not far from where Cleveland eventually made his home just down Bayard Lane.

Thus began the networking that begot visitors who became legendary local residents. For example, populist senator and presidential candidate William Jennings Bryan visited then New Jersey governor Woodrow Wilson at wife Ellen Wilson's arrangement.

Of course, the presence of the university, Princeton Theological Seminary, Institute for Advanced Study, and other major centers of inquiry continued to keep Princeton firmly on the world stage.

As a result, simply working in Princeton could mean encounters with history and, by association, moments on that stage. An outstanding example is longtime resident Emma King. While serving as a hostess at the Nassau Inn in Palmer Square central in the 1950s and 1960s, King met and waited upon numerous distinguished visitors, including seven US presidents, Soviet party chairman Nikita Khrushchev, and Cuban premiere Fidel Castro.

Some locals seemed destined for greatness. Some brought their stature with them. Others were success stories of a most delightfully unlikely sort. All are embraced today as legends of Princeton's role in national and world events.

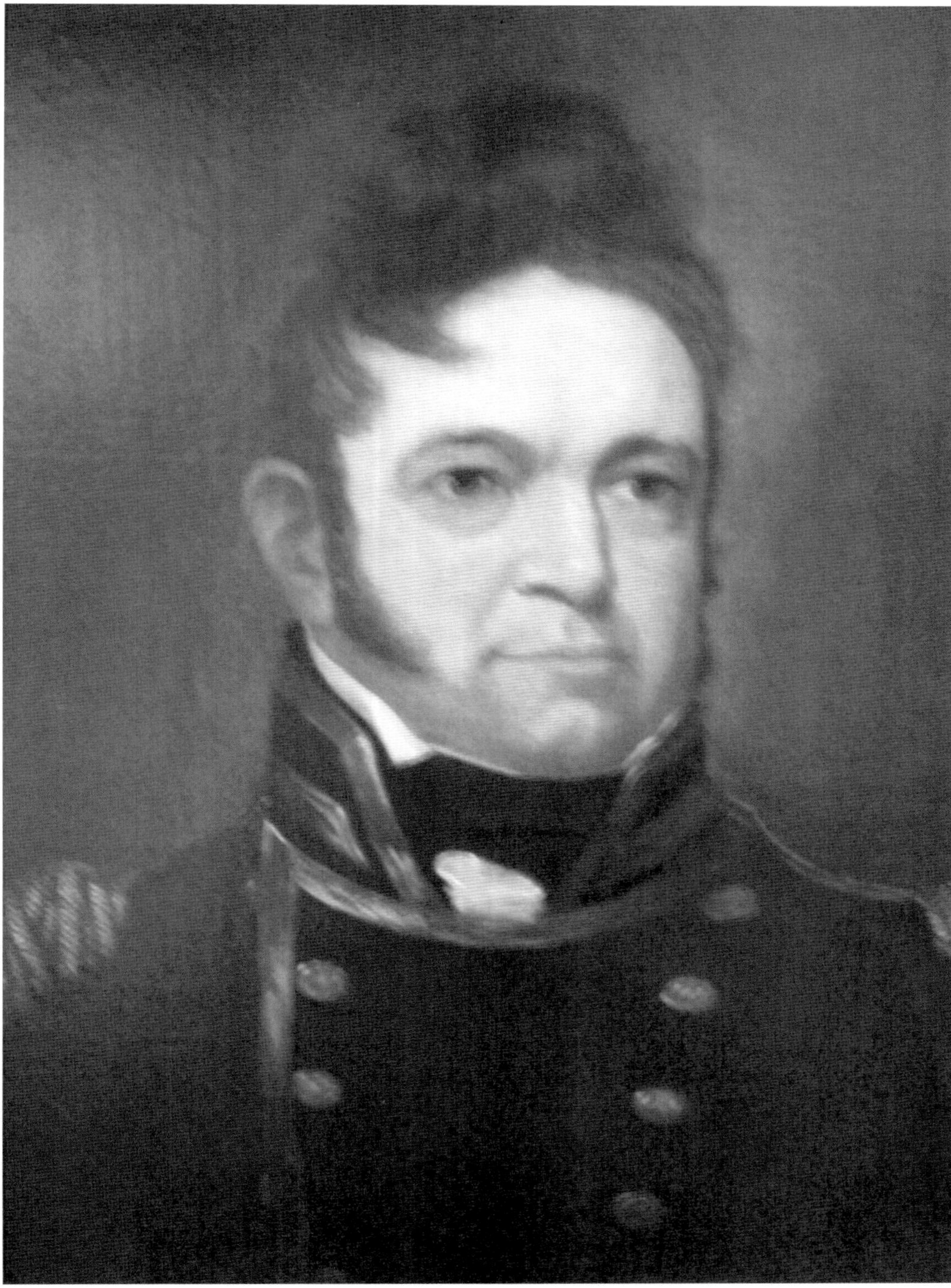

Commodore William Bainbridge (1774–1833)
Commander of the USS *Constitution* ("Old Ironsides") in the War of 1812, Bainbridge was born in Princeton. His birthplace, now called Bainbridge House, is currently headquarters of the Historical Society of Princeton. (HSP.)

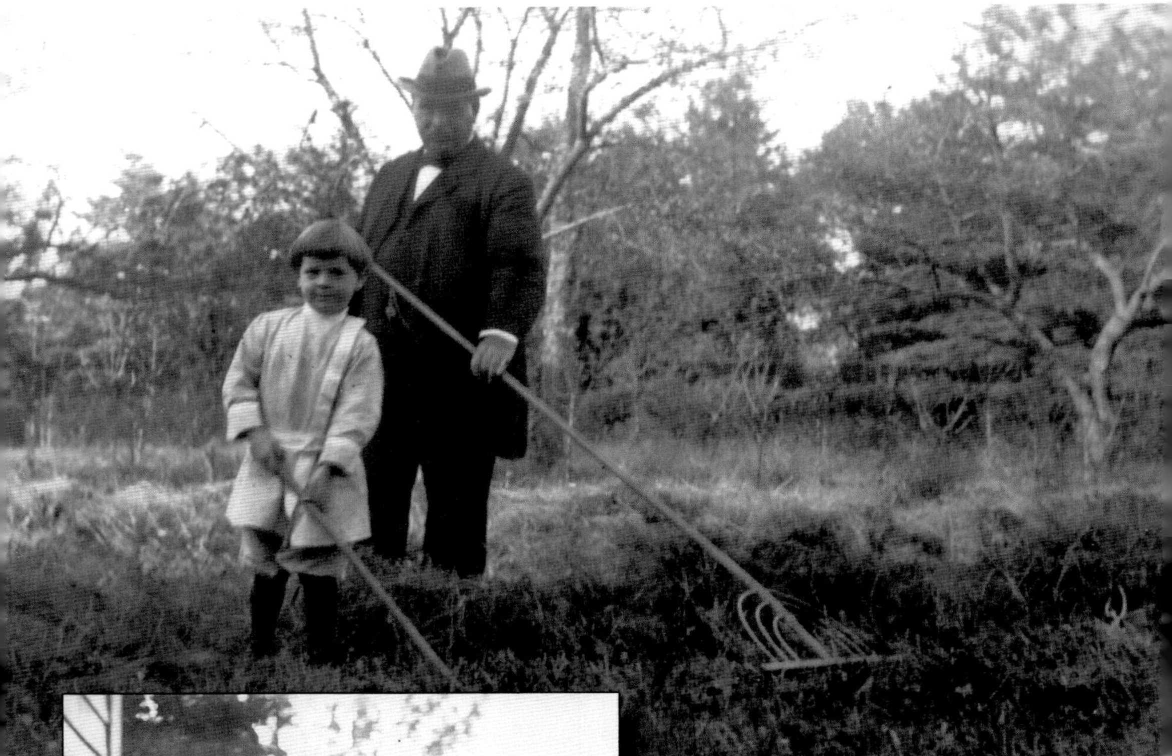

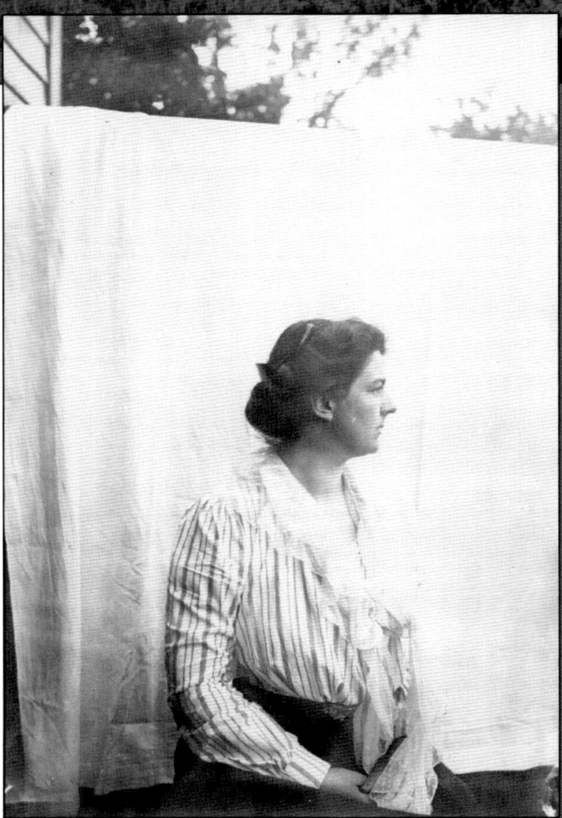

Grover Cleveland (1837–1908)

A New Jersey native and a lawyer, Cleveland was mayor of Buffalo, governor of New York, and twice president of the United States from 1885 to 1889 and from 1893 to 1897. He is shown here playing with his son by his second marriage. His birthday (March 18) is celebrated at the Princeton Cemetery with a short eulogy and wreath-laying ceremony by a military honor guard from Fort Dix. (HSP.)

Frances Folsom Cleveland Preston (1864–1947)

The lovely, young second Mrs. Cleveland remained in Princeton after Grover's death and remarried. She is shown here in a rare backyard portrait, with a sheet serving as an impromptu photographic backdrop. She was not only a darling of the town's well-heeled society but beloved by the humble shopkeepers and serving persons, to whom she always spoke with friendliness and genuine courtesy. (HSP.)

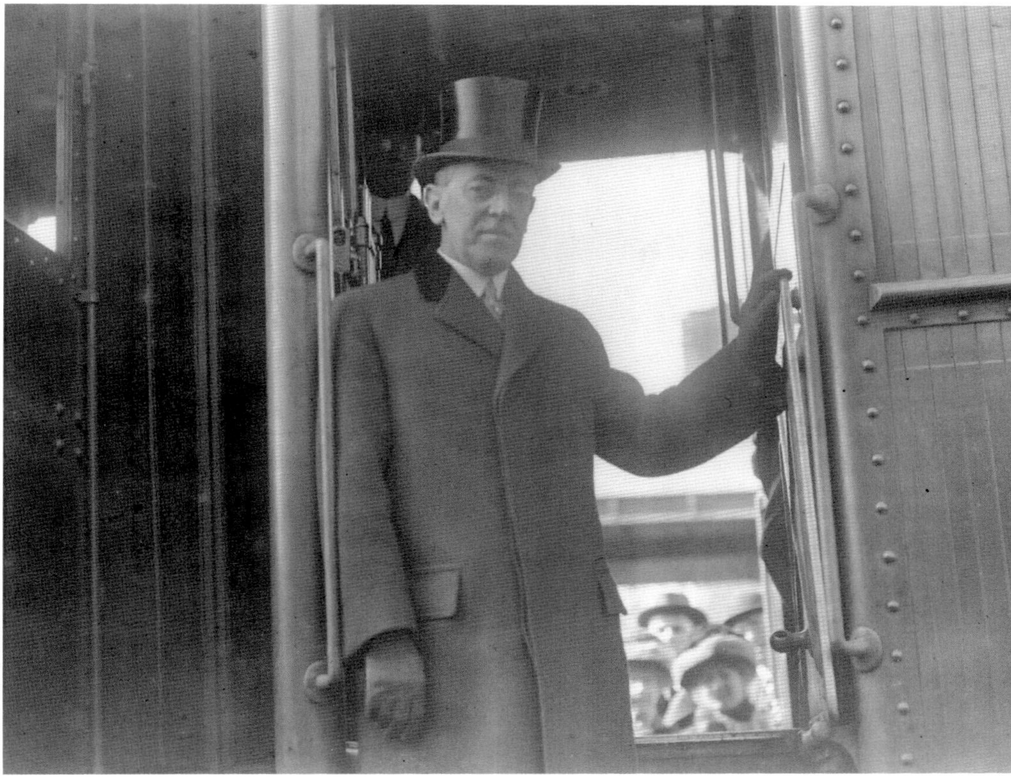

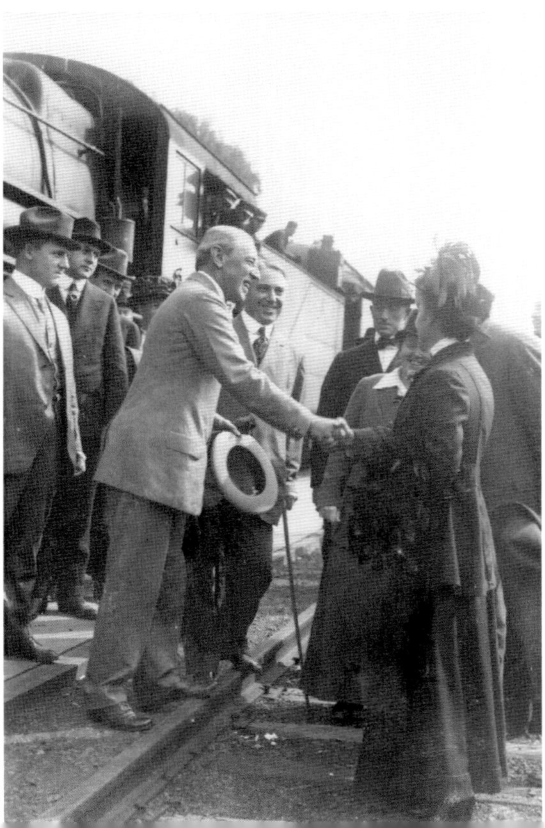

Woodrow Wilson (1856–1924)
Wilson was among the first sons of Virginian families to again be sent north to college after the Civil War, as Southern resentments over defeat and Reconstruction began to ease. Wilson graduated from the College of New Jersey (Princeton) in 1879 and eventually returned, becoming professor, the school's president, governor of New Jersey, and, finally, the 28th president of the United States. So strong was Wilson's affection for the area that, while living in the White House, he retained Princeton as his legal residence. Here, he is seen arriving from Washington to vote in Princeton during an election, thus making Wilson not only an American political legend but also a true Princeton local. (Both, HSP.)

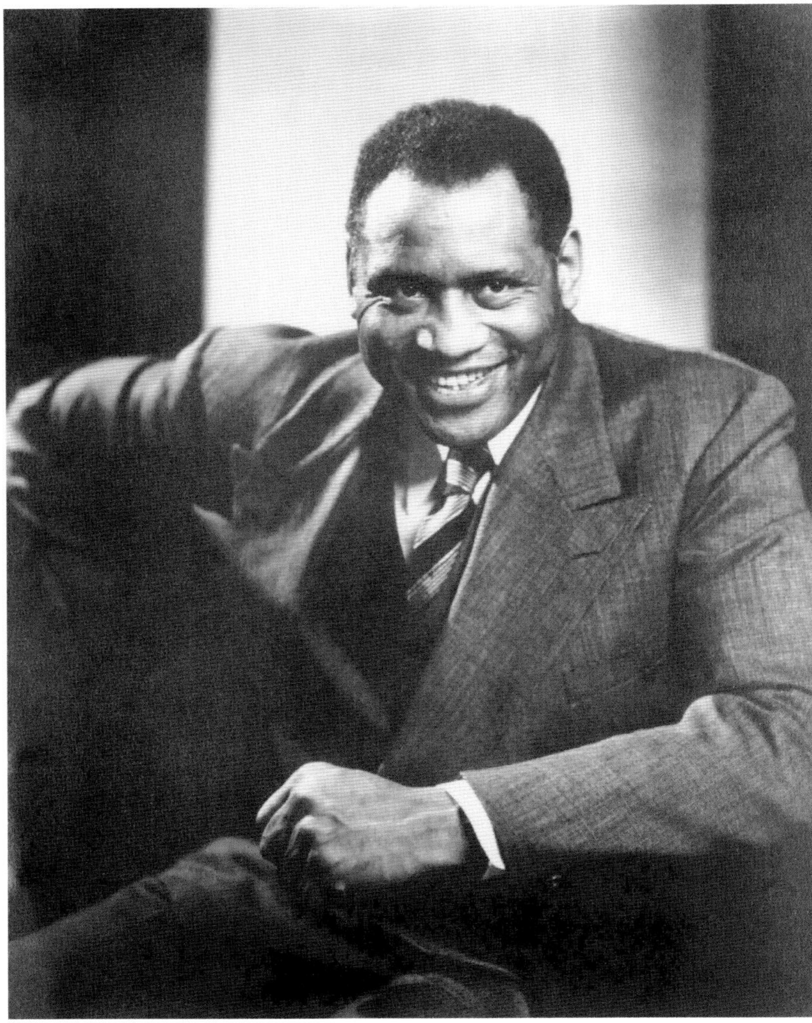

Paul Robeson (1898–1976)

Paul Leroy Robeson is largely recalled as a concert singer and stage actor, famed for his stage roles in *Emperor Jones* and *Showboat* (also starring in the memorable film versions) and his stunning realization of the title role in Shakespeare's *Othello*. But Robeson is presented here as a world figure—so colossal were his talents, so global was his acclaim, and so impassioned were his efforts internationally for social justice.

He was born in Princeton to William Drew Robeson (1845–1918), then minister of the local AME church, and Maria Louisa Bustill Robeson. The family moved to New Brunswick when Paul was eight. He graduated from New Brunswick High School with the highest academic honors and then attended Rutgers University, where he was an All-American football player in 1917 and 1918. He earned a law degree at Columbia University. But Robeson's formidable stage presence and resonant bass voice established him firmly as an actor and singer. He was tremendously popular in Europe. The adoration and lack of prejudice he enjoyed in the Soviet Union during a 1934 concert tour (and a nearly nightmarish experience in Nazi Germany immediately prior) gave him a lifelong, outspoken affection for the Russian people. This affection and his uncompromising support of civil rights and labor law reform brought him suspicion and hostility during the McCarthy era, during which time he was banned from traveling abroad. (Corbis.)

Paul Robeson Place

Paul Robeson is buried in Ferncliff Cemetery in Hartsdale, New York, but the intersection of Witherspoon and Wiggins Streets was renamed Paul Robeson Place in his honor the year he died. This memorial bust (by British sculptor Jacob Epstein with a base by local architect and designer Michael Graves, page 90) stands outside the former "colored" YMCA building, now the beautifully refurbished home of the Arts Society of Princeton and known as the Paul Robeson Center. It is fitting because Robeson retained affection for the town of his birth. Emma Green, a longtime resident and contemporary of Robeson's, recalled one of his last visits when a mutual friend had passed away. Robeson came down from New York on the train with one of his brothers, Rev. Benjamin Robeson, and sang during the interment at Princeton cemetery. "His voice rang out and was heard all around the neighborhood," Green related to the Princeton History Project. "He never forgot Princeton." (Author.)

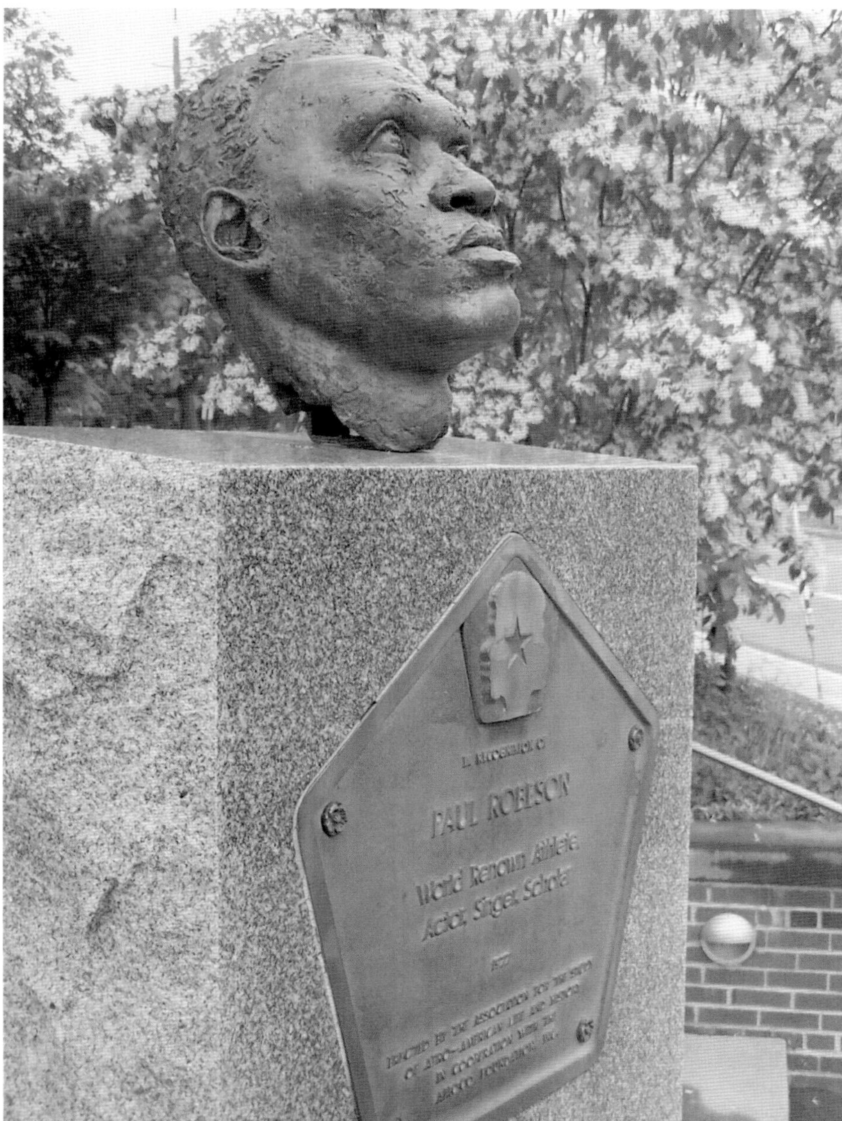

William Milligan Sloane (1850–1928)

A longtime professor of history and political science at Princeton and later at Columbia University, Sloane served for some 30 years on the International Olympic Committee. A friend of Baron deCoubertin, reviver of the Olympic Games, Sloane became founder and first president of the US Olympic Committee. He escorted the American contingent to Athens for the first modern games in 1896. A lifelong resident of Princeton, he was buried in the town cemetery. When the Olympic torch passed through America on its 1996 relay run toward the centennial games, it stopped at Sloane's grave for a special ceremony. (Bill Sloane.)

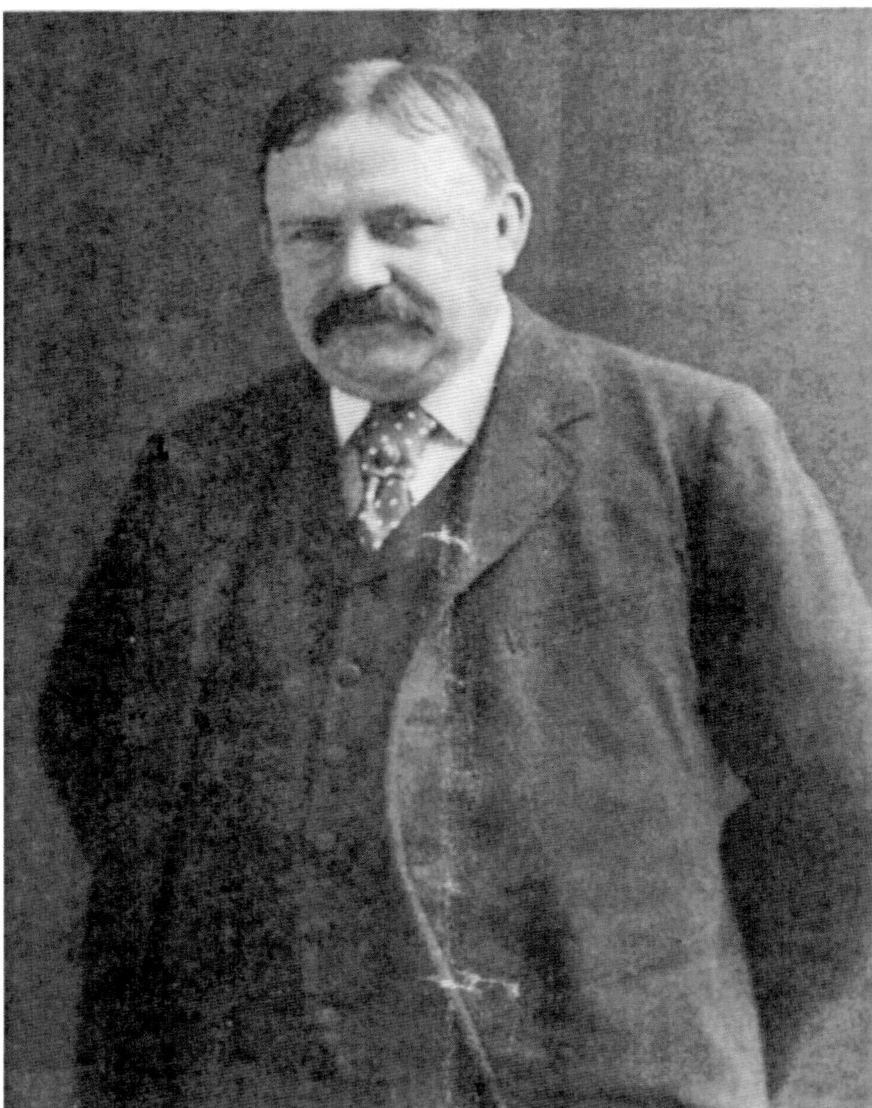

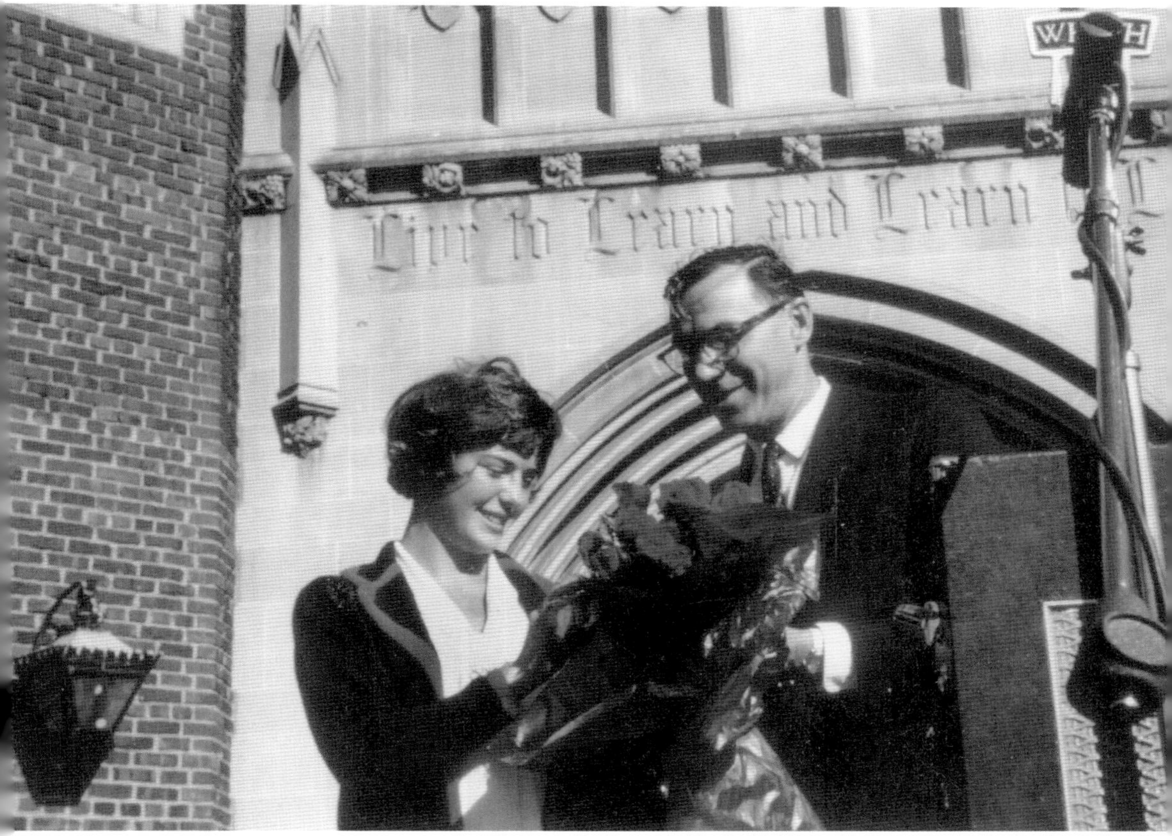

Lesley Bush

A member of the Princeton High School class of 1965, Bush, born in 1947, became the darling of Princeton and America when she won the 1964 Olympic gold medal in 10-meter platform diving. "It was such a surprise to me and everyone else that I was in a semi-daze," she admits. (She followed up this triumph with a 1967 Pan American Games gold). Born in Orange, New Jersey, her father's work took the family to Arizona, where Lesley first experienced national-level competitive swimming and diving. The family came to Princeton when she was a high school sophomore. At a time when amateur rules severely restricted American Olympians from accepting support, she was extremely grateful to be invited to train at Princeton University with its coaches and facilities. Bush, who retired recently as a teacher in the West Windsor school system, does not regret missing the late era of multimillion-dollar endorsement deals and media megastardom for Olympic champions. Recalling "Lesley Bush Day," at the conclusion of which she received roses in front of Princeton High (pictured), she reflects, "I had a lovely reception. It wasn't commercial. It was loving. I had a Princeton parade." (PR.)

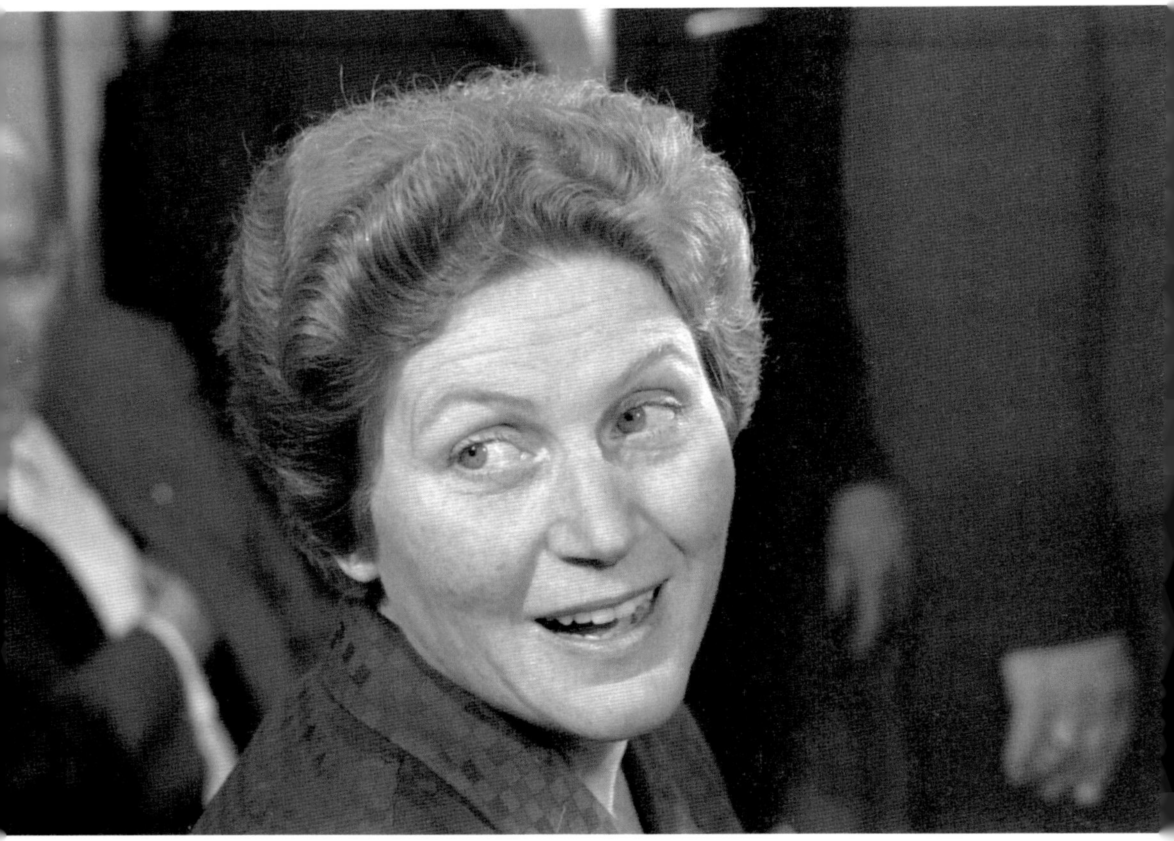

Svetlana Iosifovna Alliluyeva (1926–2011)
Born in Moscow to fame—or perhaps infamy—as the only daughter of dictator Joseph Stalin, little Svetlana was her father's darling and, of course, no party to his brutal crimes against the Soviet people. Her 1967 defection to the West made headlines worldwide. She soon settled in Princeton where the community welcomed her. She lived here for six years as a pleasant neighbor if something of a curiosity before moving on. Interestingly, she was not the only relative of a Soviet chairman to live in Princeton. From October 1996 to August 1998, Nina Krushcheva, granddaughter of Stalin's successor Nikita Krushchev, collaborated with John Matlock, America's last ambassador to the Soviet Union, at the Institute for Advanced Study before moving to New York to work as a journalist. (Corbis)

CHAPTER THREE

Finding the Way and the Why

As previously noted, Princeton University (née the College of New Jersey) has over time created a regional atmosphere conducive to learning and inquiry. Success begets success. And (borrowing an analogy from Albert Einstein's General Theory of Relativity) just as the immense gravitation fields of stars can bend the very space surrounding them, the presence of Princeton University has drawn other centers of higher learning and research to be established near it. These centers have also acquired international reputations, as witness the Princeton Theological Seminary (founded in 1812), Westminster Choir College (1926), Bristol Myers Squibb (1931), the Institute for Advanced Study (1930), and Radio Corporation of America's David Sarnoff Laboratories. The Princeton research and development laboratory of the Radio Corporation of America (RCA), established in 1941, was later named for David Sarnoff, RCA's famed first general manager, and is now an entity of Stanford Research Institute (SRI) International. Princeton University, the Institute for Advanced Study, and Sarnoff Labs have already been the subjects of Arcadia Publishing histories; therefore, most of their leading figures will not be considered in this book. The vital point is, these institutions attracted thinkers and doers of legendary status who settled in the Princeton area and created a critical mass of research creativity. The prime example, of course, is theoretical physicist Albert Einstein, whose relocation to Princeton in 1933 attracted many other European scientific, literary, and intellectual émigrés from Nazi-dominated, war-afflicted Europe.

The growth of greater Princeton as a research nexus and the home base of internationally famed thinkers continued after World War II with tremendous vitality. The 1965 edition of *Illustrated Fact Book: Princeton, New Jersey and Surrounding Areas*, sponsored by the Greater Princeton Chamber of Commerce and Civic Council, declared that "Princeton is known the world over as the center of scientific research," specifically noting that the town "is associated with the names of many great men in the fields of science, mathematics and human motivation, Einstein, Oppenheimer, Woodrow Wilson, Wigner, von Neuman, Gallup and many others." The *Fact Book* backed up this hyperbole with statistics, noting the presence of "fifty-five or more research facilities and laboratories where dedicated men and women devote their time to basic research," listing 37 of these facilities by name. All this was two decades before the mid-1980s explosion of office parks along nearby US Highway 1, filling with information, medical, and light-industrial startups, which achieved wide recognition as the "Princeton research corridor."

This was not a solely 20th-century phenomenon. For example, John Witherspoon (1723–1794), the Scottish cleric who became the fourth president of the College of New Jersey was a dedicated experimenter in the science of agriculture. He did numerous experiments in horticulture and animal husbandry at Tusculum, his estate just outside the town, which exists to this day as a private residence. The road he traveled between the college and his farm was fittingly named Witherspoon Street.

Space does not allow in-depth consideration of every prominent finder of the way and the why who made Princeton his or her home. Two merit brief mention in hope that their interesting stories will represent others.

One contemporary Princeton-based researcher/journalist took his nom de plume from a contemporary of Witherspoon's in the Scottish Enlightenment. When skilled economic analyst George W. Goodman (born 1930) undertook the writing of hard-hitting articles about Wall Street for *New York* magazine, his editor thought that he would be most effective if his identity were kept anonymous. Hence his pen name "Adam Smith," a nod to the early proponent of laissez-faire economics. Coming out from behind his typewriter and in front of the camera, Goodman was for many years host of the public television show *Adam Smith's Money World*. He has also published fiction under his own name. His wife, Sallie, made a name for herself in the arts as a successful play director at Theater Intime on the Princeton University campus.

Of course, women have stood out quite well from their husbands or fathers. Helen Crossley was the daughter of Archibald M. Crossley, who, like George Gallup, was a towering figure in early opinion polling. Helen Crossley made her place in what was then largely a man's world. She started at age nine doing radio audience counts for her father and then graduated from Radcliffe in 1942, earning her master's in 1948 at the University of Denver's Opinion Research Center. She distinguished herself in government work during World War II. In 1955, she began a long career with the US Information Agency, working with Leo P. Crespi (another prominent Princeton-based pollster) to measure overseas attitudes about America. Helen Crossley was included in the first edition of *Who's Who of American Women*, served as an officer of several professional polling organizations, and, by the time of her retirement, had won international respect among her colleagues. A specialist in applying survey research to human communication and conflict resolution, she found an agreeable home in multicultural Princeton.

Contrary to popular belief, some of Princeton's greatest research legends never calculated to boost their careers by the reflected glory of an association with the town or the university. Some just happened to be living here when a seedling of sideline initiative blossomed into a fully branched business of world renown.

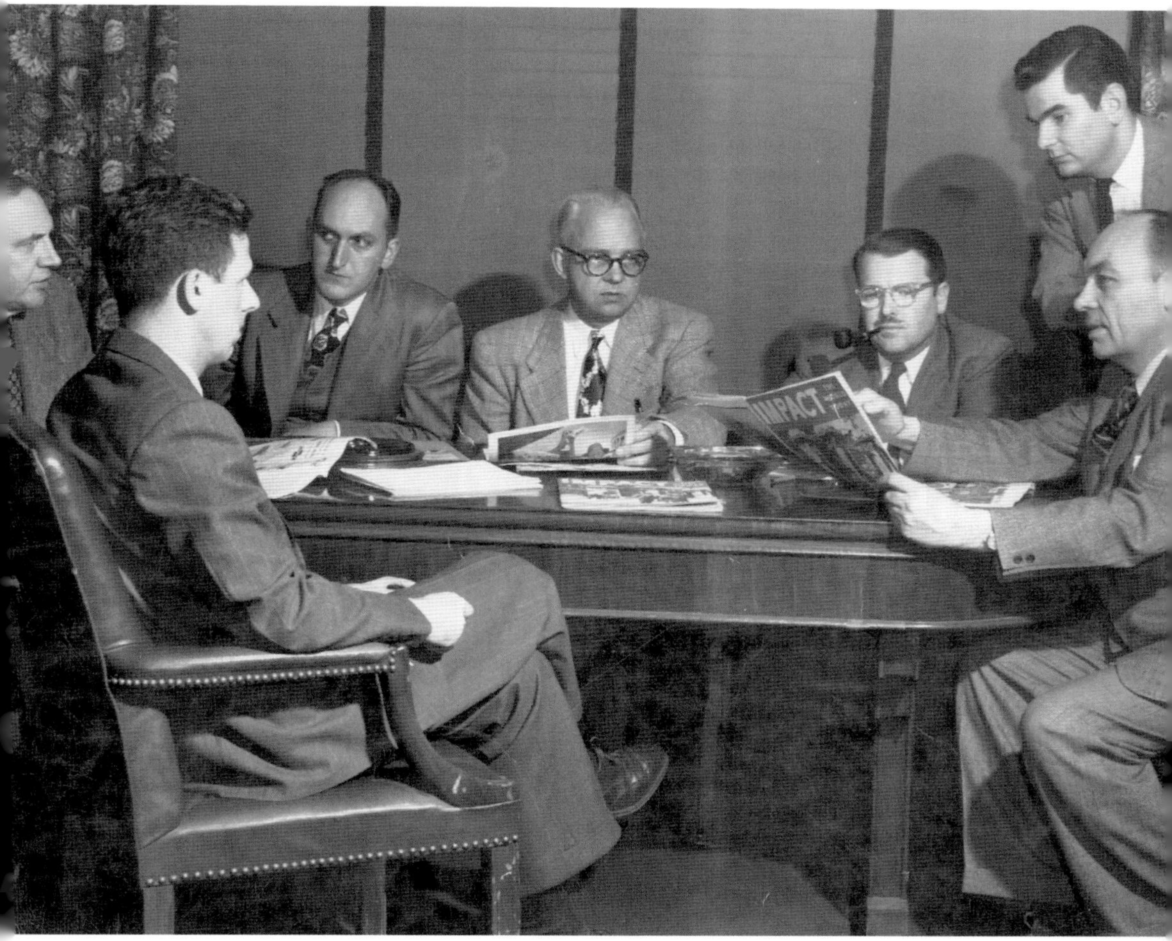

George H. Gallup (1901–1984)
Gallup was a distinguished statistician and journalist whose pioneering work in public-opinion and market research set new standards. Founder of the American Institute of Public Opinion in 1935, he is especially remembered for his Gallup Poll of the American electorate. Originally from Iowa, Gallup purchased a large farm on Great Road (later well known locally for its black Angus cattle) as a base for commuting to New York where he was doing in-house surveys for a major advertising firm. He applied his highly accurate respondent sampling and survey framing techniques to a little sideline business, the Institute for Public Opinion, which first occupied a small office on Nassau Street. Its syndicated newspaper feature "America Speaks" was almost an overnight success, and the little institute soon flourished as the world-famous Gallup Poll. A professorial and professionally generous man, Gallup encouraged his executives as they started their own companies, looking on them not as competitors but colleagues. (Several are seen gathered with Gallup, who sits at far right). Princeton soon became a world center for polling research. (Corbis.)

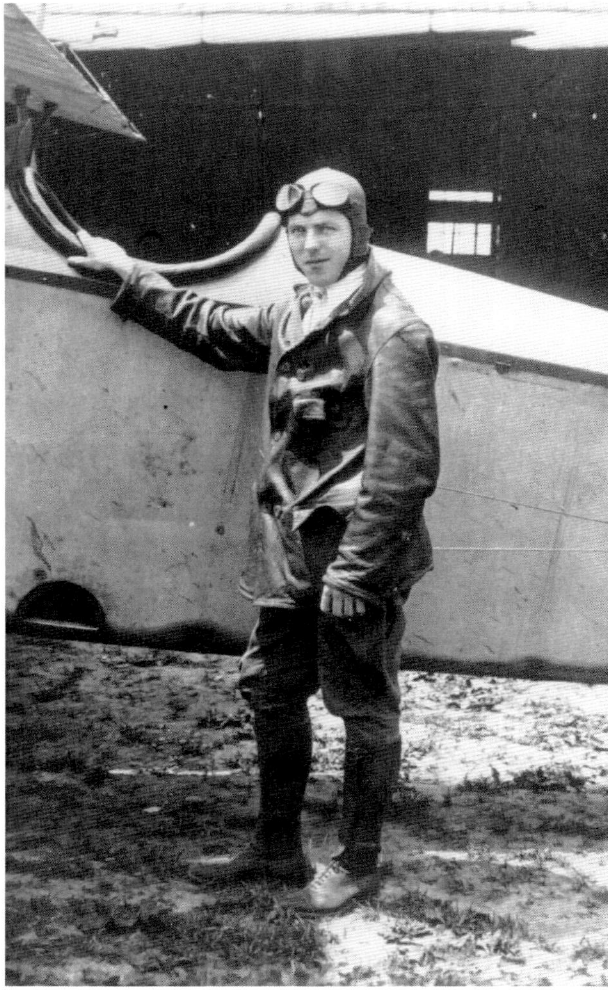

Francis Callery

In 1911, a mere eight years after the Wright Brothers built and operated the first heavier-than-air vehicle in sustained, controlled flight, German émigré and draftsman-engineer Richard A. Newhouse (originally Neuhaus) began designing and building the Princeton area's first airplanes in nearby Rocky Hill. His first biplane featured innovative banking-ailerons of his own creation, and Newhouse improved the designs of other manufacturers. His friend George Schmitt flew the 1911 vehicle immense distances but, sadly, was killed when it crashed in Vermont. This tragedy and a need to support his growing family caused Newhouse to suspend his hobby. But other aviation pioneers continued to fly and experiment. Bolmer's Field, on what was then called Route 31, became increasingly active during and after World War I as Francis Callery (pictured here) and other pilots trained for the aerial combat or airmail delivery, all the while learning and improving aviation science. Callery went on to a career with the Consolidated Vultee Aircraft Corporation of California and Texas (later known as Convair), for which he authored a seminal 1943 report "Aviation Faces the Future." In 1929, Richard Newhouse and son Werner inaugurated the Newhouse Flying Service at Bolmer's Field—now Princeton Airport on what is modern-day Route 206—and operated it successfully and safely through the 1930s. Princeton never became a national aviation research center because no full-scale aircraft manufacturing facilities were ever established here. But the pioneering roles of the Callerys, Newhouses, and others should not be forgotten. (PR.)

Freeman Dyson

The British-born (1923) scientist has had an influence beyond his primary fields of theoretical physics and mathematics, having contributed significantly to thinking about space colonization and biotechnology. A champion of science to the general public, his is also widely respected for his insights into the relations of metaphysics and religion to the life of the intellect. A Princeton resident for more than half a century, Dyson has observed that here "I have the freedom to do what I want [and] bright people to talk to every day." (Douglas Kirkland/Corbis.)

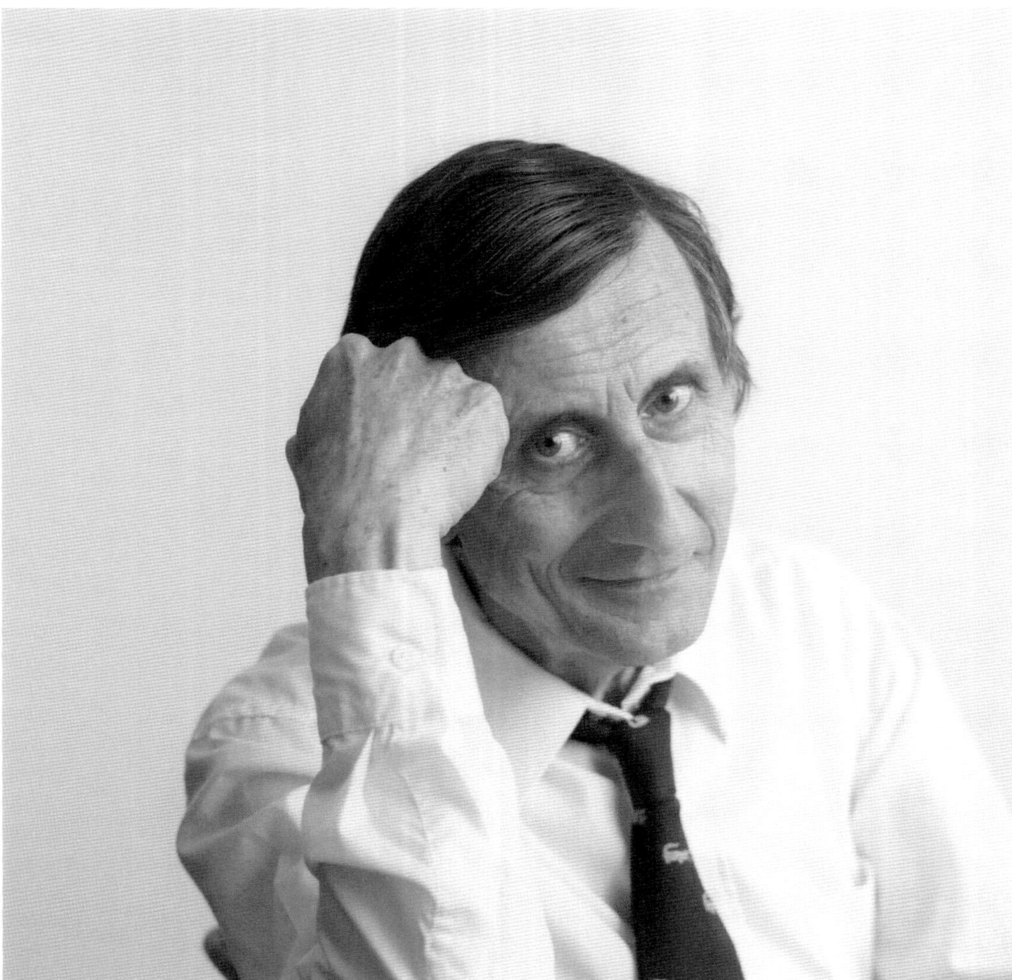

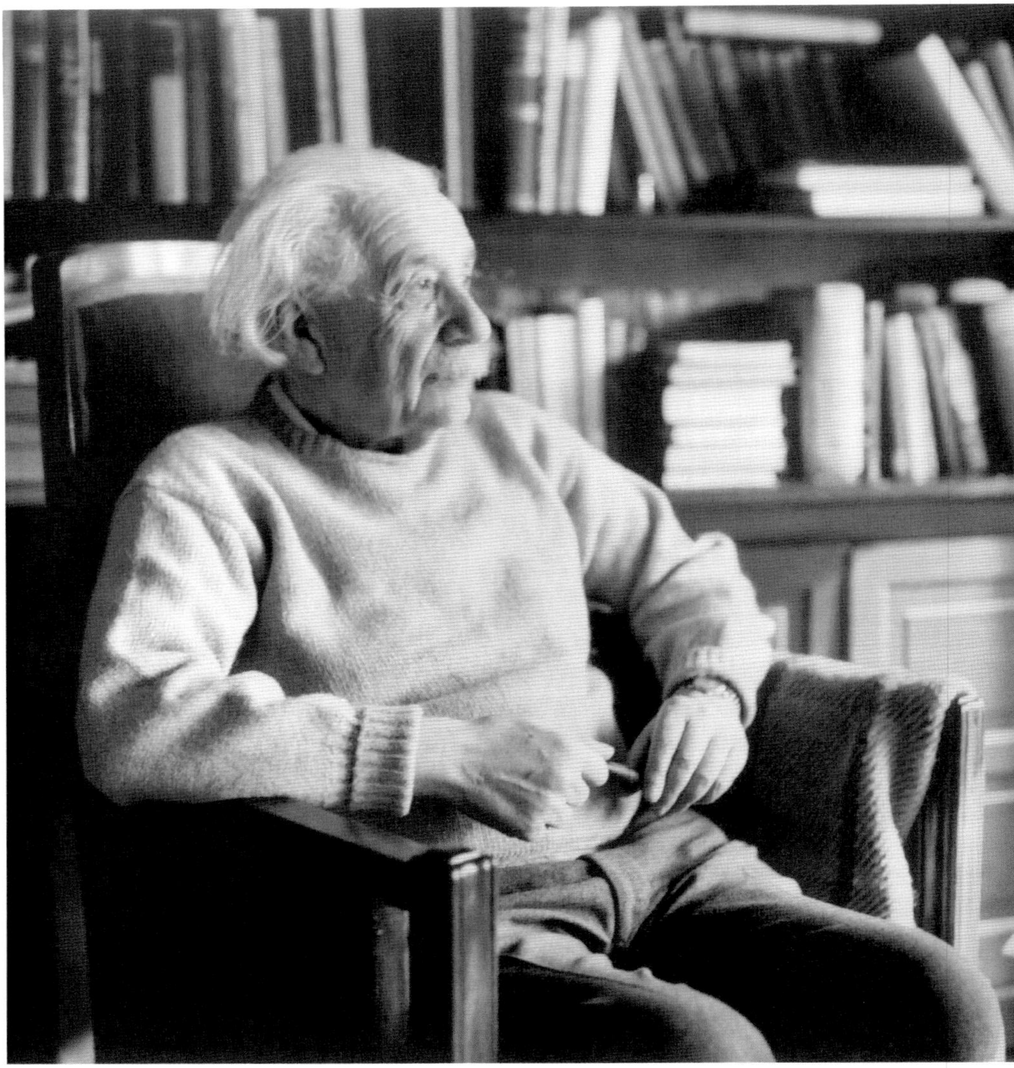

Albert Einstein (1879–1955)
The 20th century's most famous genius spent the last 22 years of his life living in Princeton and working at the Institute for Advanced Study. Not only was he a beloved local figure, but his personal advocacy of Jewish scientists settling in Princeton after fleeing Nazi Europe helped turn the town almost overnight into a world center for mathematics and theoretical physics. What had been initially conceived in 1933 as a six-month-per-year working schedule in Princeton at the newly founded Institute for Advanced Study became full time when the Nazis added his books to those of other Jewish scientists and intellectuals being burned at rallies.

Einstein often remarked the following to European visitors over the contrast between his international fame and the quiet isolation in which he now lived and worked: "I wished for this isolation all my life, and now I have finally achieved it, here in Princeton." (Corbis.)

Humble Scientist

Einstein was a genuinely humble human being. He pointed out that he had not invented or created anything, merely discovered existing laws of the universe. He was especially regretful that he was not especially good at building or repairs. In 1954, the year before his passing, the aged physicist was greatly touched when Zvi Gezari, an industrial engineer and avid amateur astronomer with access to facilities at the Hayden Planetarium, presented him with a telescope that Gezari had personally made, right down to its hand-ground optics. "I envy you," the modest Einstein told Gezari (seen here to the scientist's left). "I've never been good with my hands." The instrument was later donated to Hebrew University in Jerusalem where it was restored, put on display, and—as per Einstein's wish—made available for use by young science students. (Corbis.)

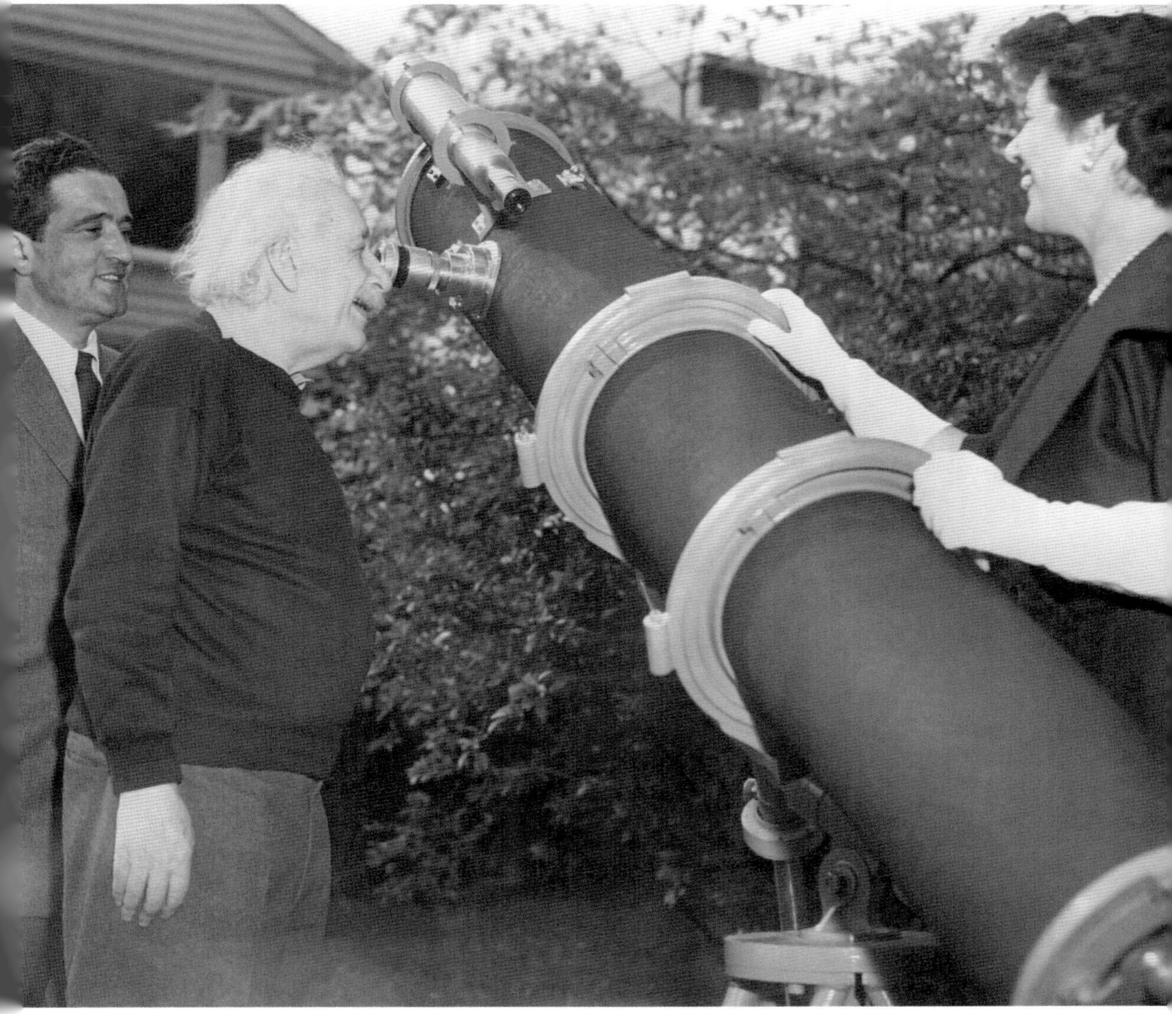

Immanuel Velikovsky (1895–1979)

Settling in town in his later years, the Russian-born scientist author was already highly controversial for the theories he presented in such bestselling books as *Worlds in Collision*. Velikovsky postulated that past close encounters with immense comets and asteroids had dramatically affected the Earth's geological and even astronomical history. Supporters contend that Velikovsky was decades ahead of his time in raising the issue of disastrous (literally, "of an evil star") close encounters with celestial objects. Critics charged that his interpretations of cataclysmic Biblical events as evidence for his theories amounted to dangerously misleading pseudoscience. The controversy is far from over, but Veliokovsky might have gained satisfaction from one posthumous development—his daughter succeeded in donating his papers to Princeton University. (Corbis.)

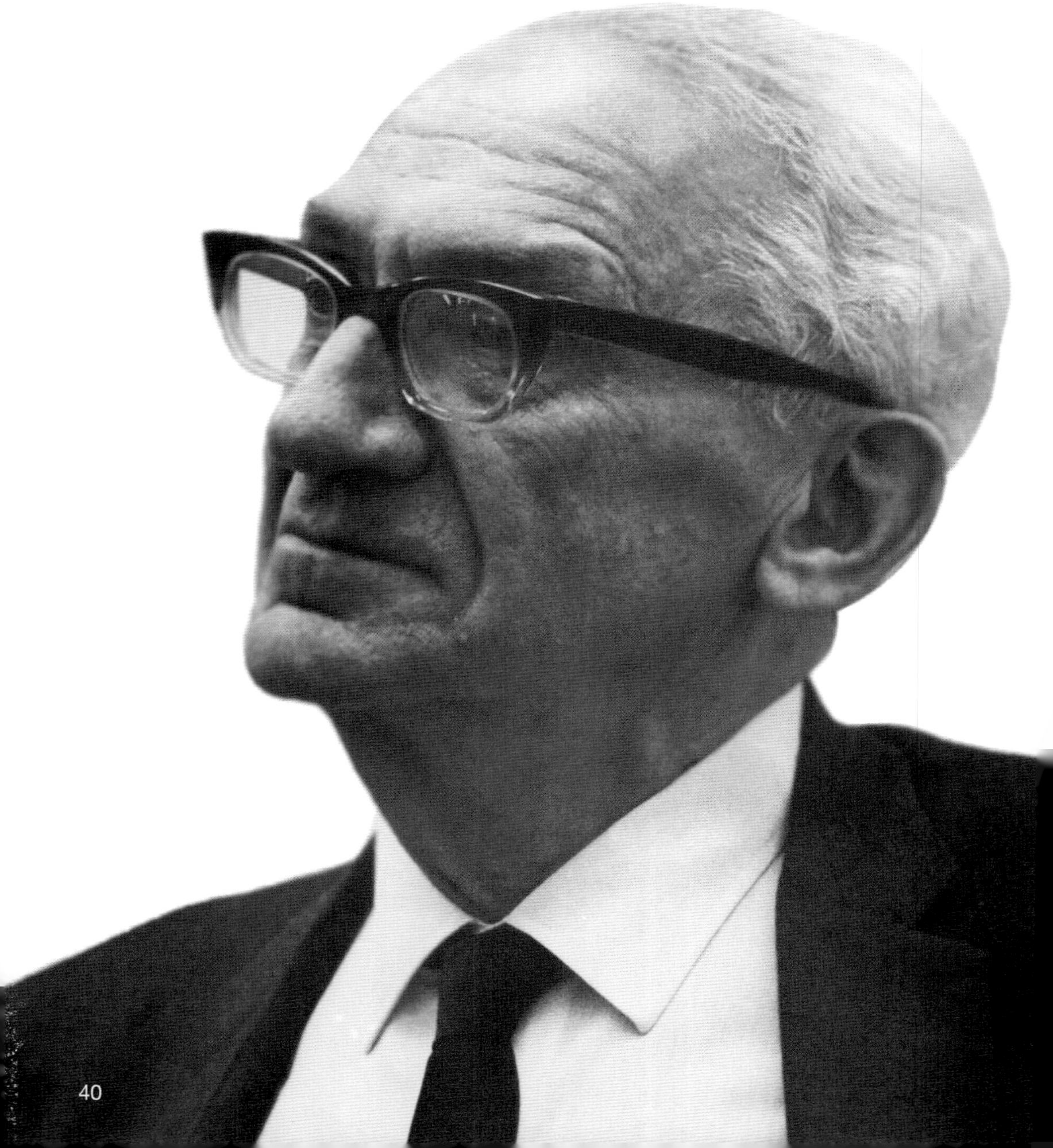

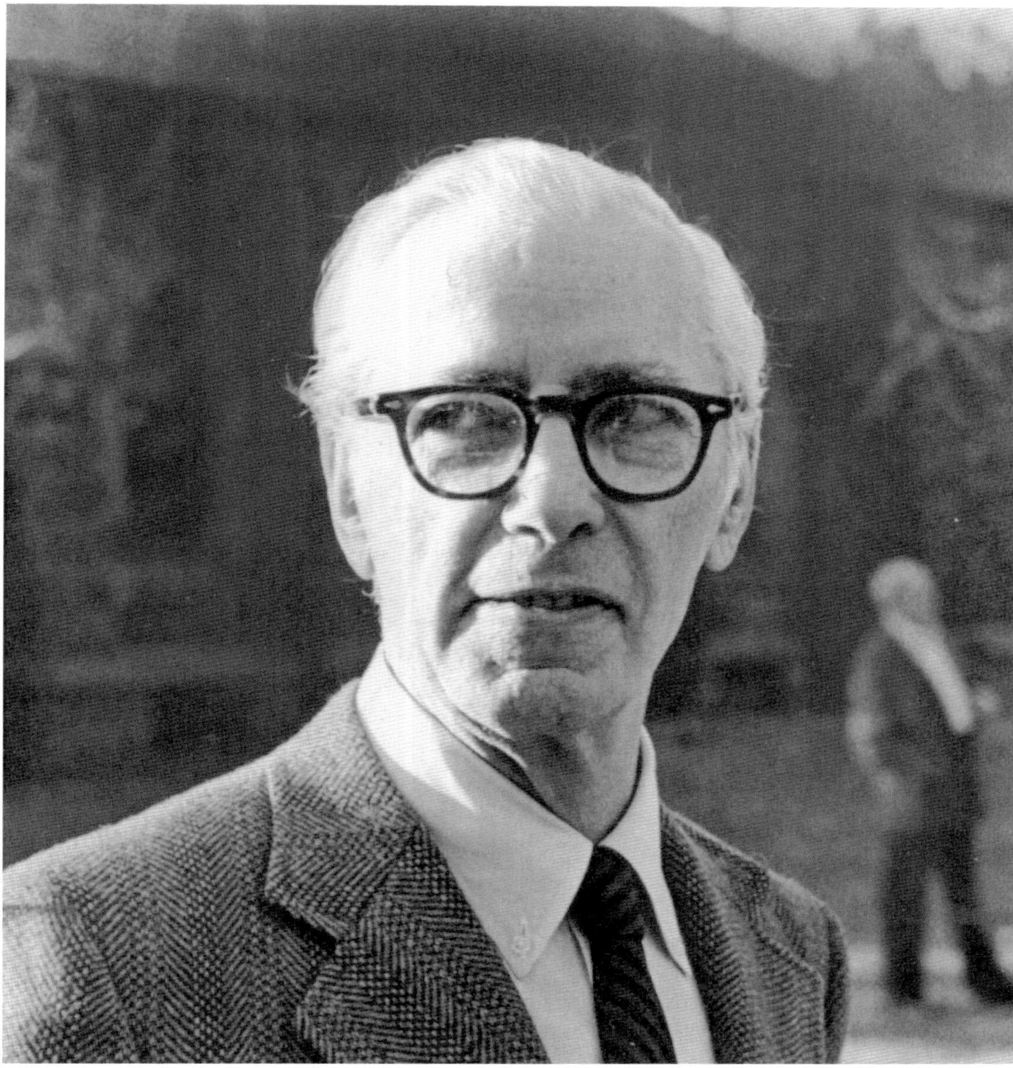

Ashley Montagu (1905–1999)

The British-born anthropologist was one of many prominent scientists and researchers who made Princeton their home while not having an appointment at the university. Dismissed from Rutgers University due to suspicions about his political views, Montagu moved to Princeton in 1955 and continued to thrive both as an intellectual force and popularizer of anthropology. He was a frequent guest on *The Tonight Show Starring Johnny Carson*; his bestselling books include *The Natural Superiority of Women* and *The Elephant Man: A Study in Human Dignity.* An influential academic theorist on the roles of gender and racial concepts in shaping human societies, he was also a dedicated humanist who spoke out against the culturally dictated genital mutilation of children. (Ashley Montagu Institute.)

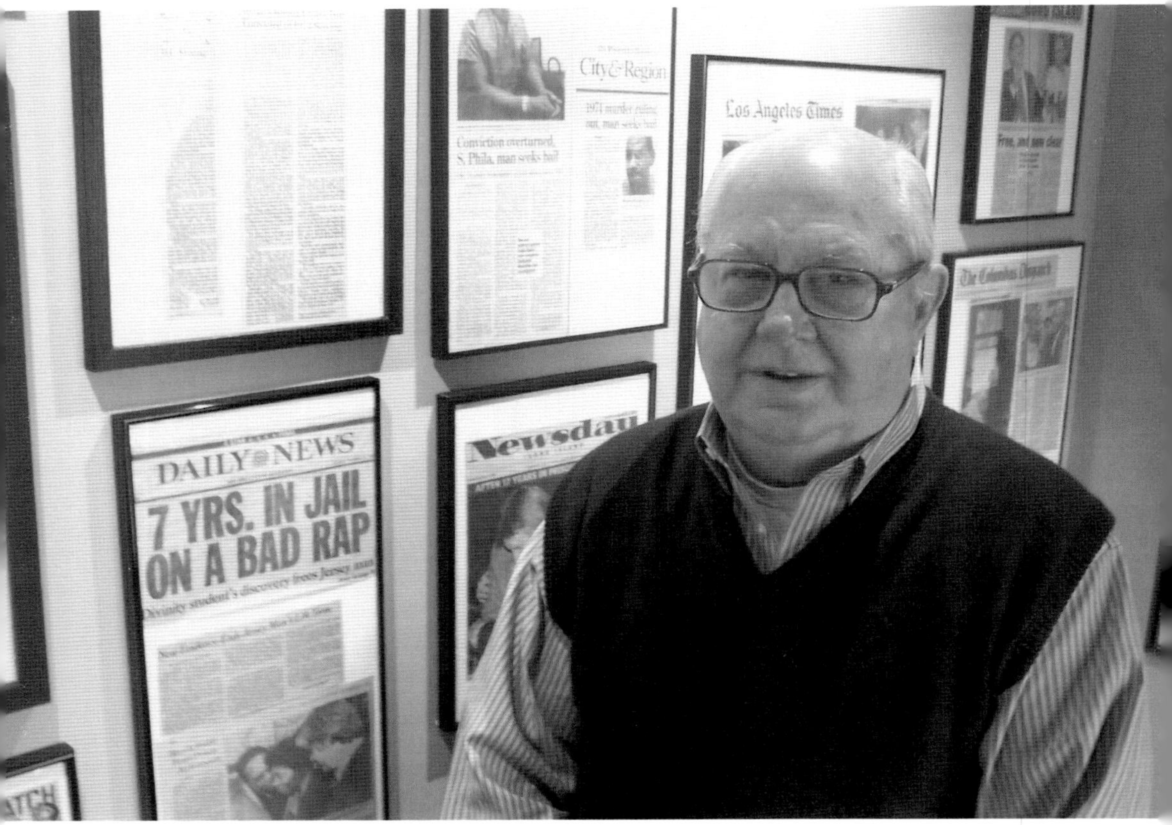

James McCloskey, Founder of Centurion Ministries
James McCloskey's research is not done with particle accelerators, by compiling public opinion questionnaires, or by crunching immense mathematical formulas. McCloskey and his assistants labor in court records, police reports, legal depositions, eyewitness statements and DNA analyses. His Princeton-based Centurion Ministries is dedicated to freeing prisoners sentenced to life imprisonment or even execution for crimes they demonstrably did not commit.

Born and raised in Havertown near Philadelphia to a prosperous family (his father's construction business was a contractor on major Philadelphia sports stadiums), McCloskey eventually felt called to spiritual pursuits. He entered Princeton Theological Seminary in 1979, at age of 37. As part of required fieldwork toward his master of divinity degree, McCloskey became a student chaplain at Trenton State Prison. There, his first-person contacts convinced him that some prisoners were the victims of terrible miscarriages of justice. He first succeeded in freeing Jorge de los Santos, an inmate convicted of murder. From there has come an impressive history of salvaging lives. In 1983, after receiving his degree, McCloskey founded Centurion Ministries as a nonsectarian organization ("I'm the only Princeton resident who made this their home because it's halfway between Trenton and Rahway state prisons," he observes with a smile). Centurion Ministries does not accept every appeal; it carefully examines the hundreds of inquiries it receives annually and has only about 20 cases under review at any time. As of this writing, it has taken up 87 cases in which 53 wrongfully convicted men and women in the United States and Canada have been freed. (Author.)

CHAPTER FOUR

Telling the Story

In his introduction to "Literary Landmarks of Princeton" (an article in the *Princeton University Library Chronicle* of autumn 1967 that encapsulated a landmark Firestone Library exhibit of the same name), Alfred L. Bush noted that a colleague of his had "recently . . . surmised that one out every three passers-by on Nassau Street is the author of a book."

Whether that was more accurate in 1967 before Princeton's population greatly expanded and diversified—or whether it was ever accurate at all—there has indeed been and continues to be a local mystique about books, bookstores, writing, and publishing. (This author, for one, is exceedingly grateful for such an atmosphere!)

Again, the presence of the university and the educational institutions that followed it historically has been vital. By publishing, academe and the local literary world have not perished but persisted and proliferated. As noted in Chapter Two, Princeton became a congenial location for writing, removed from the noisy distractions of a city but not so isolated that it is without resources. Indeed, several authors have gratefully noted that the university's formidable research collection (housed beginning in 1873 in the Chancellor Green Building and in the Firestone Memorial Library in 1948) provided decisive resources for their best work.

But it would be shortsighted to think of literary Princeton only in terms of higher learning. Publishing and education have thrived here at the most basic levels, as early as 1786 when Scottish immigrant James Tod moved from Philadelphia, where he had been running a school, to set up the first printing press and newspaper, the original *Princeton Packet*, which lasted but two years before Tod moved on to what is now Brooklyn and resumed teaching.

Over the years, public and private schools at the grade and secondary level have thrived. The figures associated with many of them are legendary in their own right but too numerous to allow all to have individual profiles. But many living Princetonians will recognize, especially in connection with independent schools, such names as Miss (Laura) Gildner, Miss (Mary) Mason, Miss (May Margaret) Fine, and John Gale Hun.

Worthy successors to James Tod include the next printer in Princeton, Daniel Borrenstein, from London who arrived in the spring of 1824. Printing in the late 19th and early 20th centuries went type-in-press with newspaper publication. Charles LaTourette revived the name *Princeton Packet*. As an elderly man, LaTourette was convinced by Bernard Kilgore (1908–1967), who was then commuting from Princeton to New York where he headed up Dow Jones & Company and was editor/publisher of the *Wall*

Street Journal, to sell the operation; Kilgore proceeded to turn it into a modern periodical of influential streamlined layout, eventually the flagship of a group of community newspapers. The Stuart family, until recently longtime publishers of the *Town Topics*, made their weekly a true Princeton institution, which it remains today. Meanwhile Richard K. Rein (born 1947) attended Princeton University, where he was editor of the *Daily Princetonian*. After his 1969 graduation, Rein moved quickly into a position as a writer for *Time* magazine and, later, its successful celebrity-oriented sister *People*. He returned to Princeton as a freelance writer, where he soon recognized that the business and office park boom along Route 1 had created a new community, which, although spread across several municipalities, shared a common "Princeton" mental map. Seeing a market for a newspaper to serve this readership, in 1984, he founded *U.S. 1: Princeton's Business & Entertainment Journal*, which recently completed a synergistic merger with the Community Newspaper Group.

But it is with authors this chapter concludes. Again, a legion of worthy writers on the faculties of Princeton University and the Institute for Advanced Study have been featured in other Arcadia volumes and must regretfully be left out here due to space limitations. In addition, there have been numerous authors who did major work while temporarily living in Princeton and serving as guest lecturers at the university, such as T.S. Eliot, who wrote most of his 1949 play *The Cocktail Party* while living in a small house off Alexander Street.

But this humble author hopes that the reader will be intrigued enough to pick up works by those profiled—or simply be pleasantly surprised by the many famous writers whose close connections to the town of Princeton might be little known.

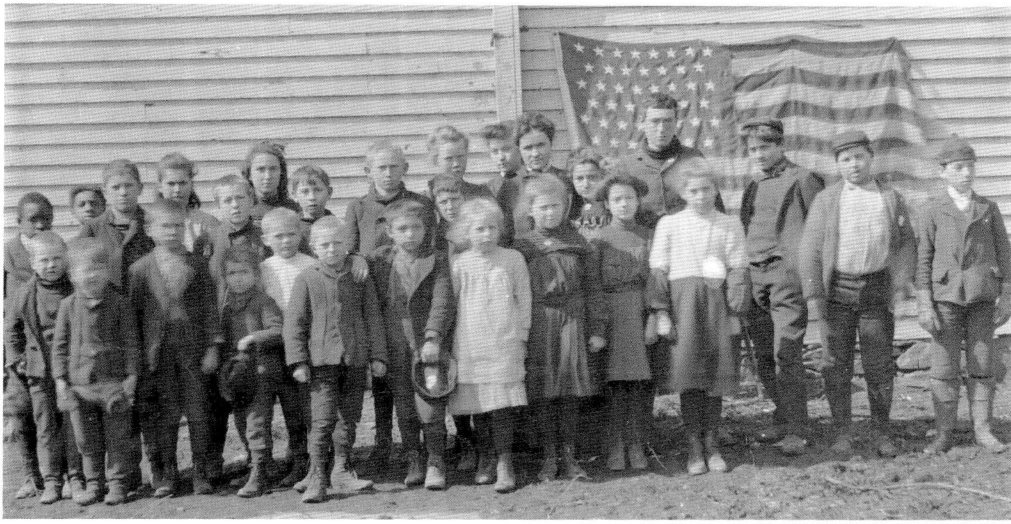

Stony Brook Public School

As noted earlier, that the Stony Brook neighborhood west of town saw habitation long before what is now Princeton, with Native American encampments (see page 13) and then the farms, blacksmith shops, and meetinghouses of Quakers (see page 16). Therefore, the one-room public school at Stony Brook must be honored as one of the most historically significant educational institutions in a region that now boosts many. Presiding over generations of little learners was Mary Louise Snook, shown here near the center of a school group. She was compassionate; for example, slow-learning or nearsighted children were given seats close to the blackboard. However, she was also strict. "The fear of Miss Snooks," observed one former student, using her nickname, "is the beginning of all wisdom." (HSP.)

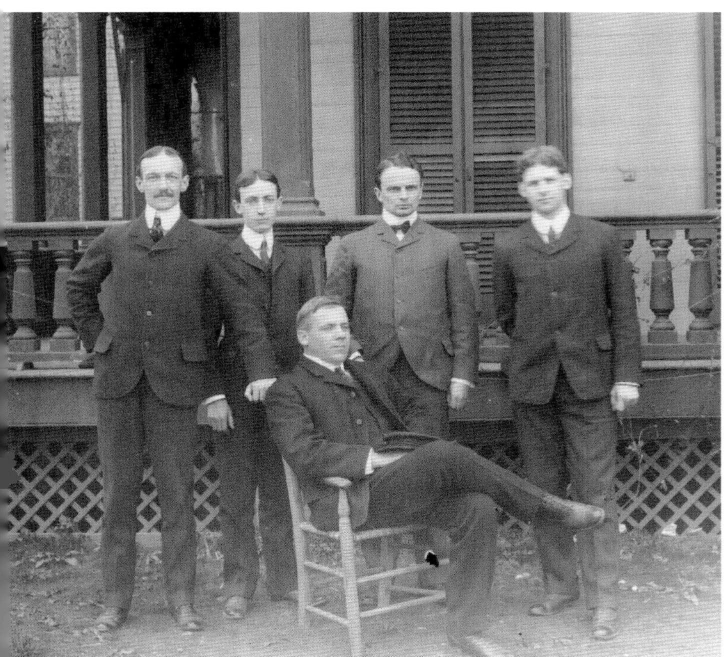

Princeton Preparatory School

This private secondary school was founded in 1873 by the College of New Jersey to successfully prepare students for admission to "Old Nassau." Financial issues caused the college to formally divest itself of Princeton Prep in the 1880s, but school founder John Burchard Fine, seated here with faculty members, continued the school successfully for many additional years. His sister May Margaret Fine founded Miss Fine's, the prestigious local private school for girls, which merged in 1965 with the Princeton Country Day boys' school (one of Princeton Prep's successors) to become Princeton Country Day. (HSP.)

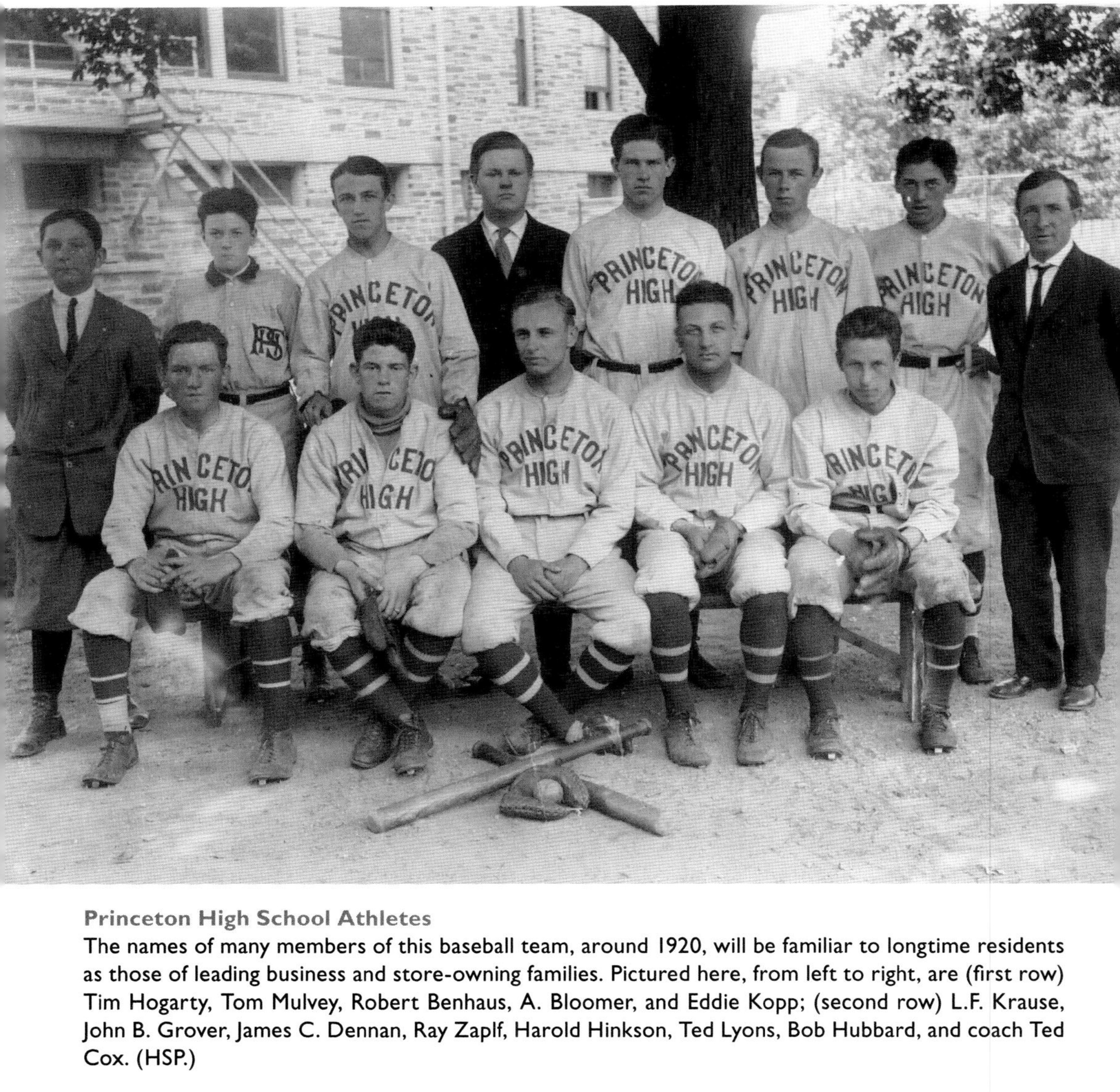

Princeton High School Athletes

The names of many members of this baseball team, around 1920, will be familiar to longtime residents as those of leading business and store-owning families. Pictured here, from left to right, are (first row) Tim Hogarty, Tom Mulvey, Robert Benhaus, A. Bloomer, and Eddie Kopp; (second row) L.F. Krause, John B. Grover, James C. Dennan, Ray Zaplf, Harold Hinkson, Ted Lyons, Bob Hubbard, and coach Ted Cox. (HSP.)

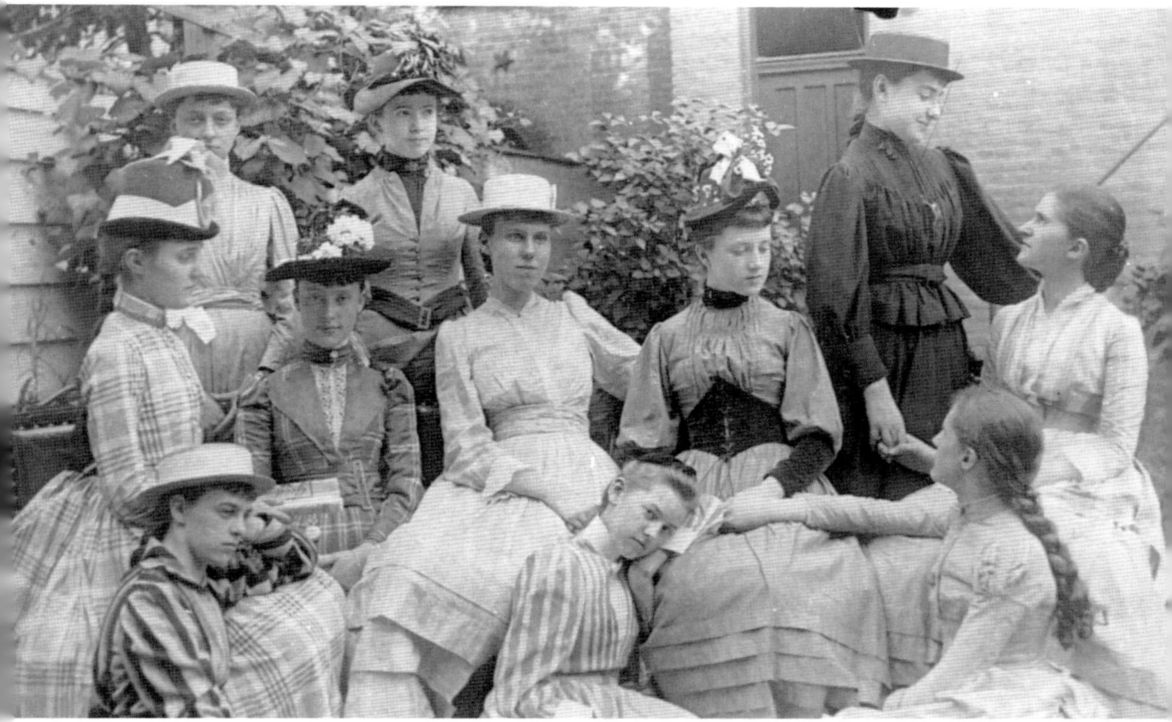

Evelyn College for Women

From 1876 to 1886, a small center of higher education attended by these female scholars was housed in "The Pines," named for the trees shading it. The house, now divided into apartments and condominiums, still stands on Evelyn Place (pronounced "EEV a linn"). Founder and chief instructor Joshua Hall McIlvaine envisioned not a finishing school for husband hunters but a serious experience in higher education for women when few were available—an institution that could become for Princeton University what Radcliffe was to Harvard. *Harper's Magazine* noted some Princeton faculty members (all male, of course) were skeptical that "a woman's mind could grasp learning heretofore supposed to be masculine property." But Evelyn College proved them wrong. Yes, the dances were well chaperoned, the surroundings well advertised as healthful, and teas served every afternoon at 5:00 p.m. But the curriculum was broad based and rigorous. Sadly, McIlvanine's death and a concurrent national recession, causing college tuition for daughters to be suddenly considered an expensive luxury, ended this noble experiment. (HSP.)

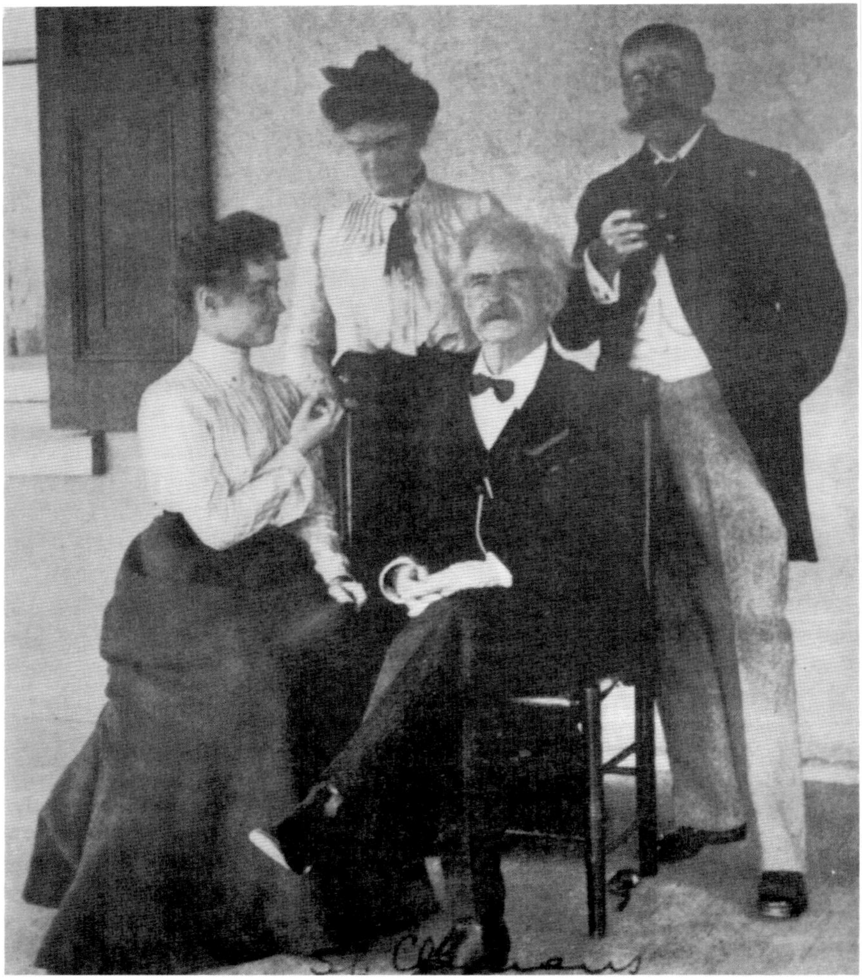

Laurence Hutton (1843–1904)

Hutton, literary editor of *Harper's Magazine* in New York for 12 years and lecturer on English literature at the university, was known for his series of books on "literary landmarks" of various major cities of the world. A tall and red-headed Scotsman, Laurence Hutton moved to Princeton, becoming an early commuter to New York for work. Mark Twain and Helen Keller, with her teacher Annie Sullivan (shown here with Hutton, who stands on the right), were among the distinguished visitors at Hutton's home in Princeton, the former Princeton Inn on the site of the Borough Hall, which he renamed "Peep O' Day." Hutton introduced Twain and Keller at the end of March 1895. Twain himself even seriously considered moving here. After returning from a Europe sojourn, Hutton wrote the following to a friend: "Hereafter my address will be Peep O'Day, Princeton, and so it is going to keep on being—until it is Princeton Cemetery." When Hutton died in June 1904, traditional, simple Scottish custom was observed. There were no honorary pallbearers, and his loyal employees, a coachman, two horse-cab drivers, a gardener, and two farmhands, carried his casket. (PR.)

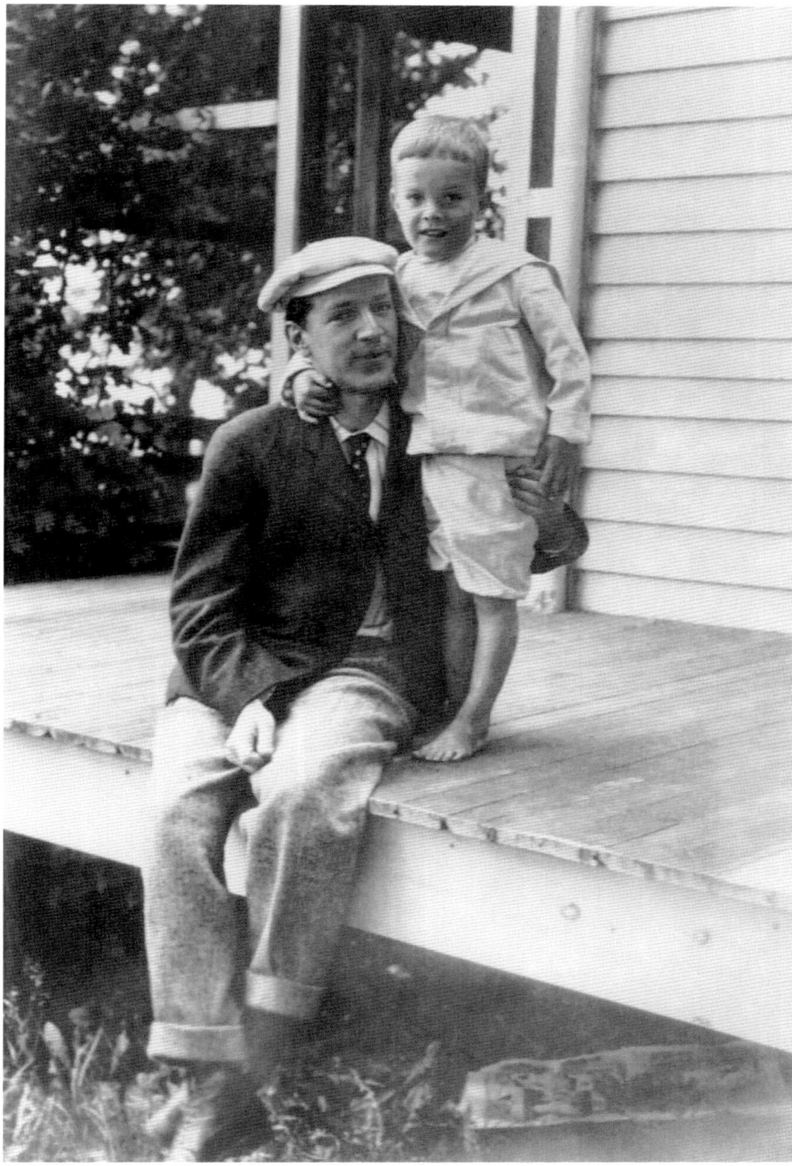

Upton Sinclair (1878 –1968)
Sinclair spent several productive summers in the Princeton Township countryside on Ridgeview Road in the Cedar Grove section near Province Line Road. He lived with his wife, Meta, in a tent on a corner of land rented from farmers Isaac and Caroline Leigh. Sinclair describes the tent in the first chapter of his autobiography. It was in this humble shelter that he found peace, quiet, and concentration to write his novel *Manassas*. Sinclair noted with gratitude that his research material came from "the Civil War collection at Princeton College Library; they let me take home armfuls of books." He later constructed a humble bungalow with a veranda. Here, he wrote his 1906 "muckraking" best seller *The Jungle* whose fact-based descriptions of deplorably filthy conditions in the nation's meatpacking industry (in which Sinclair himself had worked for a year gathering secret first-person observations) shocked America and helped pass major consumer protection laws. (Corbis.)

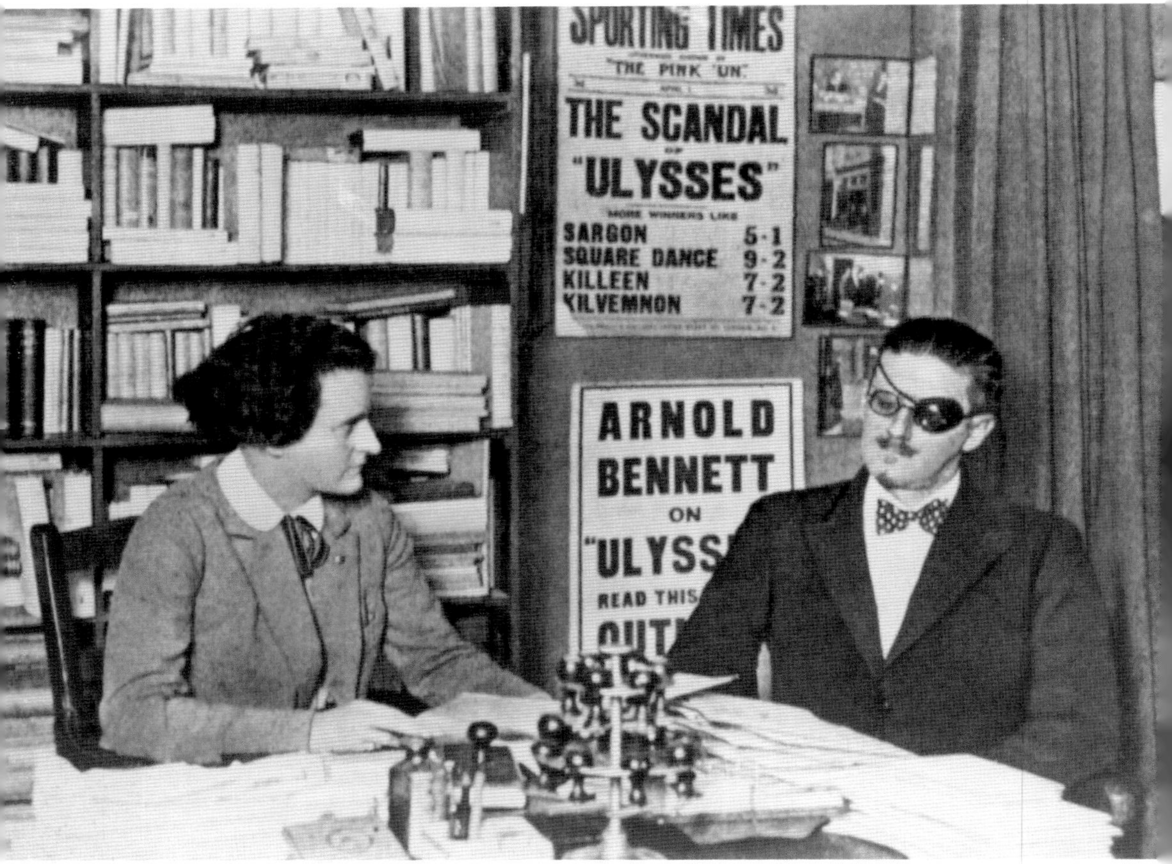

Sylvia Beach (1887–1962)

The daughter of the pastor of the staid First Presbyterian Church of Princeton, Beach is revered today by literati as an avant-garde figure and cultural rebel. She was the founder of Shakespeare & Company, the legendary Paris bookshop, which became a focus and refuge for struggling expatriate writers. In 1922, she published *Ulysses* by James Joyce (shown here visiting Beach). Now regarded as a literary masterpiece, this rather surrealistic novel was at the time widely considered obscene, as witness posters about the controversy on the wall behind Beach and Joyce. In 1941, Beach closed her store in protest against the Nazi occupation of France. (Corbis.)

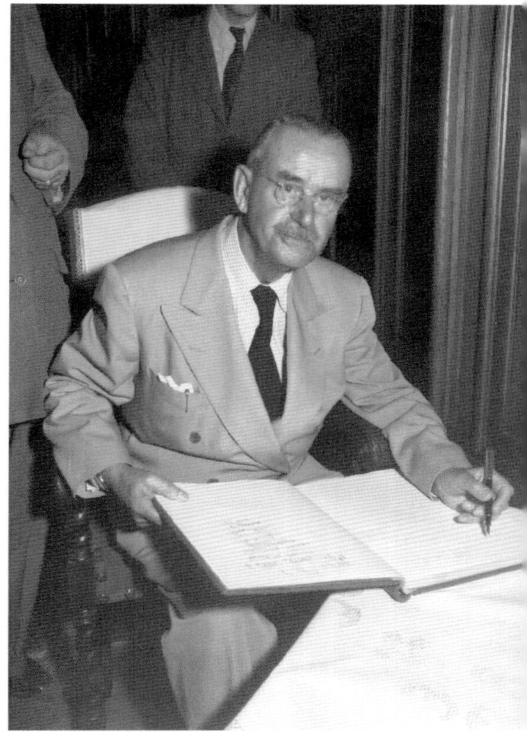

Thomas Mann (1875–1955)

The German-born Nobel Prize–winning author of *The Magic Mountain*, *The Glass Bead Game*, and other major early-20th-century novels was among the most prominent intellectual émigrés who fled Nazi-dominated Europe. Mann's repeated protests and warnings about Fascism succeeded only in raising Nazi ire, and he left his native Germany in 1933. Accepting an invitation to lecture at Princeton University, he arrived in 1938 and lived at 65 Stockton Street (now the Aquinas Institute). His three years in town were nearly idyllic. One autumn, in a letter to a friend, Mann described the setting as "parklike, well suited to walks, with amazingly beautiful trees which now, in the Indian summer, glow in the most magnificent colors." (Corbis.)

Mann and Einstein

Thomas Mann and Albert Einstein were good friends and visited each other frequently. Coincidentally, upon first coming to Princeton in 1932, Einstein had first rented an apartment in the brick building directly across Library Place from what became Mann's residence. In 1938, right at the beginning of Mann's Princeton period, they attended the New York premiere of an antiwar film. (Corbis.)

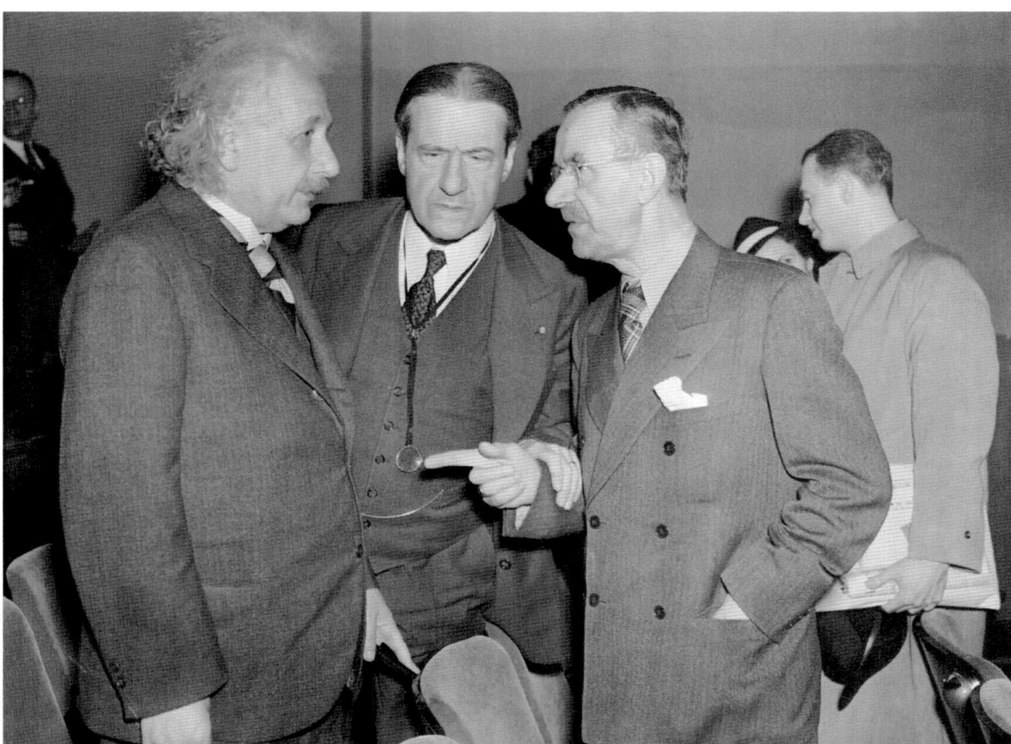

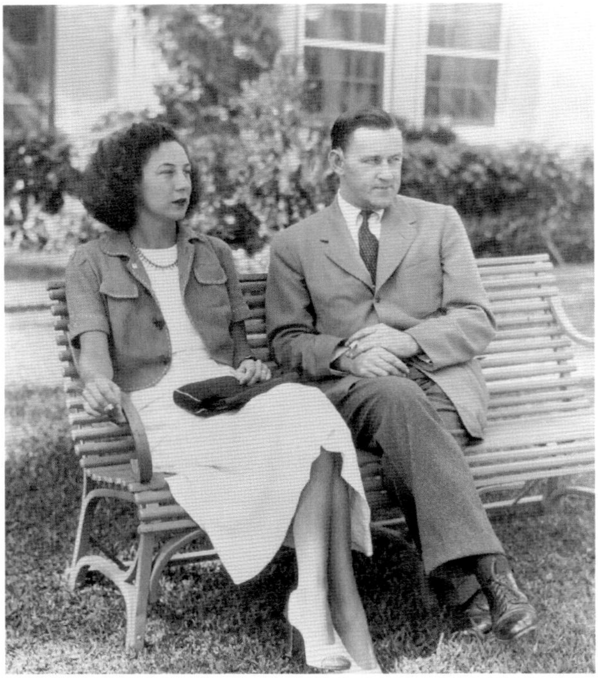

John O'Hara (1905–1970)
Bestselling writer O'Hara was a voluminous and much-honored talent. His novels *Appointment in Samarra* (1934) and *Ten North Frederick* (1955) and his collection of short stories *Pal Joey* (1940) are among his many critical and commercial successes. Moving to Princeton in 1949, O'Hara and his second wife, Belle Wylie (shown here), found a congenial home on scenic and exclusive Pretty Brook Road. (Corbis.)

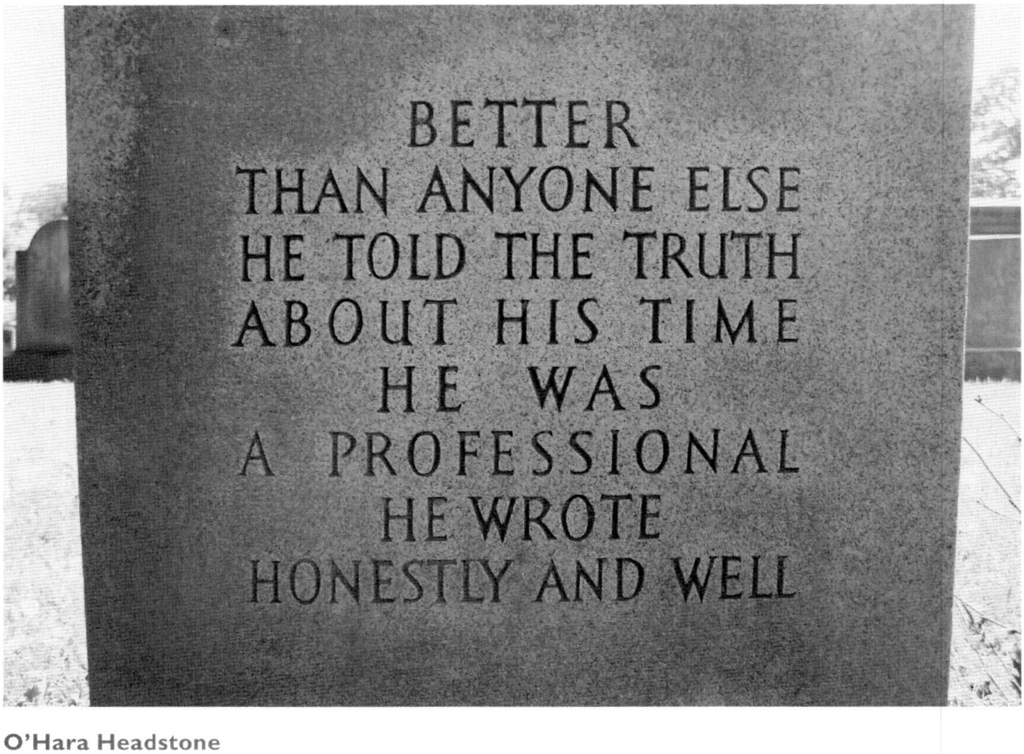

O'Hara Headstone
O'Hara and third wife, Katharine Barnes, are buried together in the Princeton cemetery. The inscription on his headstone was self-composed but reflects his greatness and legacy. (Author.)

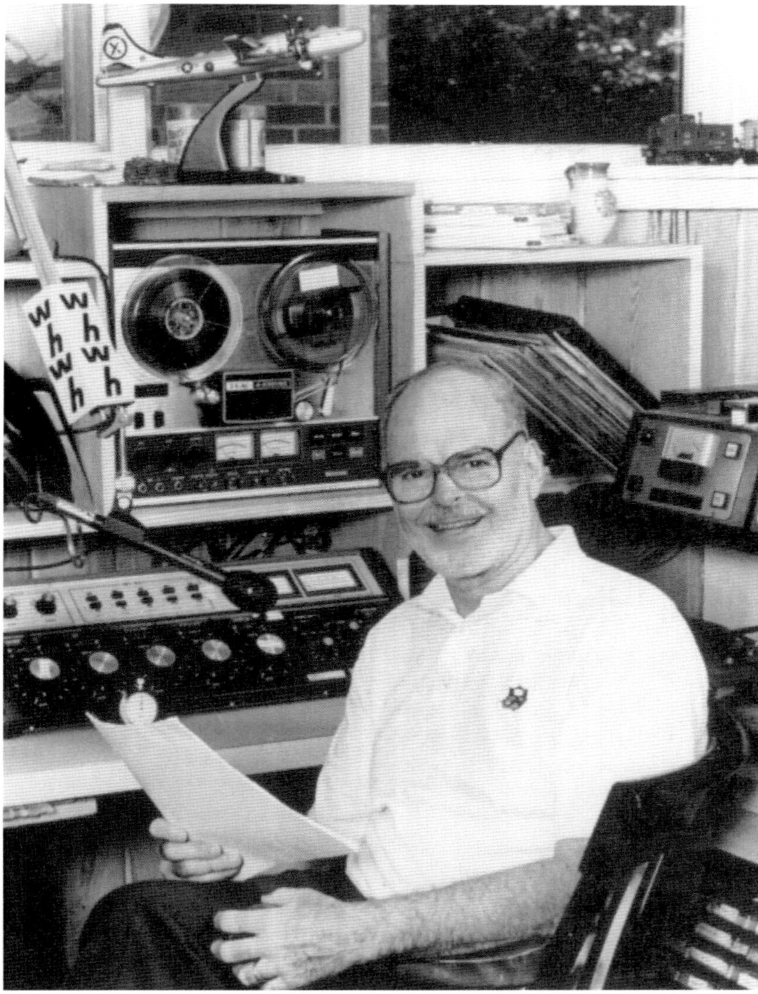

Herb Hobler

Born in 1925, Hobler is a stalwart member of the Princeton University class of 1946, whose education was delayed only by his World War II service. He settled here and became a commuting veteran of another great force, the National Broadcasting Corporation in New York. Hobler sold the first commercial spot on the original *Tonight* show on NBC television. Going out on his own, he founded the Nassau Broadcasting Company, a nod to Princeton University, also known as "Old Nassau" and the town's main street; the initials "NBC" were of course also the same as those of his former company. In 1963, he put on the air Princeton AM radio station WHWH (whose call letters contained the initials of his name). The station served Central New Jersey and nearby Pennsylvania with not only news and music but also valued public services, such as the daily "Pet Patrol" segment that reunited lost animals with their anxious owners. Hobler later started a sister FM station, WPST. His energy and enthusiasm have been a life constant, as witness his innumerable business and charitable ventures. A notable example is his involvement in the Spirit of Princeton's 20th Century Recognition Walk (see page 122–123). He once characteristically achieved a multiyear stretch of walking a mile every morning, even if it meant doing his "roadwork" in the aisle of a transcontinental flight. This personal stamina serves him well in a "retirement" filled with projects and a continuing love of Princeton. "It's a one of a kind town," Hobler says, "and people are proud to live here." (Herbert W. Hobler.)

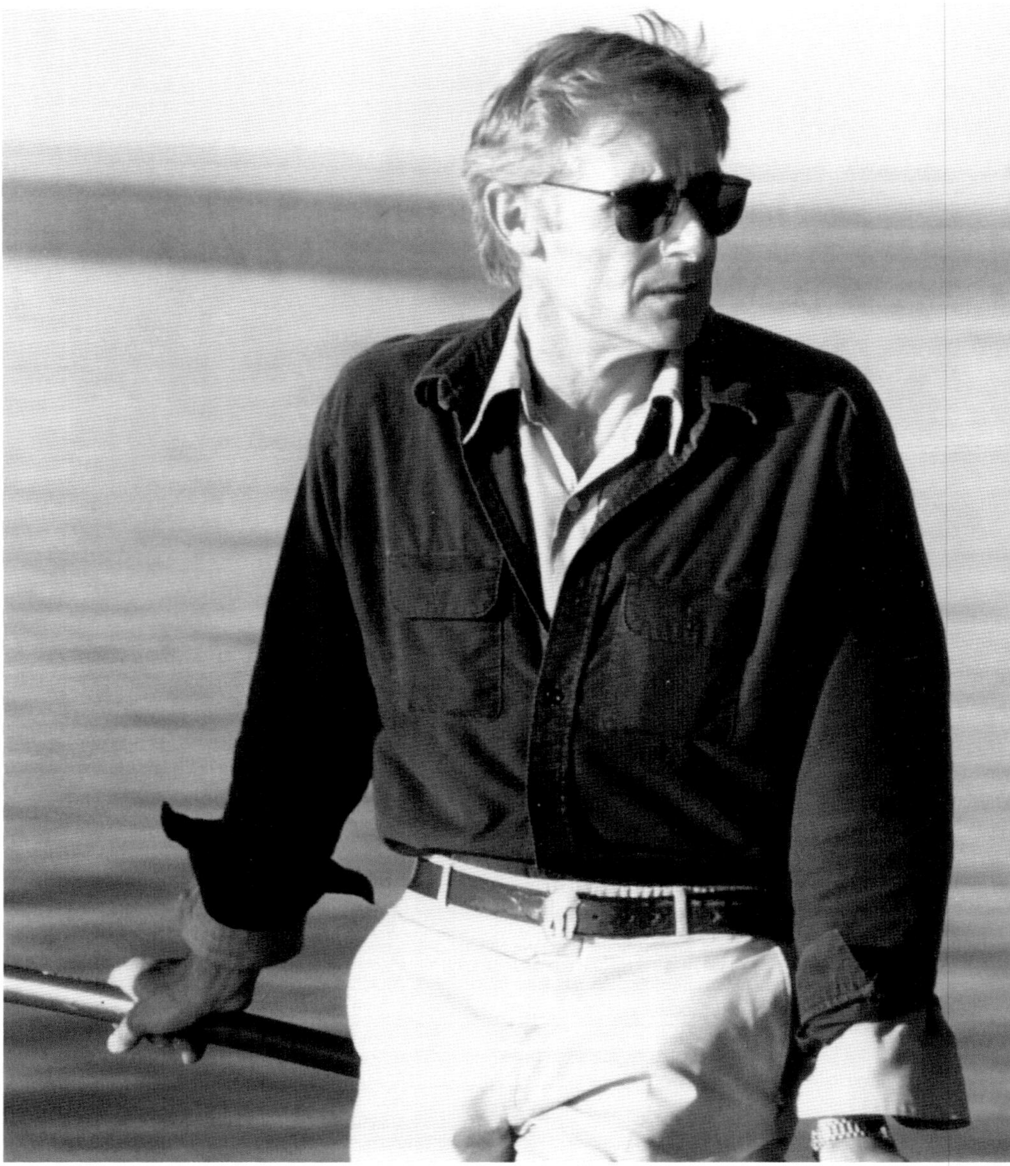

Peter Benchley (1940–2006)
Benchley continued a family history of literary creativity—his father was author Nathaniel Benchley, his grandfather was humorist and Algonquin Round Table founder Robert Benchley. Peter did a stint as a speechwriter for Pres. Lyndon Johnson. Then, his wife, Wendy recalls, "we searched for a town with a mix of people, an active community and cultural life and, most of all, a heart and soul. Princeton had it all." Of his many novels, Peter is especially remembered for *Jaws*, a best-seller about a rampaging great white shark that became a blockbuster movie. But he strongly opposed the macho culture of hunting these magnificent and increasingly threatened sea creatures. Until his passing, Peter Benchley was an eloquent activist for the conservation of great whites and the oceans in which they live. (Scott Stallard.)

Gina Kolata

The *New York Times* science/medical reporter, her mathematician husband, Bill, who works at a nonprofit professional society for industrial and applied mathematics, and their family have found an ideal base of operations in Princeton. Kolata modestly declines to be referred to as "a Princeton writer." But like other creative residents, this enthusiastic runner and cyclist values being able to find herself on untrafficked byways within minutes after leaving her house: "When I'm out in the country I can be the only person on the road," she says. "It's like an oasis."

The couple's convenient commute from "lovely, centrally placed" Princeton to offices in New York and Philadelphia is another plus widely reported by others. Kolata is also a staunch supporter of buying locally; Princeton store owners, she says, "know me and I love them."

"We've talked about where to go when we retire," says Kolata. "But why move? We're in paradise." (Gina Kolata.)

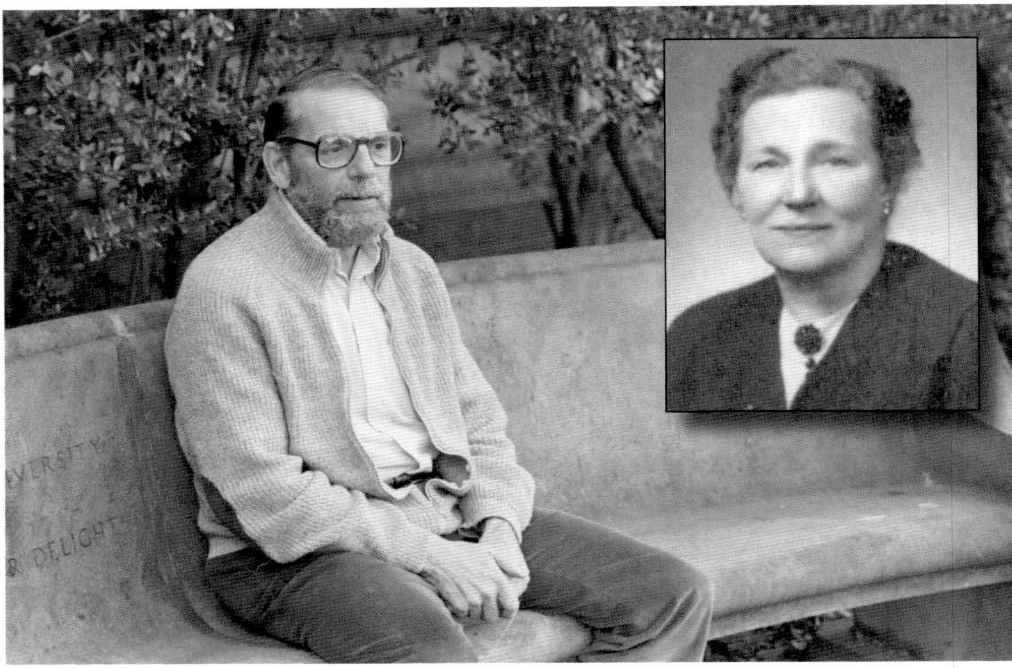

John McPhee

Winner of a Pulitzer Prize for general nonfiction and a longtime *New Yorker* contributor, McPhee, born in 1931, is a Princeton native who "grew up right in the middle of town" and, from kindergarten through eighth grade, attended public grammar school at 185 Nassau Street.

His Ohio-born physician father, Harry, was an early specialist in what is now called sports medicine. In 1928, he came from Iowa State to Princeton University, where he worked with athletes and trainers and, later, served as an Olympic and Pan American Games team doctor. Perhaps not surprisingly, John developed an international outlook and became an active basketball and tennis player at Princeton High School. As an adult, he became an avid cyclist and fly-fisher. He caddied locally at the Springdale Golf Course. An after-school job working with Princeton University biological specimens boosted his interest in natural history. Matriculating from Princeton High School in 1948, he studied for a year at Deerfield Academy and then graduated from Princeton in 1953.

The university's capacious Firestone Library eventually decided him on establishing a professional base in his hometown. He says, "I knew if I ever got to do the work I wanted, this would be the resource." Skilled at making even arcane subjects accessible, McPhee often unfolds his topics through the engaging stories of their central participants, with a renowned ability to organize a chaos of information and anecdotes into a flowing narrative. He credits this skill to the late Olive McKee (inset), a legendary Princeton High School English teacher who staunchly schooled her students in sentence and story outlining. (Above, Corbis; inset, Princeton High School.)

CHAPTER FIVE

Creative Legends

As with its multitudinous researchers, educators and writers, Princeton has had a surfeit of famous artists—painters, sculptors, photographers, actors, directors, and musicians—and for probably similar reasons. Granted, numerous among these became legendary after they were local. But many independently comment about the creative atmosphere and encouragement they enjoyed during their formative years in town.

It may seem contradictory, and perhaps unfair, that a pictorial history of Princeton would have a dearth of images of photographers. This writer will, in his own defense, point out that painters may delight in self-portraits (sometimes overly so), but photographers seem too busy recording others to take the time to preserve their own images. Here are some of Princeton's finest photographers: the Rose Studios, which, in the 19th century, created innumerable town and campus views as well as carte de visit studio portraits (thankfully, a large collection of Rose Studio glass negative plates survived to become part of the collection of the Historical Society of Princeton); Henry Pannell and Romus Broadway, who also served this market; Orren Jack Turner Sr. and Jr., who, after the closing of the Rose Studios, dominated commercial photography in Princeton for some 60 years; and Pryde Brown, whose deceptively informal personal portraits and wedding photographs in casual settings are, in fact, informed by a highly insightful and disciplined professional eye, evincing an instantly recognizable style.

Among local painters, Rex Goreleigh (1902–1986) became known for sympathetically depicting the lives of migrant farmworkers in the state. He was an instructor with the Princeton Art Association who inspired a new generation of African American realist artists. Goreleigh is represented on page 81 with his evocative rendition of Mary Watts's country store. Another artist who found inspiration in local scenes and whose work provides valuable information as well as visual delight records was Vinton Duffield who created framed, detailed bas-relief models of historical local buildings. His renditions of Nassau Hall, Princeton Bank & Trust Building, the Nassau Club, Bainbridge House, the original Princeton Hospital, and other structures are superb, accurate records of these landmarks. His first serious miniatures project was an 11-building model of the Nassau Street structures that had been torn down to make way for Palmer Square.

Again, space regretfully does not permit inclusion of several important local creative entities and the persons who were for years their talented, dedicated directors, such as the Princeton Symphony Orchestra and Mark Laycott or the Princeton Ballet School and Mary Pat Robertson.

Among fans of amateur theatrical groups, the name PJ&B Players will bring back fond memories of rollicking, well-played musicals. Standing for "Princeton Junction and Back," this beloved and much missed musical theater group was not comprised only of commuters traveling on the "Dinky" shuttle to the main train station and back to town, but it had that happy identity and camaraderie. It was led for many years by Milton Lyon (1921–1995), longtime Triangle Show and McCarter Theatre director. PJ&B was active from the 1950s into the 1980s, by which time McCarter and its audience had grown, and there was no space in the schedules for community musical productions. A Gilbert & Sullivan Society (with George Gallup Jr. a stalwart) was led by Lee Bristol Jr., a true renaissance man who was a talented organist, pharmaceutical executive, and, later, president of Westminster Choir College. The Community Players with Herbert Mcaneny had a devoted following, as did Shakespeare '70 and the Princeton Summer Theatre, two mainstays of early outdoor public theater. Sallie B. Goodman (1928–2007) was a 1950 graduate of the Royal Academy of Dramatic Arts in London who married novelist George J.W. Goodman. They moved to Princeton in 1965 where she was active as an actress and director. The annual Sallie B. Goodman Artists Retreat, administered through the McCarter Theatre Center, a stretch of unencumbered creativity to stage talents.

Arthur Lithgow (1914–2004), father of award-winning actor John Lithgow (born 1945), served as artistic director of McCarter Theatre in Princeton from 1963 to 1972. His success there and at similar venues established him as a pioneer of the regional theater movement in America.

Among the most beautiful and influential of early Princeton aesthetic organizations was the Garden Club of Princeton, founded around 1912 and among the first such clubs in the United States. Its predominantly female membership included numerous professors' wives; serious horticulturists, they helped create Princeton's garden-like environs, so often admired by residents and visitors alike.

About this same time, a concert series was initiated that was the forerunner of today's fabulous full chart of university and town cultural offerings.

So, now please cue the music!

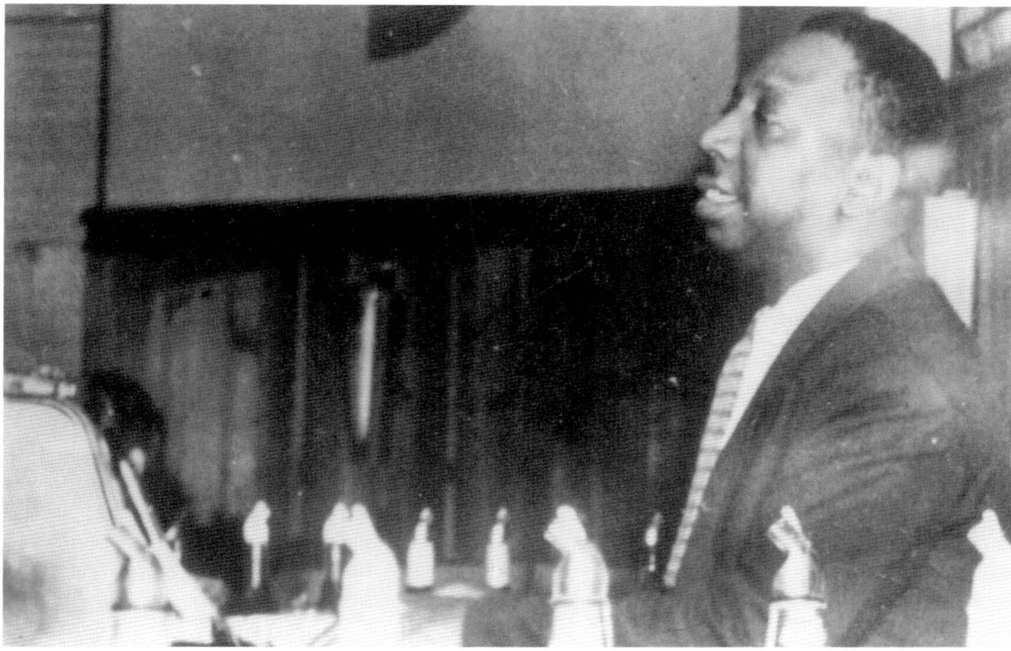

Donald Lambert (1904–1962)

Lambert, who was born in Princeton, was a popular African American jazz musician and composer who played the piano for many years in a Newark nightclub. Although his studio output was small, he was reckoned to rival the best-known "stride" pianists. Records released after his death came from informal live recordings. His appearance at the 1960 Newport Jazz Festival was a triumph, with some listeners declaring that he had outplayed even Eubie Blake and Willie "The Lion" Smith. One friend recalled that during jams, which often become fiercely competitive "cutting sessions" in jazz, Lambert "could hear chord changes coming a block away . . . He had an 'ear' in every fingertip . . . he could play the horseteeth like nobody else in the whole bloody world."

Lambert's headstone in the Princeton cemetery, donated and dedicated by admirers in 1982, is engraved with the musical notation of one of his signature riffs. (Above, PR; below, author.)

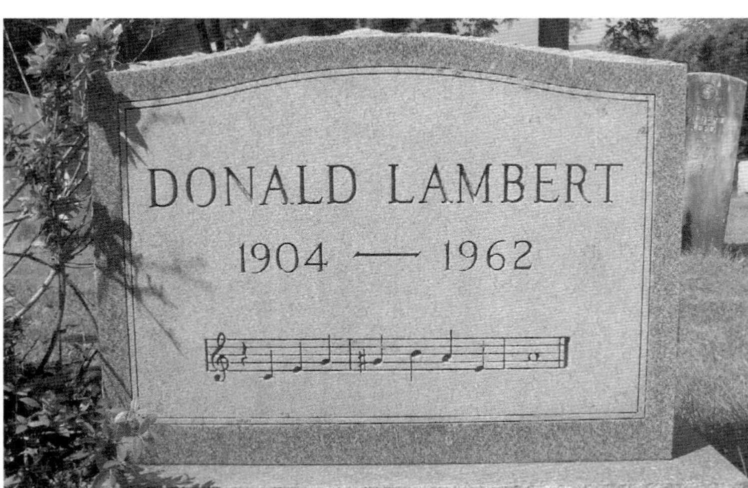

William H. Lockwood Jr.

For more than five decades, William Lockwood has booked music, dance, and other entertainments at the McCarter Theatre Center. "Institutionally, I kind of come with the building," he wryly observes.

Born in New York in 1937, his family relocated to Princeton in 1941. His father joined the university's faculty, and his mother taught for many years at Miss Fine's School and, later, Princeton Day School. A member of the Princeton University class of 1959, he founded Dana Productions in his senior year primarily to promote music shows on campus and in the region. A trip to California after graduation was satisfying, but to Lockwood even Los Angeles could not match New York City as the epicenter of entertainment. "In the business of the performing arts, it all emanates from New York," Lockwood says. So when Milt Lyon, then McCarter Theatre artistic director, hailed Lockwood back to Princeton, he returned; he actually worked under Lyon's successor, Arthur Lithgow. Lockwood divided his time between McCarter and Lincoln Center where he was head of programming from 1967 to 1993. "I commuted on the Dinky but managed to keep my McCarter hat," he says. Lockwood also helped open the Kimble Center and the New Jersey Performing Arts Center.

While the McCarter artistic directors have filled the stage with plays, Lockwood has produced music, including jazz and cabaret music programs; dance; and film series. In the community, his Princeton Adult School program "Second Chance Cinema" has been welcomed by cinemaphiles trying to catch great movies. One memorable coup was persuading a friend, superstar opera tenor Luciano Pavarotti, to perform at a McCarter fundraising gala. Lockwood of course escorted him into the hall, arm in arm (pictured below). It adds up to a legendary career, but what is the tally of performances? "Probably thousands," Lockwood says. (McCarter Theatre Center.)

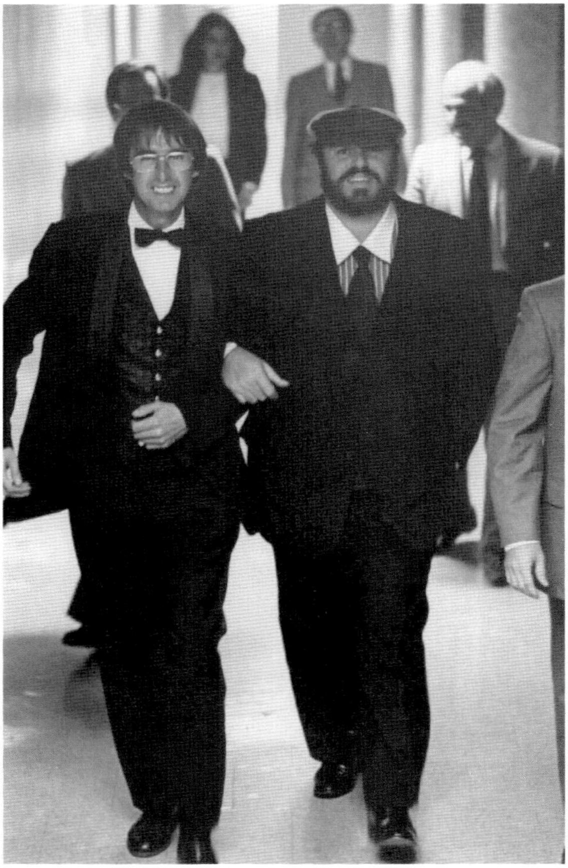

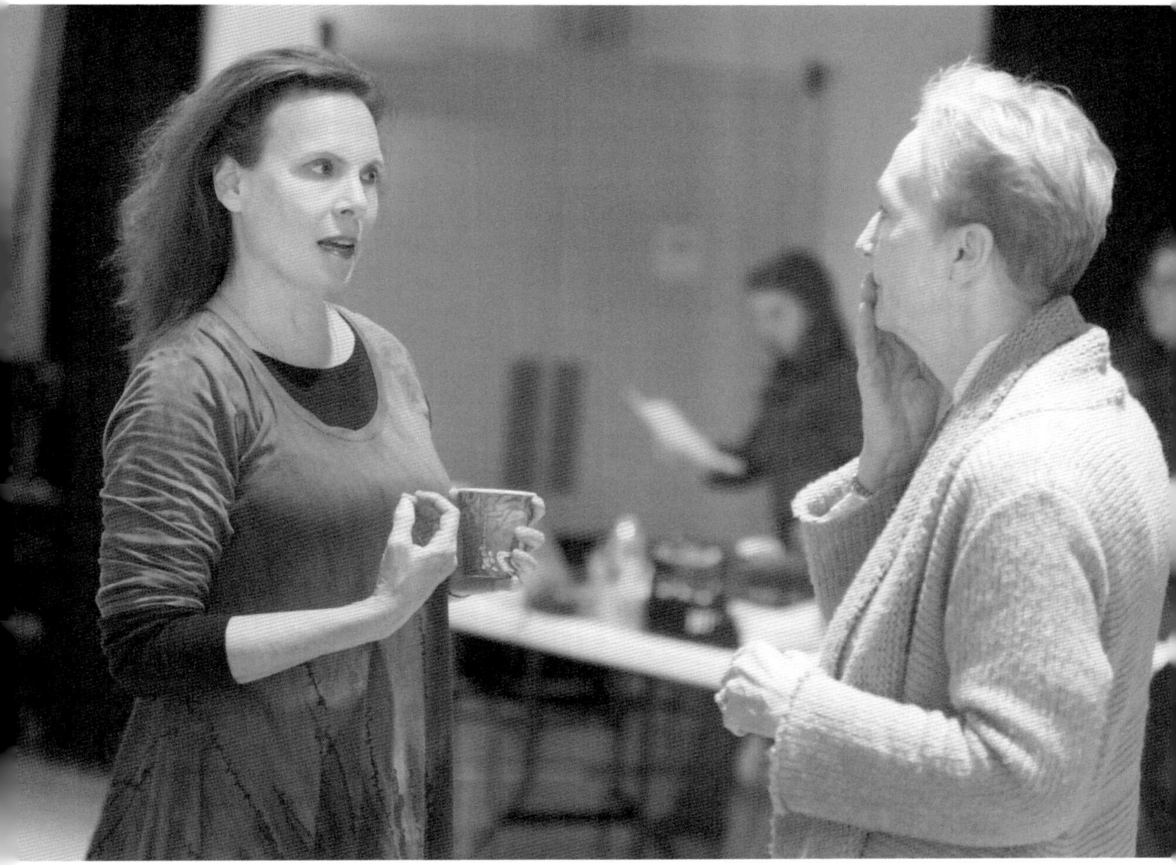

Emily Mann

Many young parents are delighted to bring up a child in the environment of Princeton. The prospect was especially pleasing in July 1990 for Emily Mann. She had been living a productive but peripathetic life as a freelance director, playwright, and screenwriter when she was offered the prestigious, but extraordinarily demanding, position of artistic director–playwright in residence at McCarter Theatre (which has historical links to Princeton University but is now an independent entity). In her 23rd McCarter season (as of this writing), Mann has overseen more than 125 productions, including world premieres of plays by such notables as Edward Albee and Christopher Durang. She is seen here directing Kathleen Chalfant in the 2013 McCarter revival of Albee's *A Delicate Balance*. Mann led the McCarter Theatre Center to a 1994 Tony Award for Outstanding Regional Theater, won the Dramatists Guild Hull-Warnier Award, and was named 2011 Person of the Year by the National Theatre Conference.

"Princeton has audiences that are open minded, intelligent and passionate," says Mann, who has built a following for thought-provoking plays that frequently evince a strong social consciousness. She likens Princeton to a European capital: "There's so much stimulation and excellence every time you turn a corner. And the beauty of the place—you're also living in a garden." (McCarter Theatre Center.)

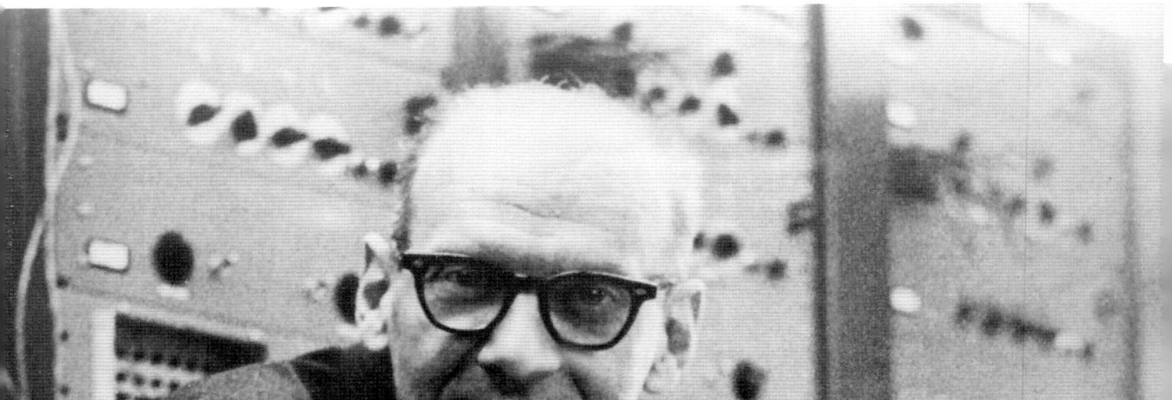

Milton Babbitt (1916–2011)

A dean of American music composers, teachers, and theorists, Babbitt studied with Roger Sessions and earned his master's of fine arts degree at Princeton in 1942, one of the first granted by the university. He later taught at the school at various times in mathematics and music, surely a unique achievement. Known for his stimulating critical writing, Babbitt was also a pioneer in electronic music, working with an early synthesizer at the Columbia-Princeton Electronic Music Center. His students ranged from legendary Broadway composer Stephen Sondheim to jazz guitarist and Princeton University graduate Stanley Jordan. (Library of Congress.)

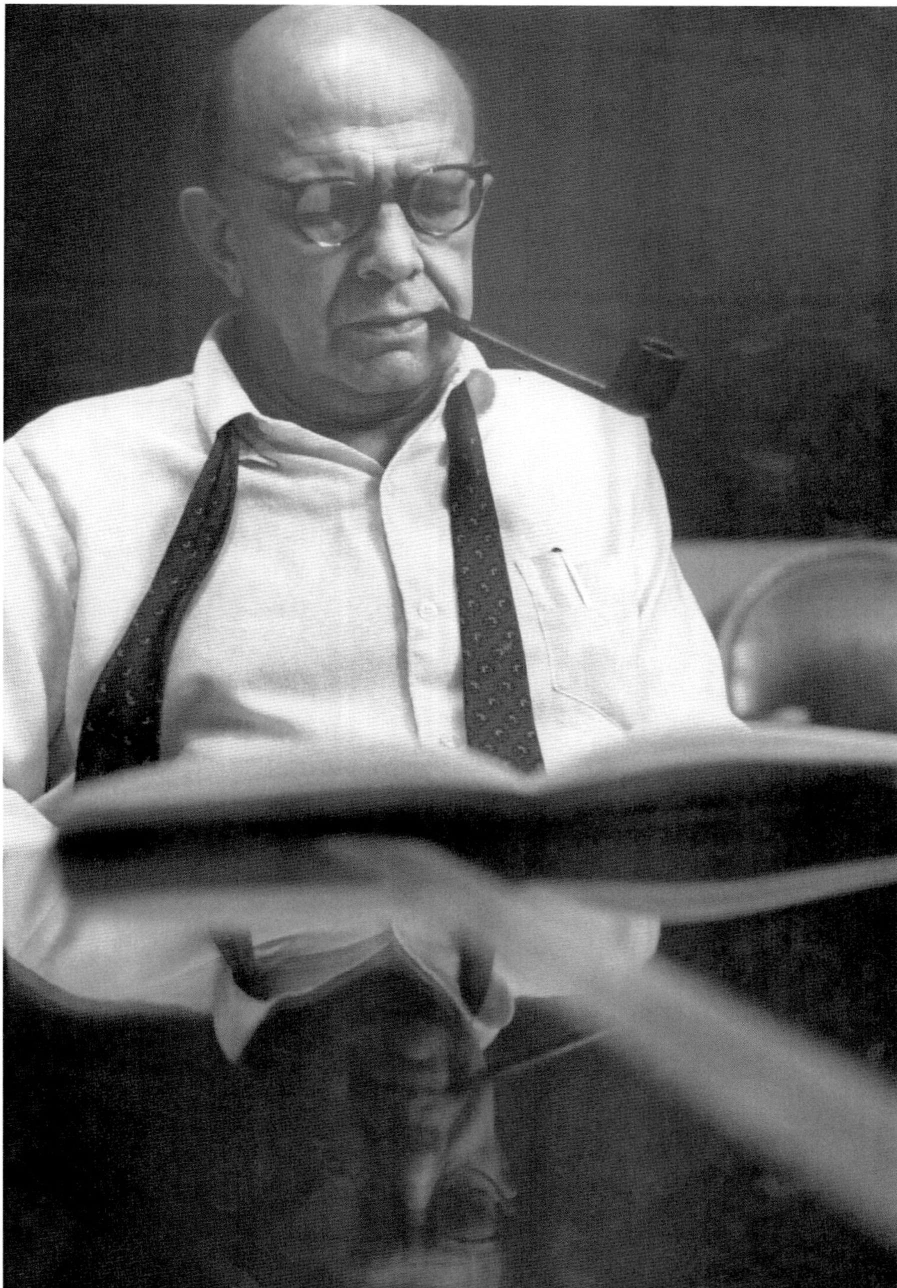

Roger Sessions (1896–1985)
This accomplished composer established himself in the classical style and later expanded into the modernist serial style. He was also a teacher with an extensive list of students and protégés that today reads like a Who's Who of American music, including Elmer Bernstein, Milton Babbitt, and Daniel Lewin. In 1953, he made Princeton his home and base of operations for lecturing and instructing at the university as well as Berkeley, Harvard, and Julliard. (Corbis.)

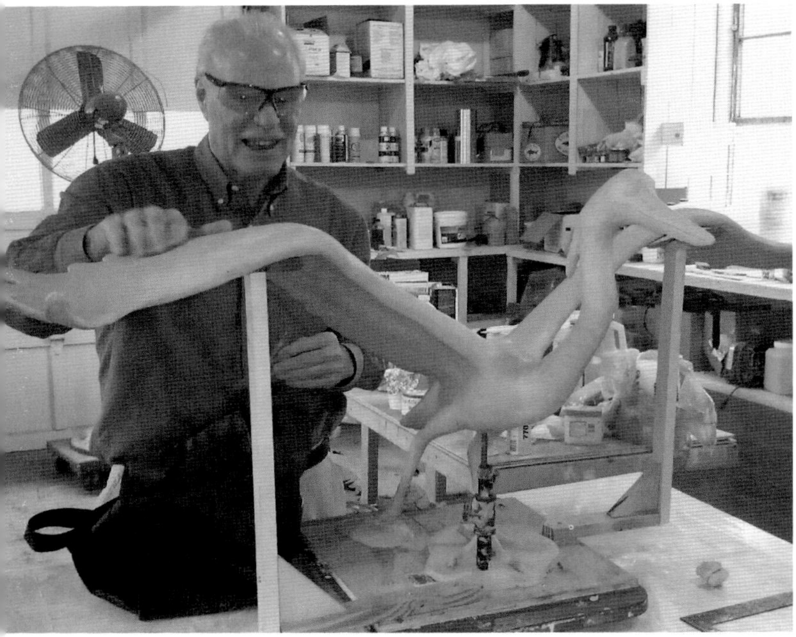

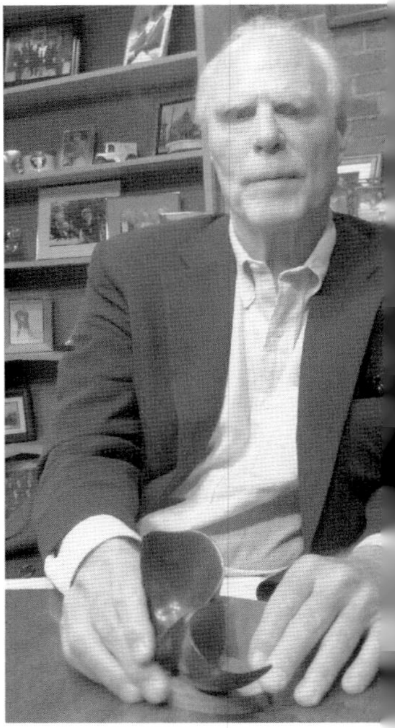

Gordon Gund

It is not at all inappropriate to say that Gordon Gund is a man of vision. His Gund Investment Corporation, founded in 1968 and now based in Princeton, ranks high in the annals of venture capital. His prescience acquisition of professional sports teams has been successful and satisfying. But when Gund's eyesight rapidly deteriorated in 1971 from macular degeneration, leaving him with mere glimpses of peripheral vision, he sought new paths of connection with the world. Today, Gordon Gund is a genuinely accomplished sculptor.

Initially introduced to woodcarving, his sense of touch became more sensitive. He began creating armature-supported clay figures that were, with the encouragement of a friend, sculptor Seward Johnson III, cast in bronze. A small bronze of a whale's tail fluke, held here by Gund during a conversation at his office, was later scaled up to full sizes. Versions have been installed at the Princeton-Plainsboro Medical Center, Grounds for Sculpture, and Philadelphia Art Museum. Gund is now exploring the contours of mounted bird specimens to create works like the seagull shown in progress in his studio.

Meanwhile, he applies his keen sense for startups to identifying promising research in vision-saving medical procedures, funded through his Foundation Fighting Blindness. Peter Benchley arranged for the *Jaws* movie to premiere at the Garden Theater as a fundraiser. Gund says, "One of the wonderful things about Princeton is that you get to know some extremely capable and successful people, but from all walks of life." (Top left, Gordon Gund; top right, author.)

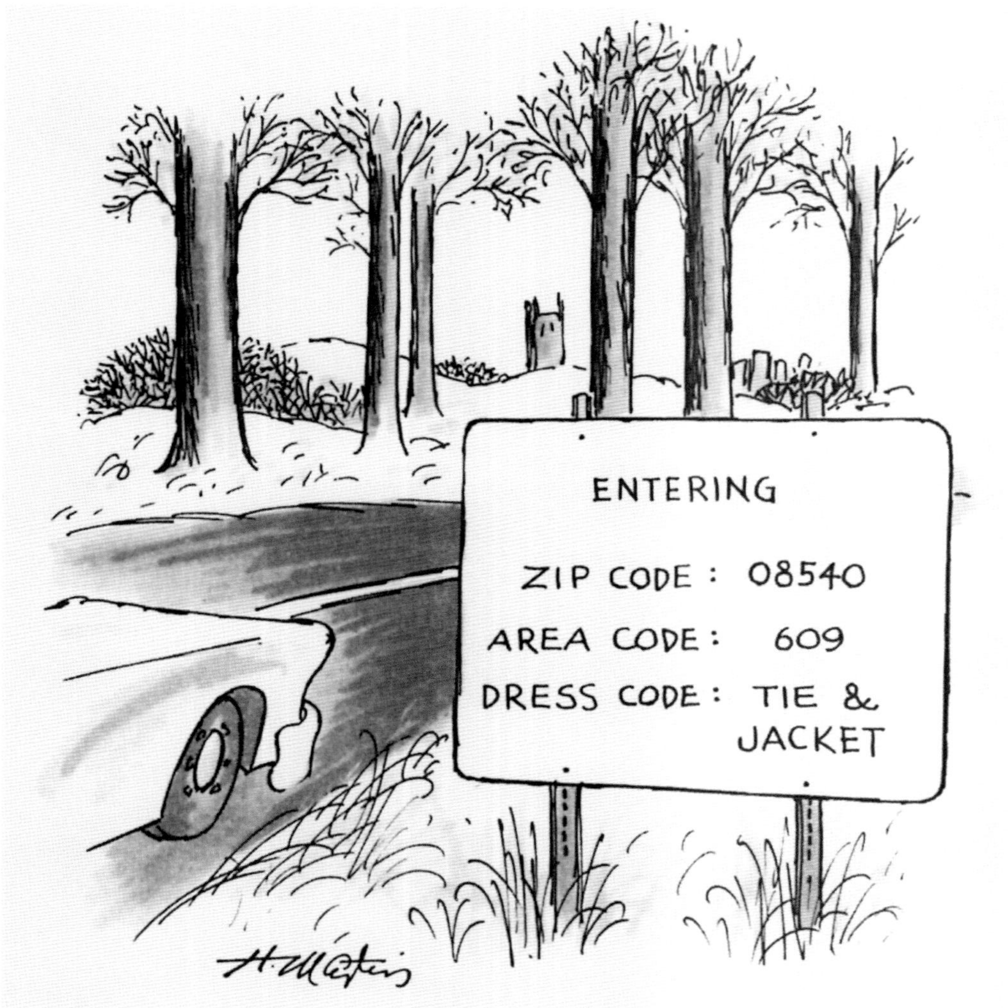

Henry Martin

One of the most beloved of the pantheons of *New Yorker* magazine cartoonists, Martin has frequently made Princeton University and the town subjects of his endearing wit, as witnessed here. A Princeton native, Martin graduated from the university in 1948. Two years later, he sold his first cartoon to the *New Yorker*. His studio for many years was an obscure one-room William Street bungalow. It made him the envy of Nassau Street colleagues beleaguered by unscheduled visitors, he recalls humorously. Now officially retired and living in Pennsylvania, Martin has contributed cartoons to the *Princeton Alumni Weekly* and other favorite periodicals. His older daughter, author Ann M. Martin, created the bestselling children's series, *The Baby-Sitters Club*. His younger daughter, Jane Martin, is an active movie producer who served early in her career as a trusted personal assistant to Woody Allen. (Condé Nast.)

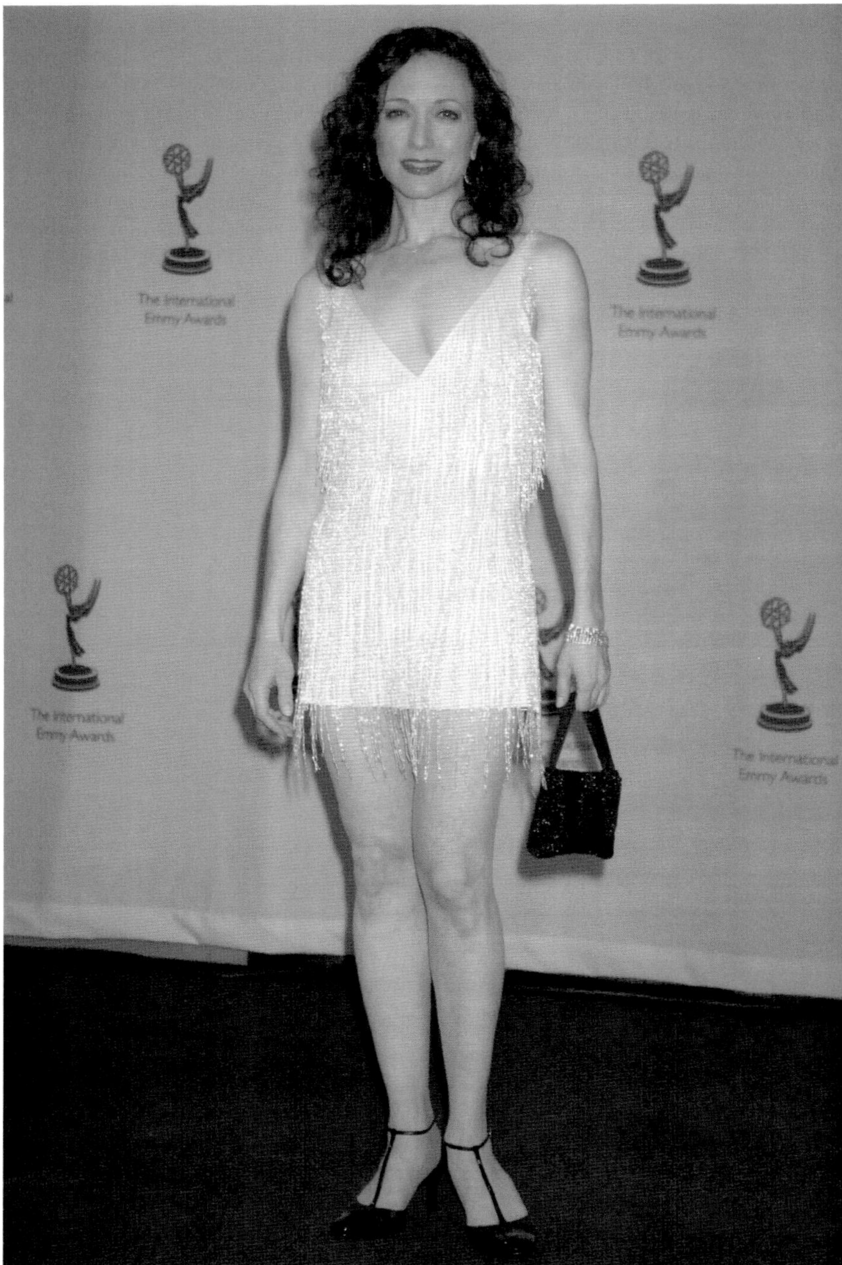

Bebe Neuwirth
Born in Princeton in 1958, Neuwirth attended the private Chapin and Princeton Day schools before graduating from Princeton High in 1976. As a child, she danced with the Princeton Ballet Company. A Tony Award–winning actress for her roles in successful revivals of the Broadway musicals of *Sweet Charity* and *Chicago*, she also had recurring roles on the popular television programs *Cheers* and *Frasier*. Although a world-renowned performer, she does not forget her roots. She has often returned to Princeton both to visit family and to appear at fundraising benefits. (The Place.)

Ethan Hawke

An Austin, Texas, native who lived for a time with his mother in New York, Hawke came to Princeton Junction as a 10 year old and graduated from the Hun School of Princeton in 1988. Hawke has had numerous successes in the movies and also in the theater, which he has described as his "first love," and—perhaps true to Princeton's literary traditions—has recently branched out successfully as a novelist. (Steven Sebring)

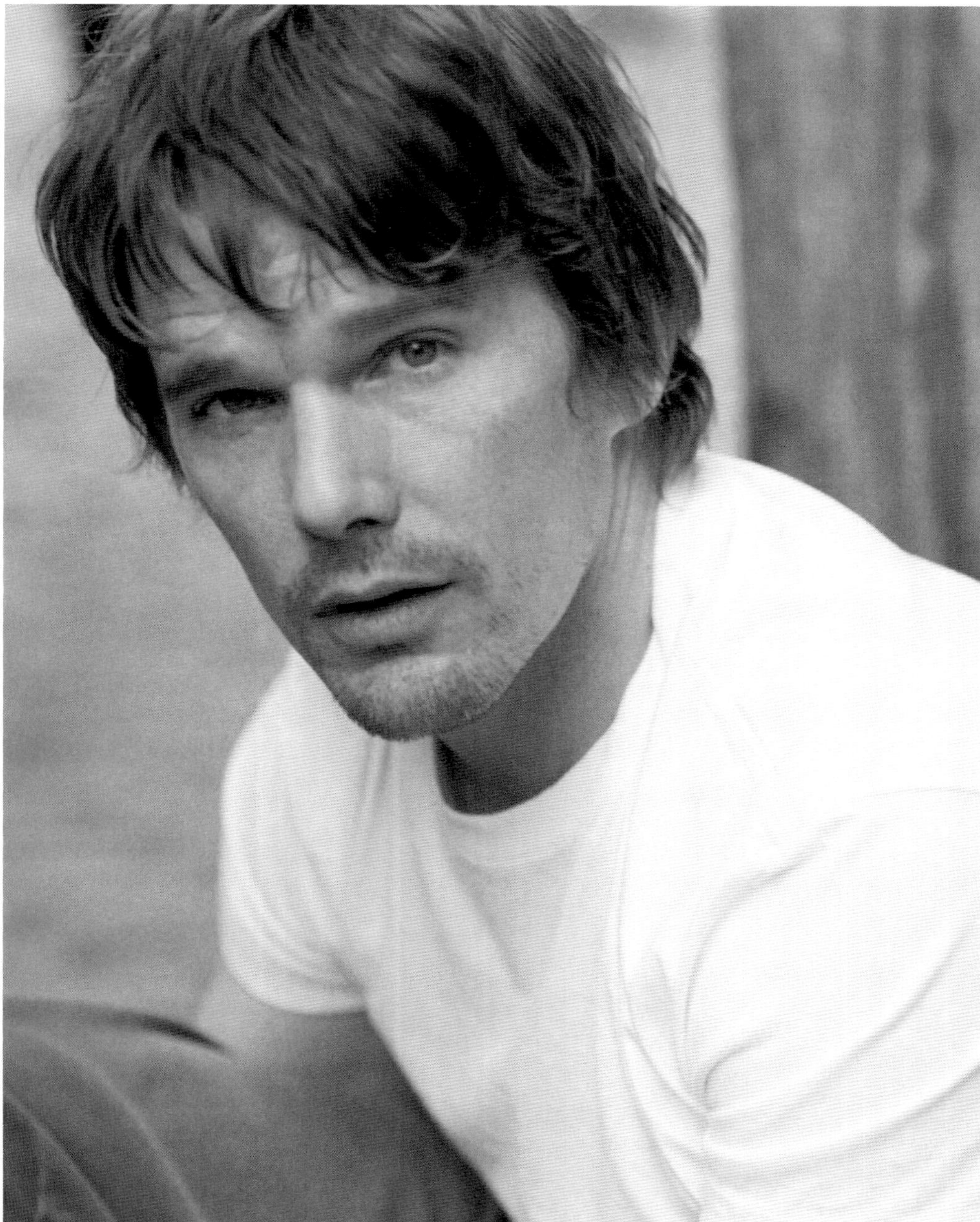

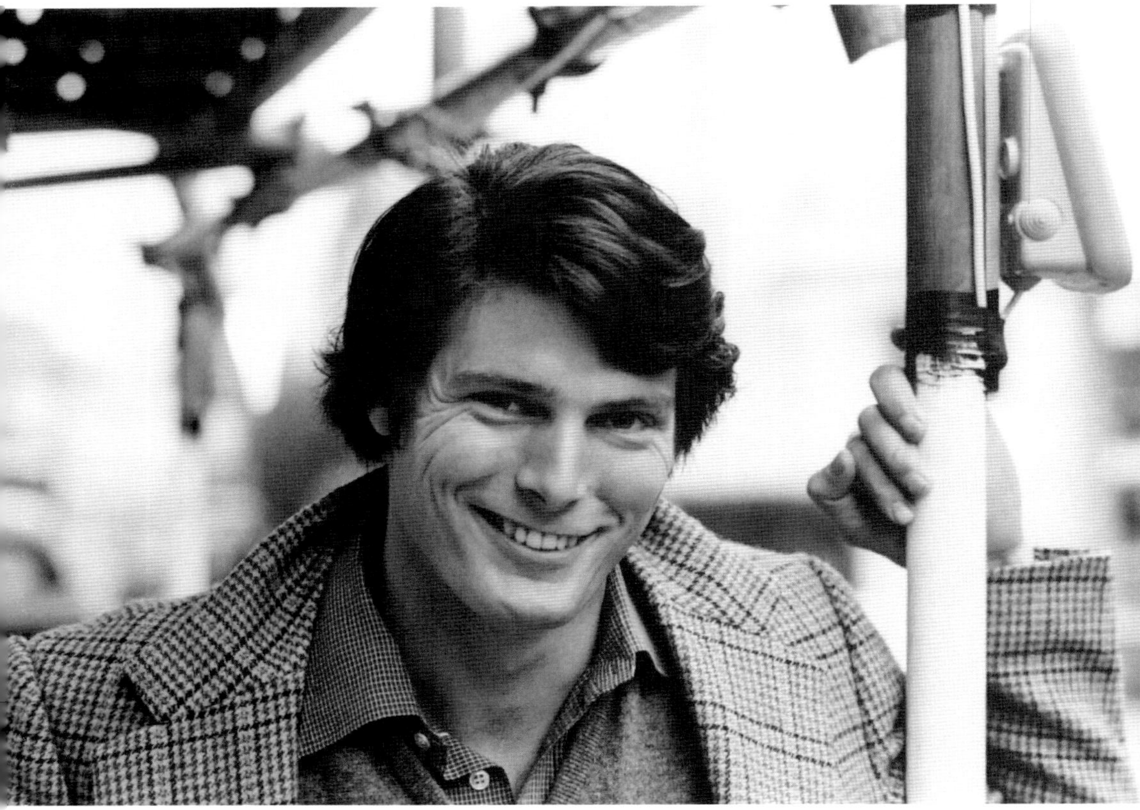

Christopher Reeve (1952–2004)
Born in New York City, the future stage and screen actor moved to Princeton in 1956 with his mother, Barbara Johnson (who was later a widely read reporter for the *Town Topics* newspaper) and his brother. By the time of his graduation from Princeton Day School in 1970, young Chris had appeared not only in PDS shows but PJ&B musicals. He graduated from Cornell in 1974 and two years later made a breakthrough in a Charles Heston film, *Grey Lady Down*. But he leaped the tall building of movie immortality in the title role of *Superman* in 1978. A tragic 1995 horse jumping accident rendered him a paraplegic, but it did not break his spirit. He turned successfully to directing. And he began the Christopher Reeve Foundation for research into spinal cord injuries. A landmark benefit for the foundation was held in January 1997, with several friends and former Princetonians in attendance, including John Lithgow and Mary Chapin Carpenter. Of course, it was Reeve's own appearance at the finale that drew a prolonged standing ovation, as the audience cheered a truly super human. (Hultan-Deutsch Collection/Corbis.)

Mary Chapin Carpenter

The country-folk singer and songwriter was born in Princeton in 1958 and lived here several years, attending Princeton Day School until relocating to Tokyo with her family in 1969. As a child, she wrote her first song about a tree in the family's yard. Returning to America, she made a name for herself in the vibrant Washington, DC, folk music scene. In the 1980s and 1990s, she won multiple Grammy awards as an artist and songwriter in folk and country music categories, also winning the prestigious Country Music Association female vocalist of the year award in 1992 and 1993. She continues to perform, the size and enthusiasm of her audiences undiminished. Of course, McCarter Theatre Center in Princeton is a frequent and popular tour stop. (SacksCo.)

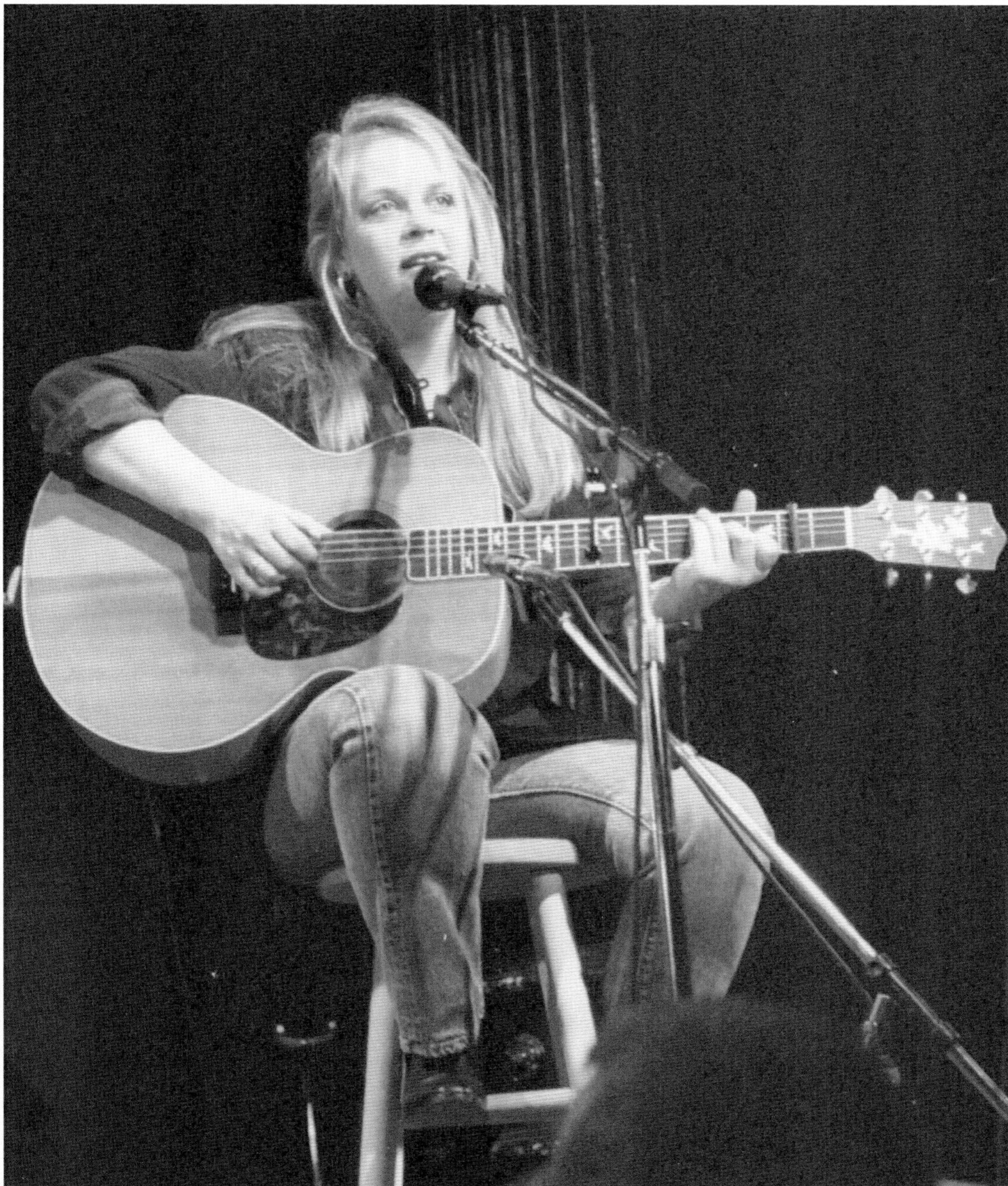

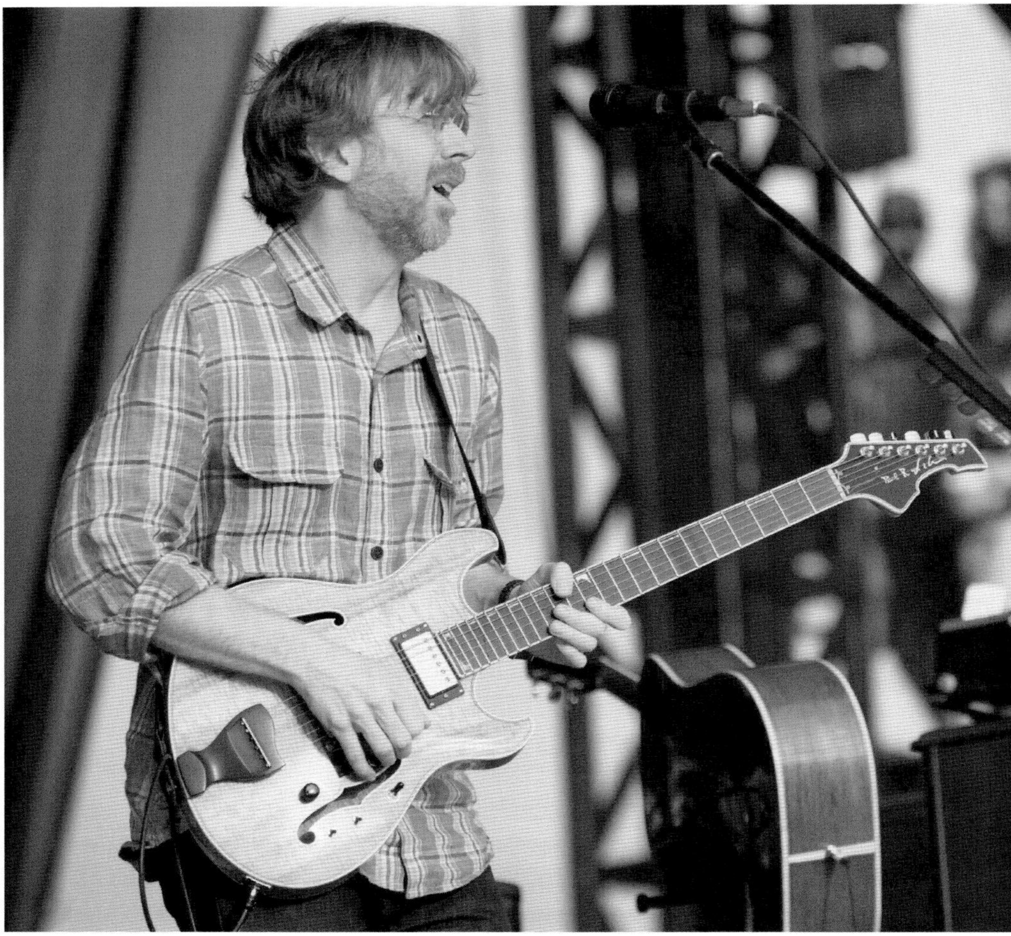

Trey Anastasio and Tom Marshall

There was nothing fishy when these future mainstays of the alternative rock "jam band" Phish first met at Princeton Day School, where they started songwriting in eighth grade. Anastasio (born 1964; pictured above) eventually became the lead singer-guitarist of Phish, and Marshall (born 1963) collaborated on much of the band's most popular original material. An outdoor sculpture in a local park was their rendezvous for jams and songwriting during their Princeton years. The sculpture's location is not given here, so not to enable fans in adding graffiti as tributary adulation. (Corbis.)

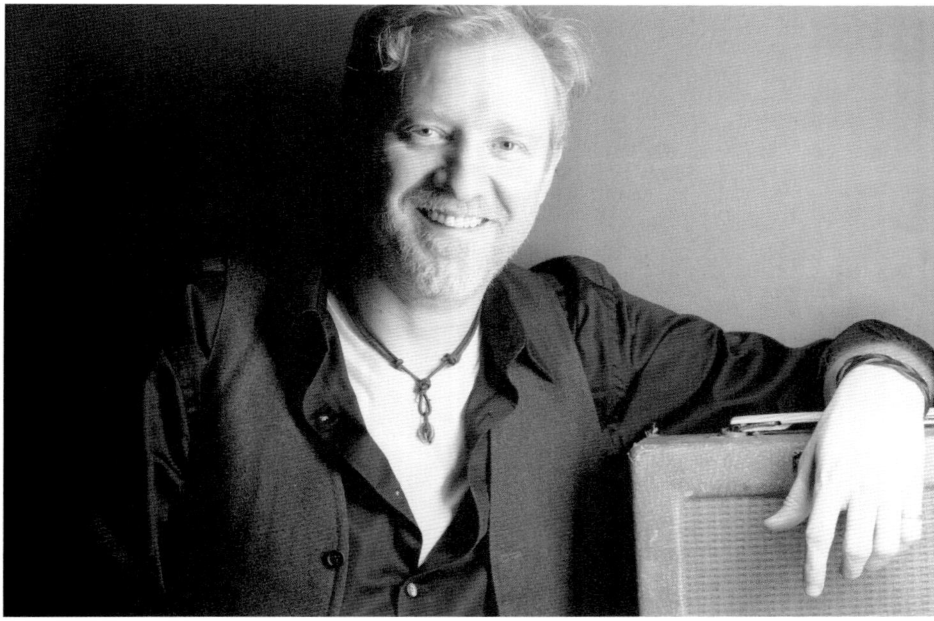

Chris Barron
Born in Honolulu in 1968 where his father was stationed at Pearl Harbor, the future lead singer of the band Spin Doctors came to Princeton with his family after stays in New York State and Australia. At Princeton High School, he became friends with John Popper (below). They later moved to New York and appeared together in the band Trucking Company. After such major radio hits as "Two Princes" and "Little Miss Can't be Wrong," Spin Doctors spun down. But Barron has participated in reunions and also established a successful new career as a solo performer and songwriter. (General Musica.)

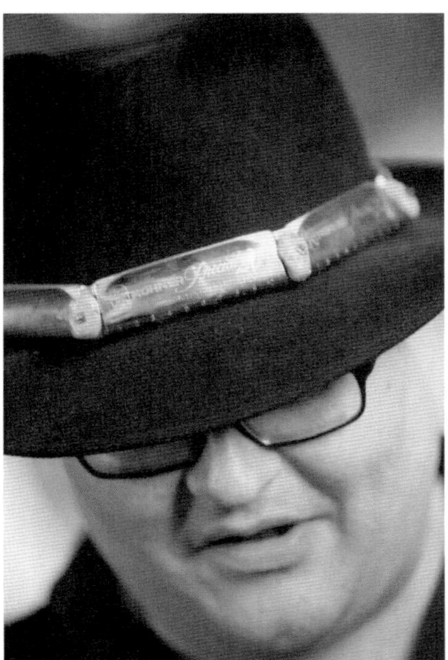

John Popper
Like alternative country star Buddy Miller (see page 72), Popper (born in 1967) is an Ohio native whose family later came to Princeton. John performed in jazz, blues, and garage rock ensembles during his Princeton High School days before traveling on to Blues Traveler fame. The band has come to town for memorable private performances at major Princeton University class reunions. (Jason Janik.)

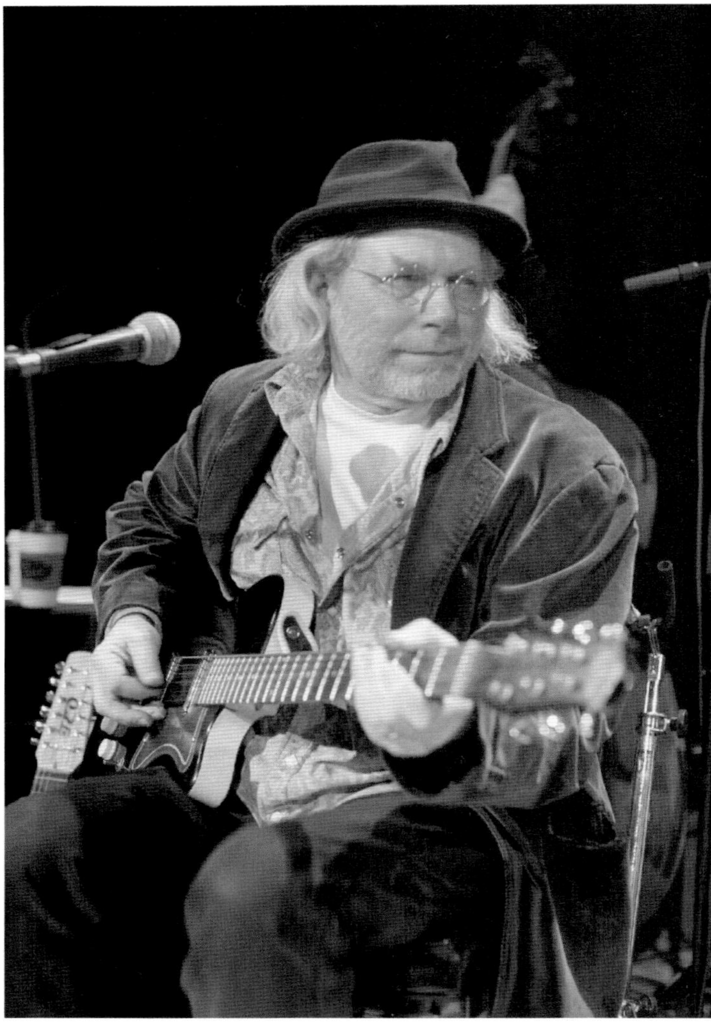

Buddy Miller
Born in 1952 in Ohio as Steve Miller, the "alternative country" singer, guitarist, songwriter, and record producer eventually took "Buddy" as his professional moniker to differentiate himself from the California rock star of the same name. His family relocated to Princeton where his father worked at RCA Sarnoff Labs as a researcher. He bought his first inexpensive guitar at the Music Shop, then in the Princeton University Store. "I rode around town with it on my back on my bike," he recalls, "until I fell off and cracked it." He took guitar lessons from the late Yvonne Aronson, a beloved Princeton Folk Music Society stalwart who encouraged dozens of aspiring young players, and hung out at the Catacombs coffeehouse in the basement of Trinity Church. Buddy graduated from Princeton High School in 1969, then moved to the Woodstock, New York, area, and blossomed as a performer-songwriter. He eventually settled in Nashville where he developed a following as a solo artist and also worked with such major figures as country/folk singer Emmylou Harris, record producer T-Bone Burnett, and rock vocalist Robert Plant, formerly of Led Zeppelin. He has garnered Americana Music Association and Grammy awards. Most recently, Buddy and T-Bone have coproduced music for the hit television series *Nashville*. "The music scene in Princeton was amazing," Miller recalls. "All these creative people in one place." (New West Records.)

CHAPTER SIX

The Entrepreneurial Spirit

Princeton, despite its share of serious fires and hard rains, has historically been spared a town-wide conflagration or flood, so many important early buildings still exist today. Similarly, the town has experienced the same recessions and outright depressions that have afflicted the rest of New Jersey and America; however, the effects were not completely devastating, and so, there has been a beneficial continuity of businesses here.

The reasons are many and cannot be examined in detail here. But Princeton's relative prosperity in the good times, the fertility of its farmlands, and its prime location for the transportation of goods and services no doubt softened economic blows. Thus, some stores and companies have achieved a longevity that has begotten renown and even a certain legendary status.

In April 1904, Frederick William Luttman opened a harness-making and saddle repair shop in a section of Nassau Street adjacent to Princeton's horse and carriage stables. Luttman was following the trade of his father, a German immigrant who had settled in Dayton, Ohio. Luttman later recalled that "when the automobiles came along, oh boy, they scared a lot of the horses. To tell the truth I felt a little bit jittery about them, myself. I began to worry about my trade." So Luttman presciently diversified into a leather goods store that sold fine suitcases, trunks, wallets, and handbags. Luttman's Luggage was a Palmer Square institution until it closed in 2005.

Princeton Nurseries was actually located in the settlement of Mapleton, near Kingston. Its owners, the Flemers, were descendants of Dutch farmers, who arrived in the late 17th and early 18th centuries from New York. William Flemer Sr. assembled land for his wholesale shrub and landscaping tree farm in 1913 in the small settlement of Mapleton. It grew to be the largest commercial nursery in America. The Flemers' land was eventually acquired by Princeton University, both for campus expansion and as a commercial investment, a section becoming the site of the Forrestal Village shopping, hotel, and restaurant complex.

Among the most versatile and colorful of Princeton entrepreneurs was Christie Whiteman. Evincing a genuine flair for showmanship, Whiteman founded a barbershop in which he began selling novelty and joke toys, magic trick kits, and postcards. Entertainment soon cut out tonsorial clipping. Whiteman expanded his entertainment offerings, showing movies in town and even becoming the official local vendor for Columbia records and phonographs.

Right in the center of Princeton was Burnett Griggs, whose Griggs's Imperial Restaurant lived up to its grand name. When offered large sums for his property on Witherspoon Street and Tulane, he turned the offers down so he could continue the business he loved. Griggs eventually agreed to a sale. The mixed-use commercial lot between what is now the Public Library of Princeton and northern Palmer Square was named Griggs's Corner in his honor.

With a well-established shoe store on Nassau Street, it is no wonder that Peter Hulitt received a call of some real urgency in the autumn of 1952. It was from Helen Dukas, secretary and housekeeper for none other than Prof. Albert Einstein. The professor's shoes were badly hurting his feet; could Hulitt come right over? "I'd never made a house call before or since," Hulitt recalled more than a half century later. "But this was Einstein." The scientist's feet were soon relieved, and Hultitt's Shoe Store still prospers.

Philadelphia native Everett Garrettson (1924–2012) came to town in 1949 to study in the university's graduate engineering program. He married Barbara Clayton Grahn, granddaughter of Henry P. Clayton, founder of the H.P. Clayton women's department store in Princeton. After a career in medical and information sampling equipment, Garrettson joined with Barbara in 1964 to run, expand, and modernize Clayton's. The firm was one of the first in town to be computerized thanks to Everett's engineering background. The Claytons sold the store and retired in 1989.

Real estate agencies and restaurants in particular have marvelous stories associated with their founders, but there are far too many to mention individually. So, presented within this chapter are some of the most charming or inspirational businesses, concluding with a tour around one strictly limited commercial block-bordered by Nassau, Witherspoon, Spring, and South Tulane Streets. Surprisingly, this small sample is quite representative of much of Princeton's retail history.

Among the many departed but still legendary Princeton businesses, perhaps the one with the most memorable slogan was Jack Honore's Barber Shop in Palmer Square—"We Make the Old Young and the Ugly Beautiful."

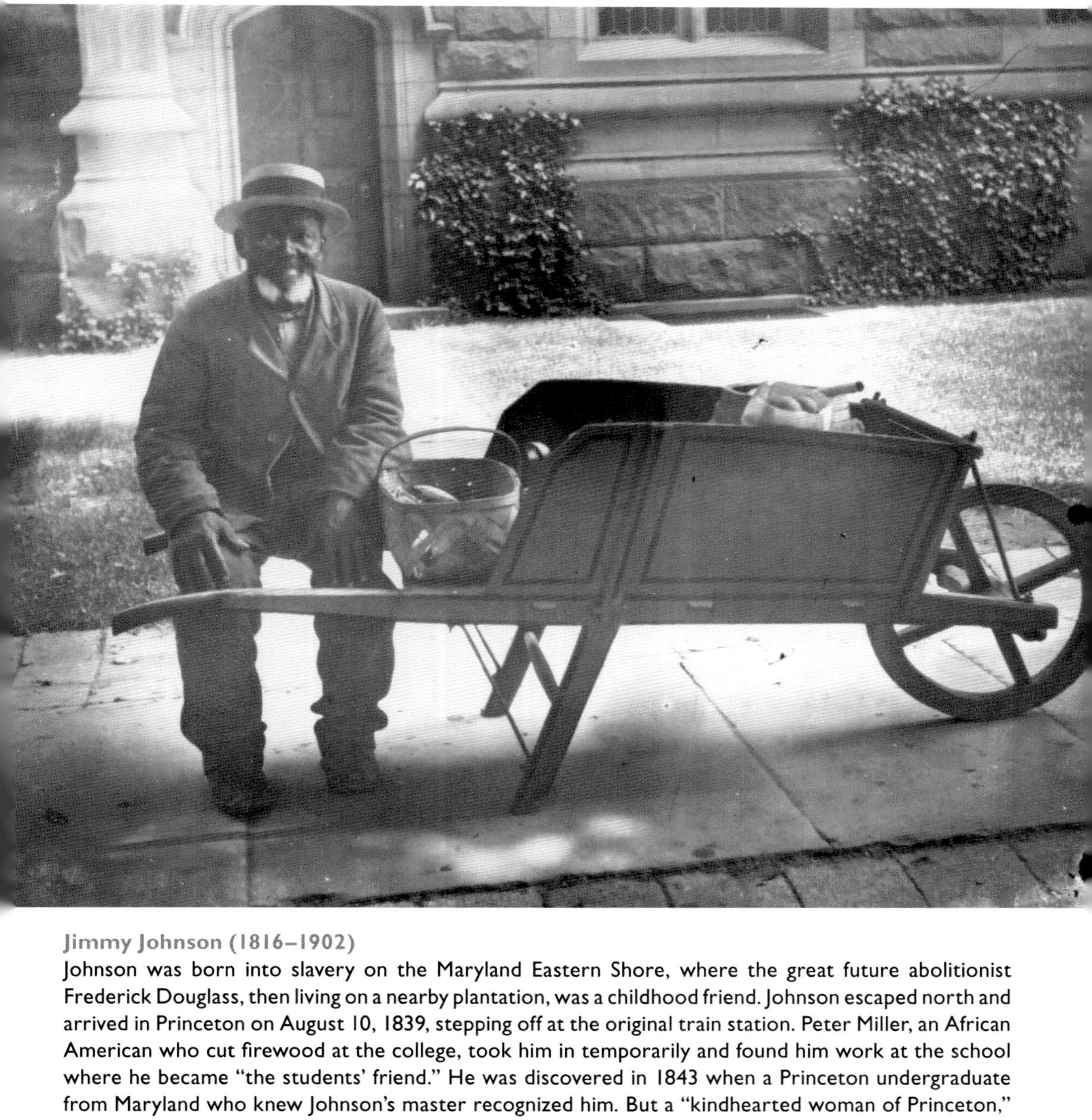

Jimmy Johnson (1816–1902)

Johnson was born into slavery on the Maryland Eastern Shore, where the great future abolitionist Frederick Douglass, then living on a nearby plantation, was a childhood friend. Johnson escaped north and arrived in Princeton on August 10, 1839, stepping off at the original train station. Peter Miller, an African American who cut firewood at the college, took him in temporarily and found him work at the school where he became "the students' friend." He was discovered in 1843 when a Princeton undergraduate from Maryland who knew Johnson's master recognized him. But a "kindhearted woman of Princeton," Theodora Prevost, bought his freedom for $550, which he insisted on repaying in installments. Students also collected money for their new friend. Johnson ran a successful if modest clothing store, which resold fine, lightly used garments purchased from college students. He later sold nuts and fruits to the college students as they rushed between classes, making him a pioneering purveyor of "fast food." His nephew Alexander "Ting" Taylor recalled helping his uncle sell peanuts and apples at university sporting events in 1900. Jimmy Johnson and his omnipresent wheelbarrow, shown here, were true campus and town icons. (HSP.)

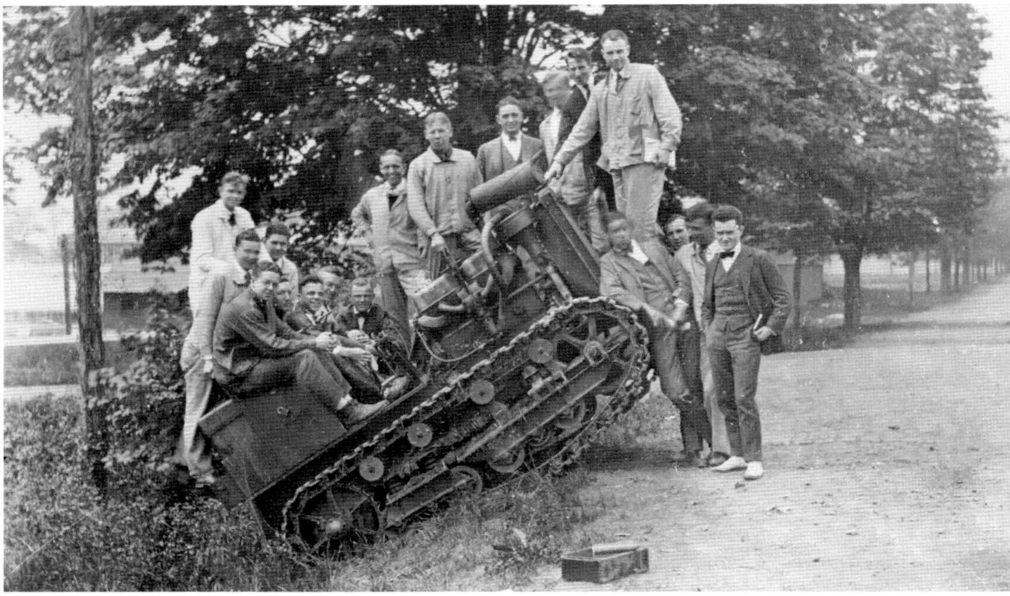

Krikor Kurkjian

A member of a prominent American family, Kurkjian (also spelled "Kurkjean" and "Kirkjian" in some sources) owned the first car dealership in town. He even sold farm and construction equipment, as shown in this photograph where Kurkjian, clipboard in hand, balances with friends and employees on an earthmover. His business success allowed him to purchase a farm estate, known for its orchards, on Mount Lucas Road in the township.

In addition to its pioneering role in Princeton automotive sales and service, the garage space operated by Krikor Kurkjian on lower Nassau Street was among the first to offer storage and parking for automobiles. (Both, HSP.)

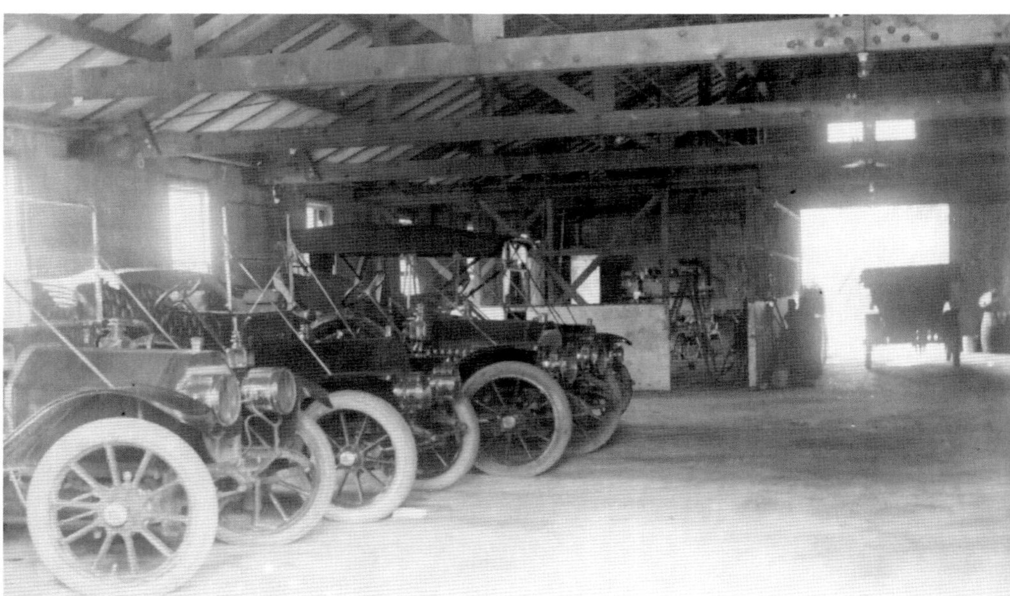

Christine Moore Howell (1899–1972)
Shown here in the 1950s, Howell provided glamour and was glamorous herself. Among the first African Americans to graduate from previously segregated Princeton High School, she studied chemistry in Paris and then operated a highly successful hairdressing salon with a wide clientele at 4–6 Spring Street. In a back room was her chemistry lab, the research and development headquarters of Christine Cosmetics, Inc., which offered "Derm Tone (Deep Pore Cleanser)," "Velvene (Complexion Vitalizer)," "Nourisheen (Helps Growing Hair)," and "Formula No. 85 (Professional Dandruff Remover)," among other popular products. "Mail orders promptly filled," her brochure assured.

Her father, William "Sport" Moore (1863–1920), a multifaceted entrepreneur and businessman, owned the building. Born in North Carolina, Moore moved to Princeton where he co-owned a clothing store (with friend Louis Kaplan) that did well by buying lightly used clothes from Princeton University students and reselling them. He also dealt in furniture and antiques. It is said that then university president Woodrow Wilson bought a desk from Moore and, later, took it to the New Jersey governor's mansion. Moore also invested in real estate, owning buildings at 4, 6, and 10 Spring Street, with some still being in the Moore family. He was a mainstay of Princeton's African American community. (Shirley A. Satterfield.)

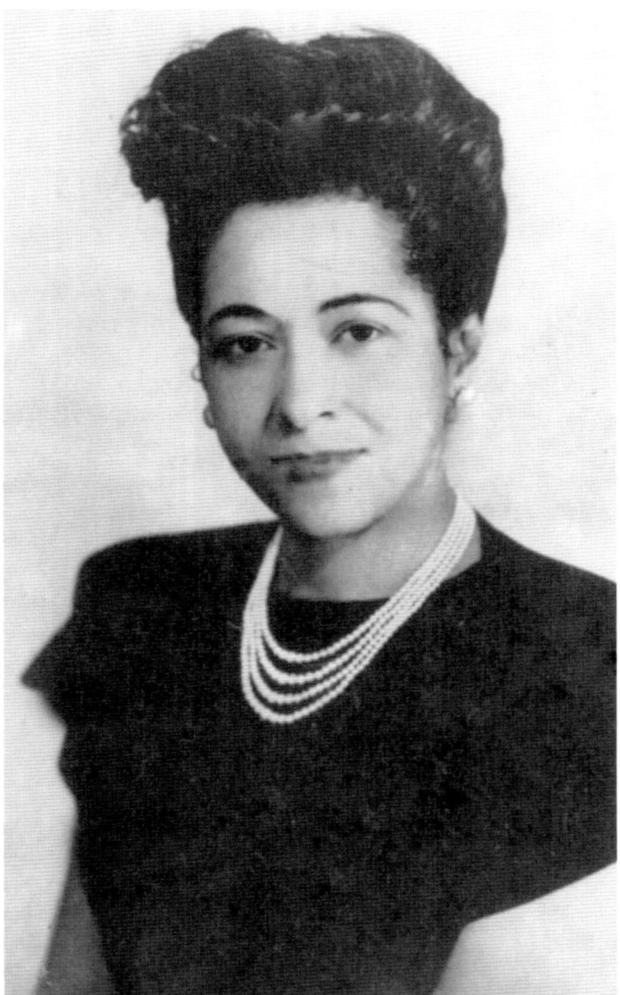

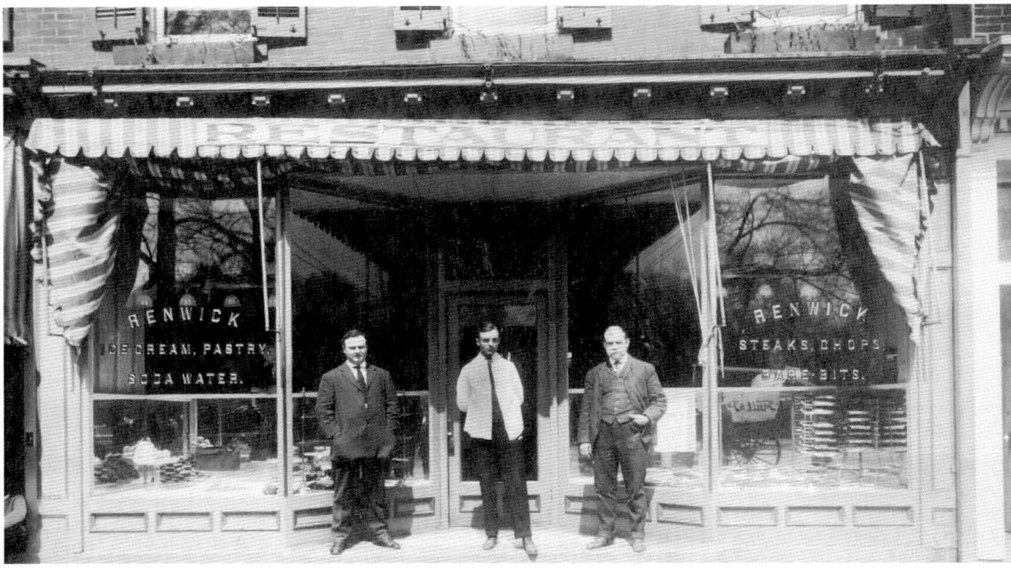

Renwick's and William "Buster" Lewis

Although he ran the Renwick restaurant and later the Nassau Inn, Lewis (left in photograph above) achieved added local renown in the early 1900s as a physical culturist and exercise coach who ran a nutritious "training table" for aspiring athletes. Later, Renwick restaurant became Renwick's, which was a legendary after-school destination for high school and university students to unwind at and grab a quick, delicious sandwich or soda. (HSP.)

Hoagie Haven

A successor of Renwick's in town-gown popularity is Hoagie Haven. It is interesting to think whether or not its hoagies would make the cut at Lewis's training table, but one thing is for sure: it is a legend, having served comfort food since the 1970s. Here, attentive and efficient Gus Liras, Georgia Liras, and Julio Ruiz make the Haven a culinary heaven for customer Adam Gormly in 1988. (PP/HSP.)

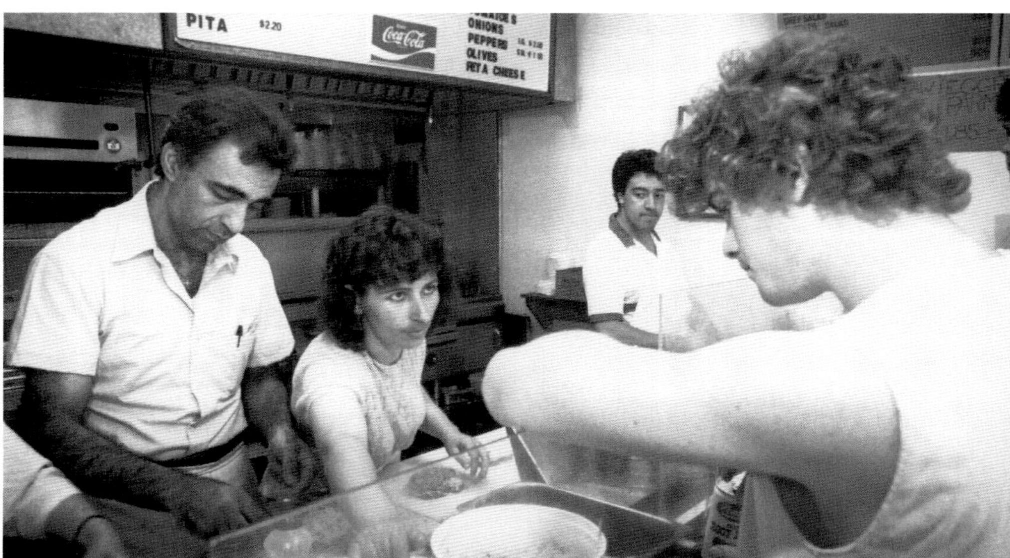

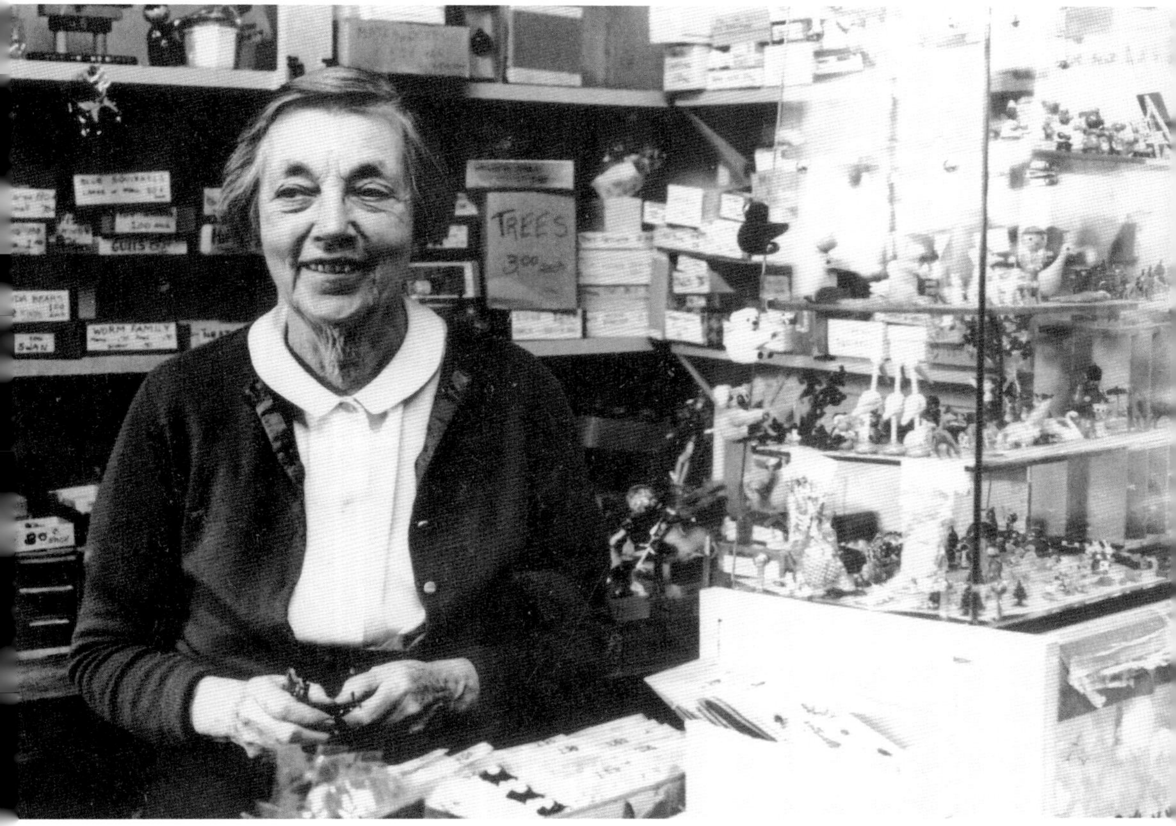

Phyllis Britcher, Stuff 'n Nonsense Shop

For nearly a quarter century, Phyllis delighted children of all ages with the dolls, toys, games, and knickknacks at her Moore Street gift store, Stuff 'n Nonsense, founded in 1954. As often happens, her discovery of her life's calling came through serendipity and the interest of a caring adult. She was born in 1900 in Syracuse, New York. Her father was a lawyer who, she recalled, "always saw the bright side of things . . . and loved to help people." At age eight, she developed a critical case of pneumonia and found herself slipping away, "swallowed up" in a huge bed. One day, her father saw in a store window a large, beautiful doll with baby clothes. He brought it home immediately to give to little Phyllis so that she had a companion to play with. She recovered and felt certain the doll had saved her life. This special appreciation for the power of toys in children's lives never left her. She studied art, including commercial illustration, first at Syracause University and then Parsons School of Design. It led to an additional career as a writer and illustrator of children's books, her first being *Corally Crothers' Birthday.* (PR.)

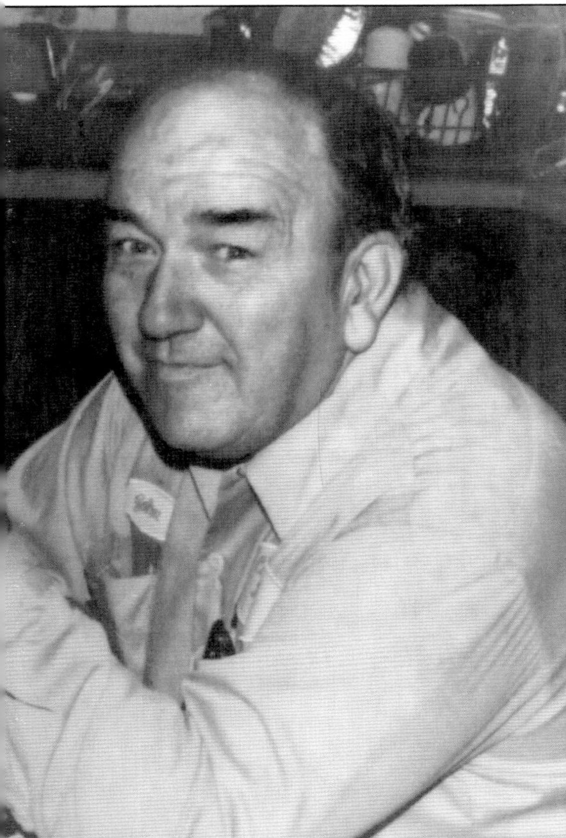

John Calhoun (1919–1979)

In the 1950s through the 1970s, if one's car broke down or the owner dared treat the Princeton University Store lot as a private parking place, chances are the driver's car was towed by Calhoun's Garage, an active AAA franchise affiliate and repair destination for Princeton motorists. Hailing from northwestern Pennsylvania, Calhoun bought a garage in nearby Rocky Hill in 1947 where he worked part time while also holding jobs at the Belle Mead Army Depot and at Mack Trucks. "He had to raise 13 kids," explains his middle son Dan. In 1958, John Calhoun relocated his business to neighboring rural Skillman and went full time. After his death, Dan stepped in to run the garage for his mother, later purchasing it.

It remains a family business. In 1990, members of the Calhoun clan gathered in the shop's yard (from right to left, Dan, his son Dan Jr., and two older brothers Bob and John Jr.). They honor their father's work ethic and his refusal to accept any assistance. "He was a hard working man," Dan says. "He didn't ask for anything from anyone." (Left, Dan Calhoun; below, Craig Terry/*U.S. 1*.)

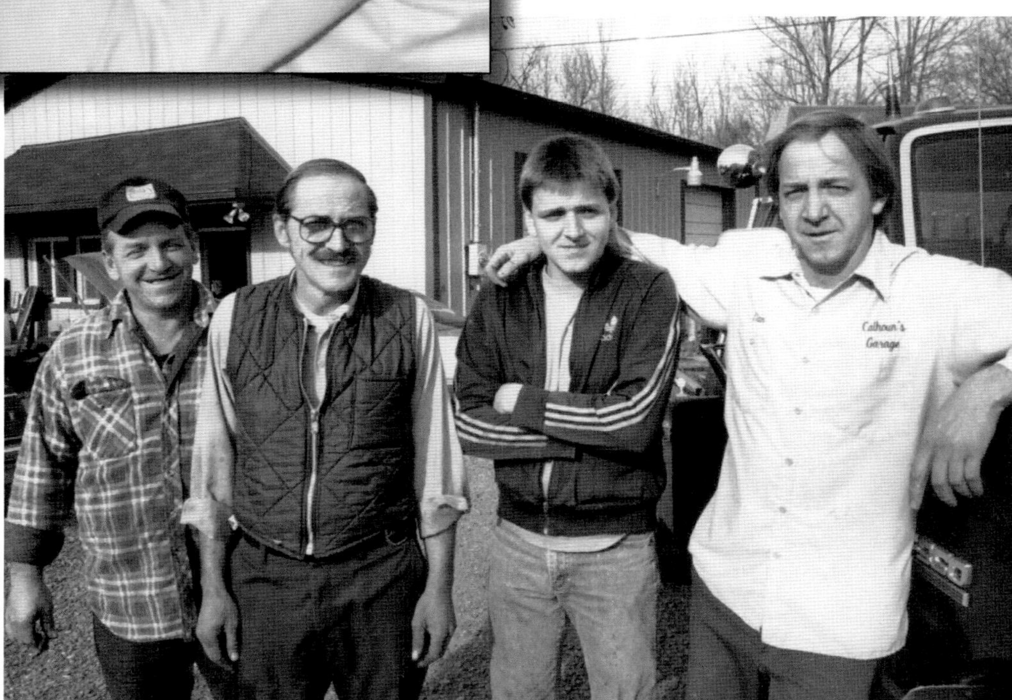

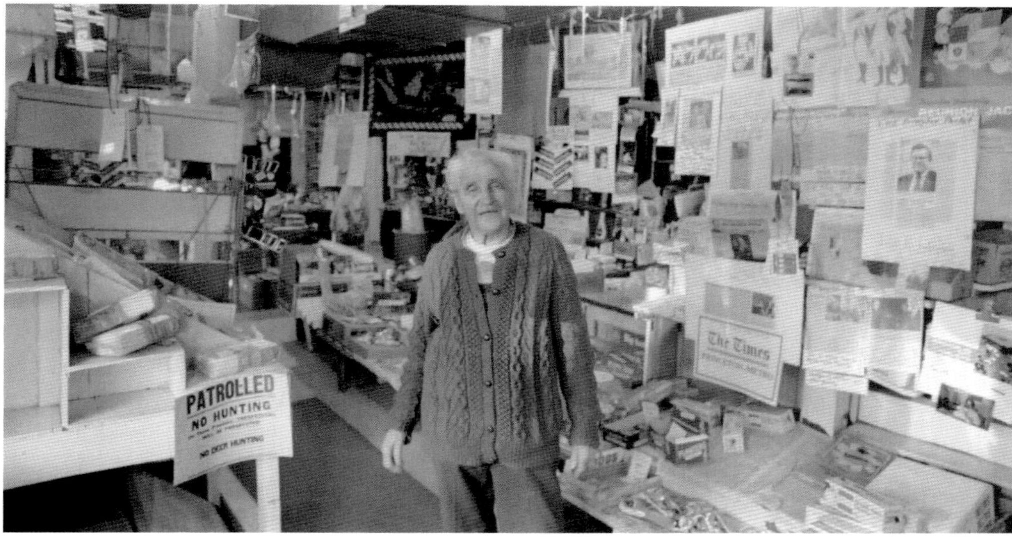

Mary Watts (1901–2001)

Mary Watts's general store was a fixture on the roadside of Route 206—and in the community's consciousness—for more than half a century. Founded with her husband, Raymond, the narrow, red Shotgun-style establishment in Princeton Township near the Montgomery line was jovially known as "hanging gardens" for its profound proliferation of stock; many items hung from the ceiling with twine when Mary's inventory overwhelmed her shelf space. She pumped gas and would prepare a sandwich lunch if asked. She sold everything from newspapers, bubble gum, sodas, and pecan pies to fly swatters, bear traps, hunting licenses, and toys. In her later years, Mary Watts was tough, wiry, and gray-haired, with the occasional salty vocabulary word but an absolute heart of gold. She loved children and addressed all youngsters with gruff affection in the form of "Hey, kid." Watts single-handedly ran the store, surviving at least two brutal late night holdups. She retired to the Merwick care unit of the Medical Center of Princeton and is buried with her husband in Princeton Cemetery. Her store defined "convenience" decades before Wawa and 7-Eleven. Local artist Rex Goreleigh immortalized it in this painting featuring Mary's annual stock of Halloween pumpkins. (Above, *New York Times*/Redux Pictures; below, HSP.)

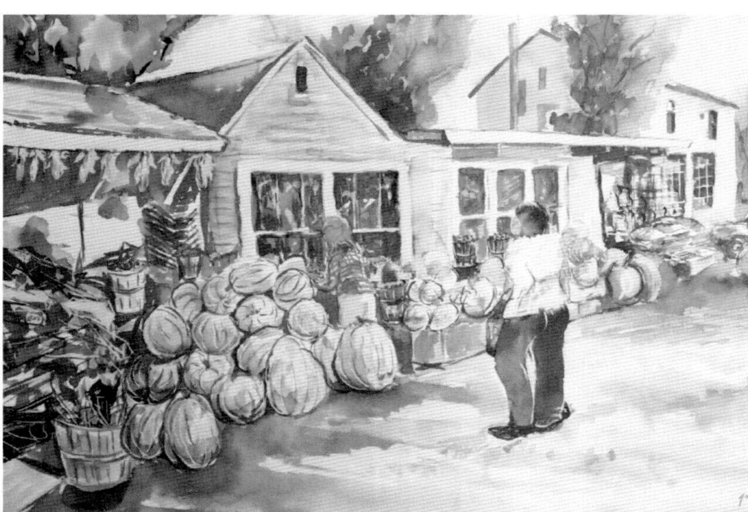

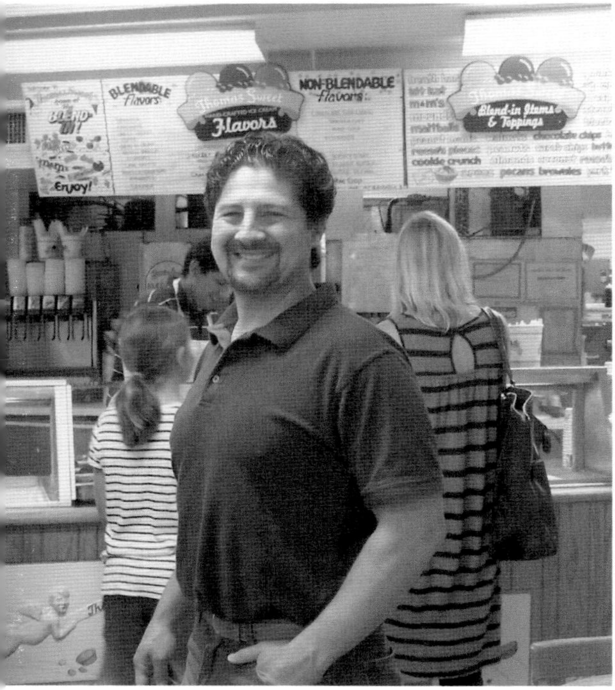

Thomas Sweet

This sweet landmark was founded by two Thomases, Tommy Block and Tom "Teddy" Grim, school chums from Buffalo, New York. They started a chocolate shop in 1978 but the next year opened a homemade-style ice cream parlor. Family-oriented, with products made in small, fresh batches, it was an instant success. Among local teens getting job experience in 1984 was Princeton High student Marco B. Cucchi, (pictured here). "I loved this store. I never forgot my experience," says Cucchi (whose name, perhaps prophetically, is pronounced "Cookie"). The memory lingered through a career as a vice president at MasterCard. By 2008, Cucchi had completed his purchase of Thomas Sweet and exchanged the corporate grind for the ice cream swirl. Thomas Sweet pioneered the option of "blend ins" of nuts, fruits, and candy. Cucchi notes, "The Princeton community has such diversity and our ice cream tapped into that." (Author.)

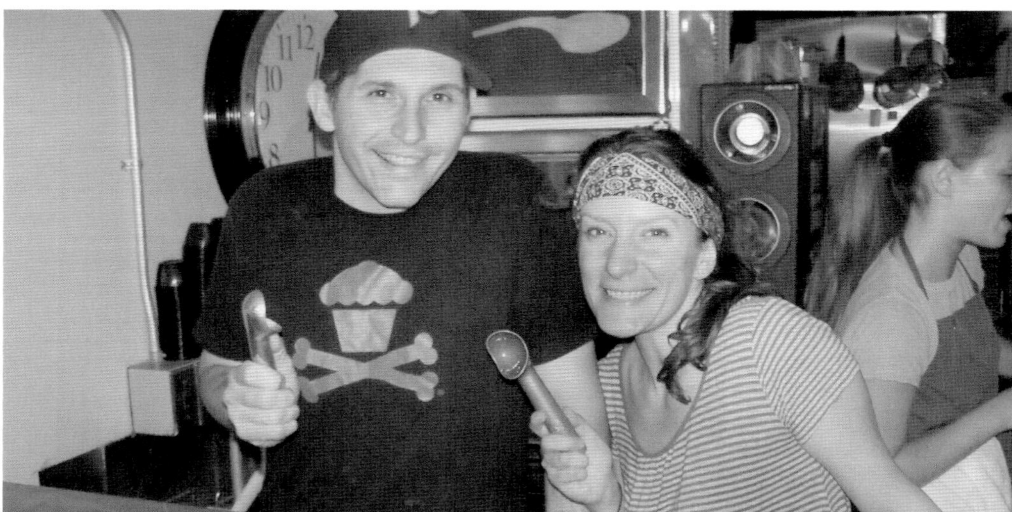

The Bent Spoon

The town was ready to enjoy another gourmet ice cream outlet, especially as the artisanal locavore food movement gained popularity. Using berries, herbs, and vegetables obtained locally, the Bent Spoon was literally an overnight success; its grand opening, totaling three hours one in evening in May 2004, offered just 12 flavors and a handful of baked goods, which all sold out. Founders and partners Gabrielle Carbone and Matthew Errico credit their passion for homemade food to their Italian heritage. "We want the quality to be what you'd get at high-end restaurant, but accessible to the general public," Errico says. They enthusiastically support gardening projects at local schools, with some harvest items coming back—to the students' delight—in their ice cream. (Author.)

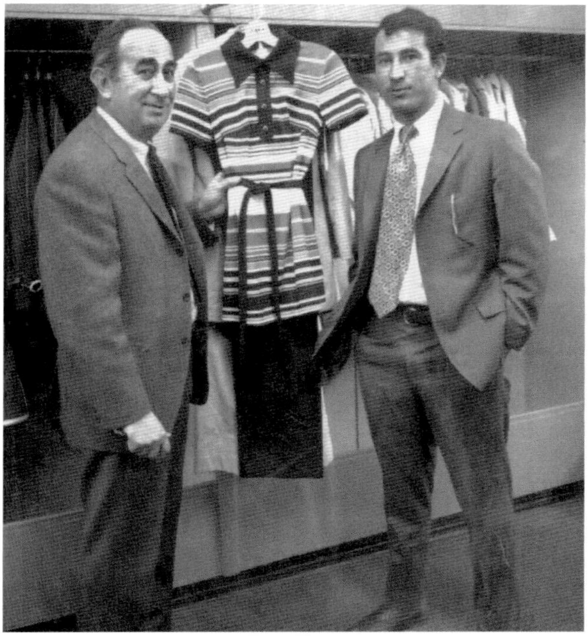

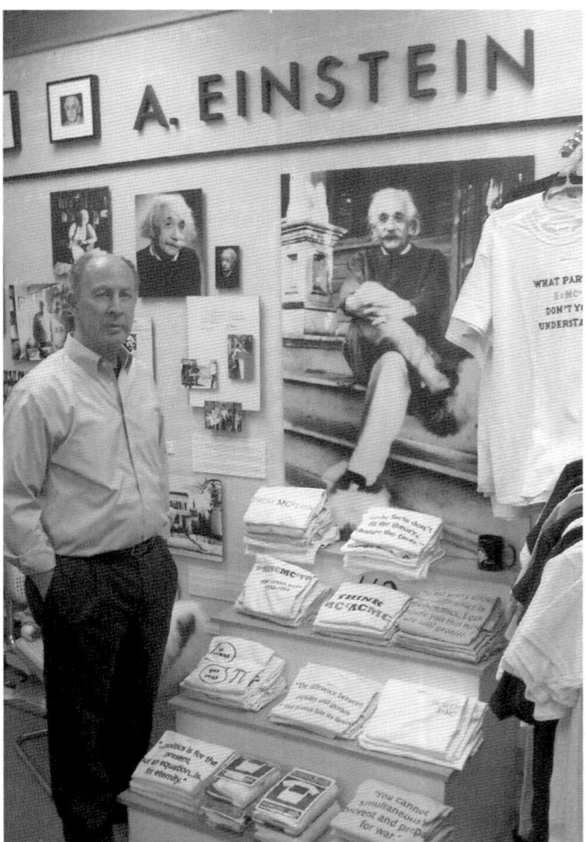

Landau

Henry Landau opened his Landau clothing store in Jersey City in 1914. But five years later, the construction of the Holland Tunnel displaced it, and it was moved to Brooklyn. Then in 1955, son David and his wife, Evelyn, arrived in Princeton. After two other locations, Landau's, as it is popularly known, settled in at 102 Nassau Street, home of the oft-remembered Zinder's newspaper and stationery store, where David and Evelyn's son Robert had some of his formative experiences in retail. Robert and his father, David, are pictured together around 1970. (Robert's brother Henry is co-owner today.) Robert of course learned the clothing trade at Landau's, purveyors of fine woolens and leisure garments. The business prospered. "We invested in the community," says Robert Landau. The store's local initiatives included an "Adopt a Neighbor" program, which granted elderly or handicapped citizens simple but heartfelt requests. (For example, a blind woman once asked for a basket of fragrant items and received it from a third-grade class.) Landau's also knew the importance of promotion: a "Come Visit Princeton" ad campaign in the *New York Times* increased out-of-town visits that benefited many businesses. Robert says, "We never wavered from policy that 'you can't sell stuff to people unless they want to buy it.'"

The Landau store houses an Einstein mini-museum, where Robert Landau is seen in a recent photograph. Family members were dear friends of the great scientist and humanitarian, often visiting him and giving him lifts to local United Jewish Appeal fundraising dinners. (Top, Robert Landau; bottom, author.)

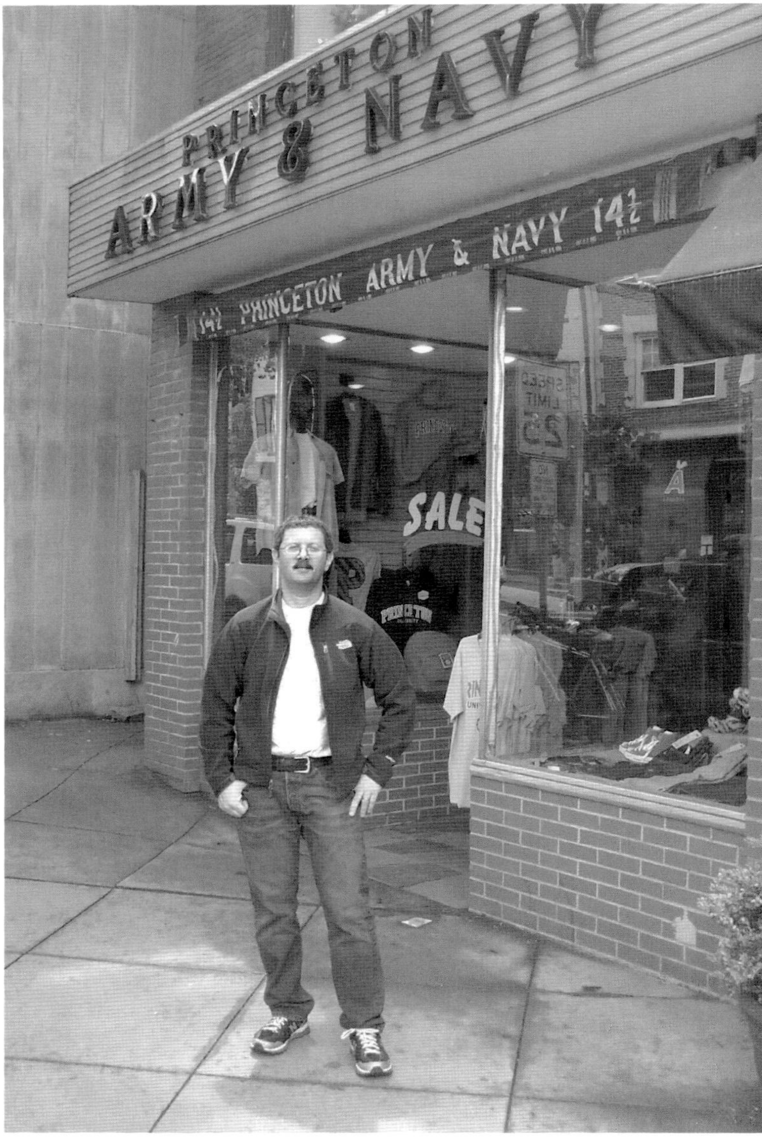

Princeton Army & Navy Store

There was an era when specialty clothing stores in America sold "Army and Navy" items. Michael Bonin, third-generation owner of the Princeton Army & Navy Store, relates how his maternal grandfather, Joseph Caplan, who already owned a gift and secondhand store in town, was among the many post–World War II merchants who bought up surplus military clothing and gear for resale to workman and outdoorsmen, as well as children eager to dress up and play soldier. Of Eastern European descent the Caplans came to America in the early 1900s. A real estate crash wiped out much of their hard-earned fortune, but the family rebuilt with retail. Caplan found himself the lone bidder for a former hook and ladder company building at 14 Witherspoon Street; today, it is still the Princeton Army & Navy Store's home. Although military surplus is no longer readily available, Bonin continues to stock backpacks, camping accessories, and popular camouflage-pattern clothing, and, of course, khaki pants; "Einstein used to buy his khakis here," says Bonin. (Author.)

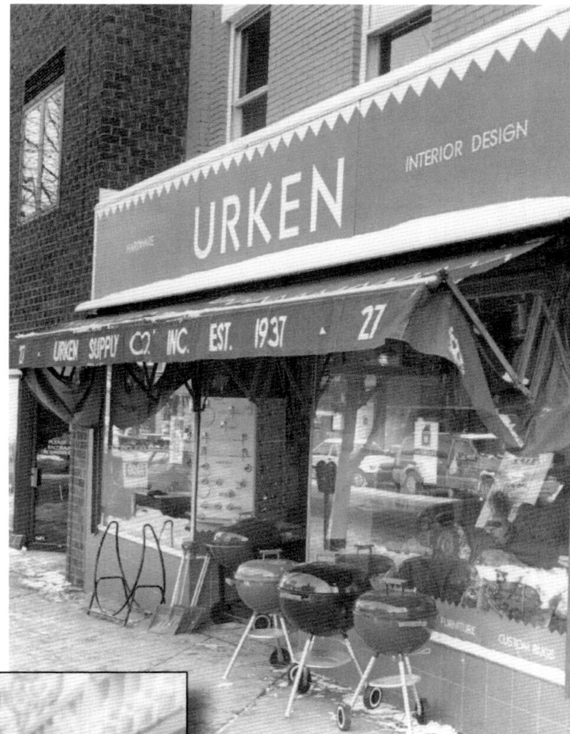

Urken Supply Company

Paul and Eunice Urken filled its bins with hardware. Customers filled the aisles in egalitarian shopping, as builders, homeowners, apartment renters, and dormitory dwellers rubbed elbows with New Jersey governors, diplomats, Nobel Prize winners, and, occasionally, visiting movie stars. Paul Urken bought the building at 27 Witherspoon Street in 1937. Initially, it was a glass shop specializing in auto windows. But over the years, "Urken's," as it was commonly called, diversified into hardware and housewares. Its al fresco displays, shown here in the 1960s, became a town retail landmark. (HSP.)

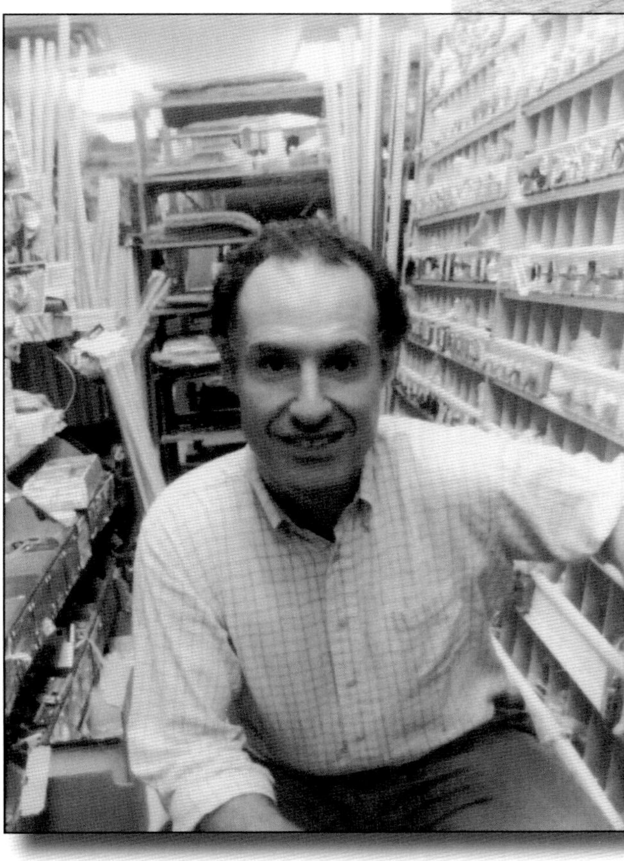

Irvin Urken

Paul Urken passed away in 1960. His son Irvin, pictured in the 1980s, came on board in 1974 after college to help his mother run and expand the business. The Urkens became adept at handling the "student rush" to outfit rooms and successfully offered increasingly popular European- and heritage-design hardware for home renovations. But the coming of big-box home improvement stores took a toll, and in 2002, the Urken Supply Company closed. "The thing I miss most are all the people," says Irvin, now a financial advisor with Northwestern Mutual. "You'd walk out in the street or get a coffee at Harry's [Luncheonette], and you'd run into people. A one minute trip would take ten minutes." (Irvin Urken.)

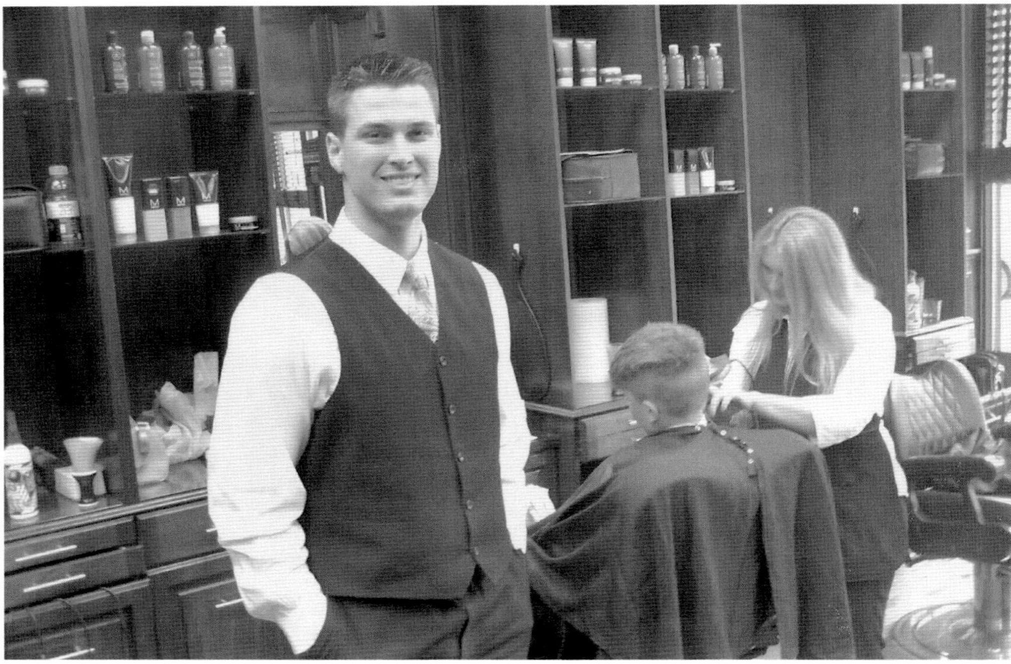

Princeton Barber Shop

The Princeton Barber Shop started as Rialto's barbershop, established in 1962, at 128 Nassau Street. The popular barber brothers Eddie Cifelli and Rich Pinelli later owned the shop. Allentown, Pennsylvania, native Travis Monahan was a barber at Rialto's when he purchased it in 2006 and renamed it Princeton Barber Shop. Five years later, he moved it around the corner to 8 South Tulane. "We just keep it a good traditional barber shop," says Monahan, shown with stylist Rachel Danley and a client. He enjoys catering to both University faculty and students and town residents. "Generally all my customers are smarter than I am," he smiles, "so I'm learning something every day." (Author.)

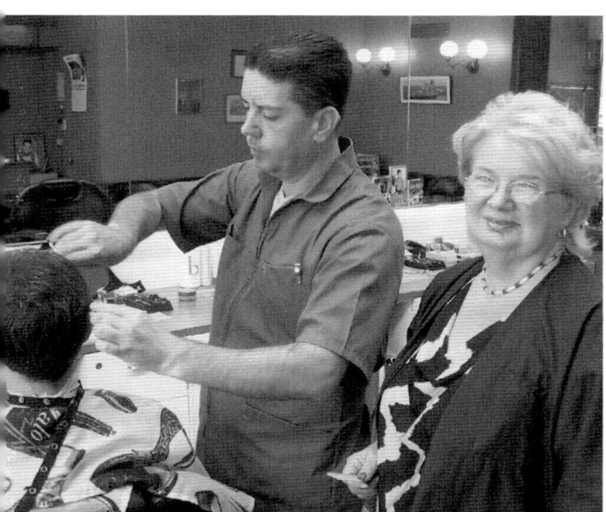

Continental Barber Shop

Also with more than 50 years of history is the Continental Barber Shop at 38 Witherspoon Street. Like many of America's beloved tonsorial destinations, it was an Italian American business, owned by Anthony and Bert Sascera. It continues to embody the tradition of immigrant success with current owner Irena Wolinski. She is seen here with barber Aliya Verlasevic and a customer. Wolinski emigrated from Poland in 1971 and was for years a popular stylist at the La Jolie Salon in Princeton where her clients included actress and then university undergrad Brooke Shields. "She was a very sweet girl," Wolinski fondly recalls. Wolinski purchased the Continental Barber Shop in 2001, fully intending to stay on at La Jolie. But her new venture proved to be a full-time success. (Author.)

E.C. Kopp

Clothing store owner as well as mechanical enthusiast, E.C. Kopp was the second person in Princeton to own a car. His Kopp's Bicycle Shop, founded in 1891, is believed to be the oldest continually operating bike store in America. Kopp is seen here on a surprisingly sophisticated racing bicycle for his time.

Edward Kopp started in business as a clerk; the 1888 *Princeton Business Directory* lists him as living at 52 University Place. Family members shared an interest in gadgets. His relative George Kopp was a jeweler and optician at 38 Nassau Street, and E.C. Kopp later had a clock repair service in his bicycle shop. Kopp passed away in 1936. The Kopp's Bicycle Shop's current owner, Charles Kuhn, believes that "if Mr. Kopp were alive today, he'd have been among the first to get into personal computers." E.C. was also proud to serve as a foreman of the Princeton Fire Company and is shown here in full company regalia. (Right, Charles Kuhn; bottom, HSP.)

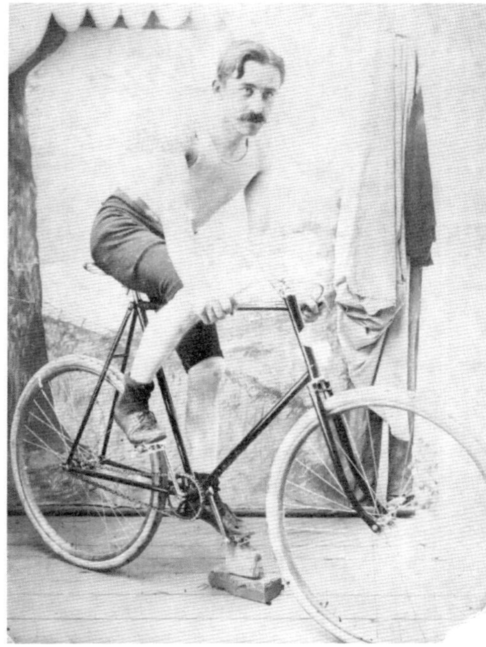

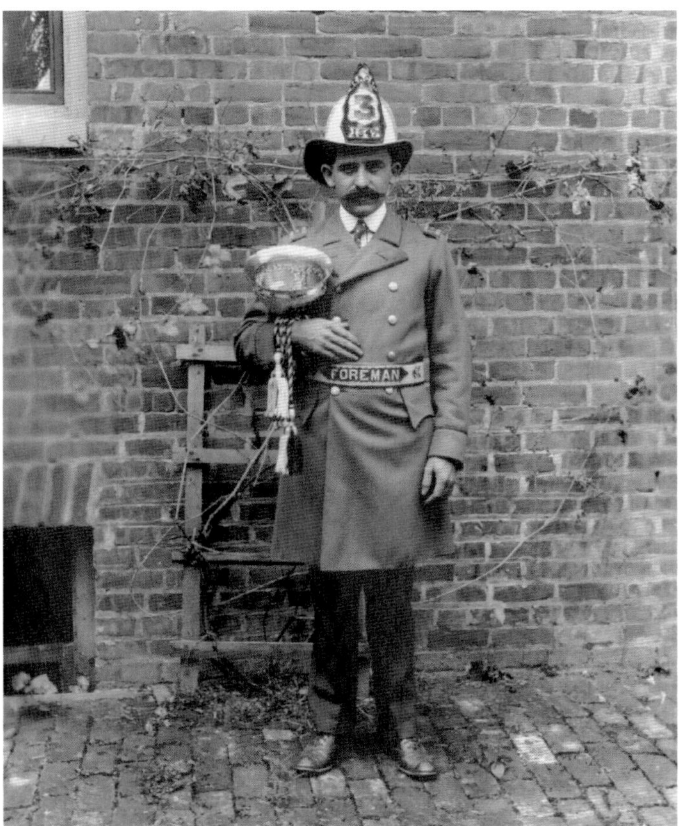

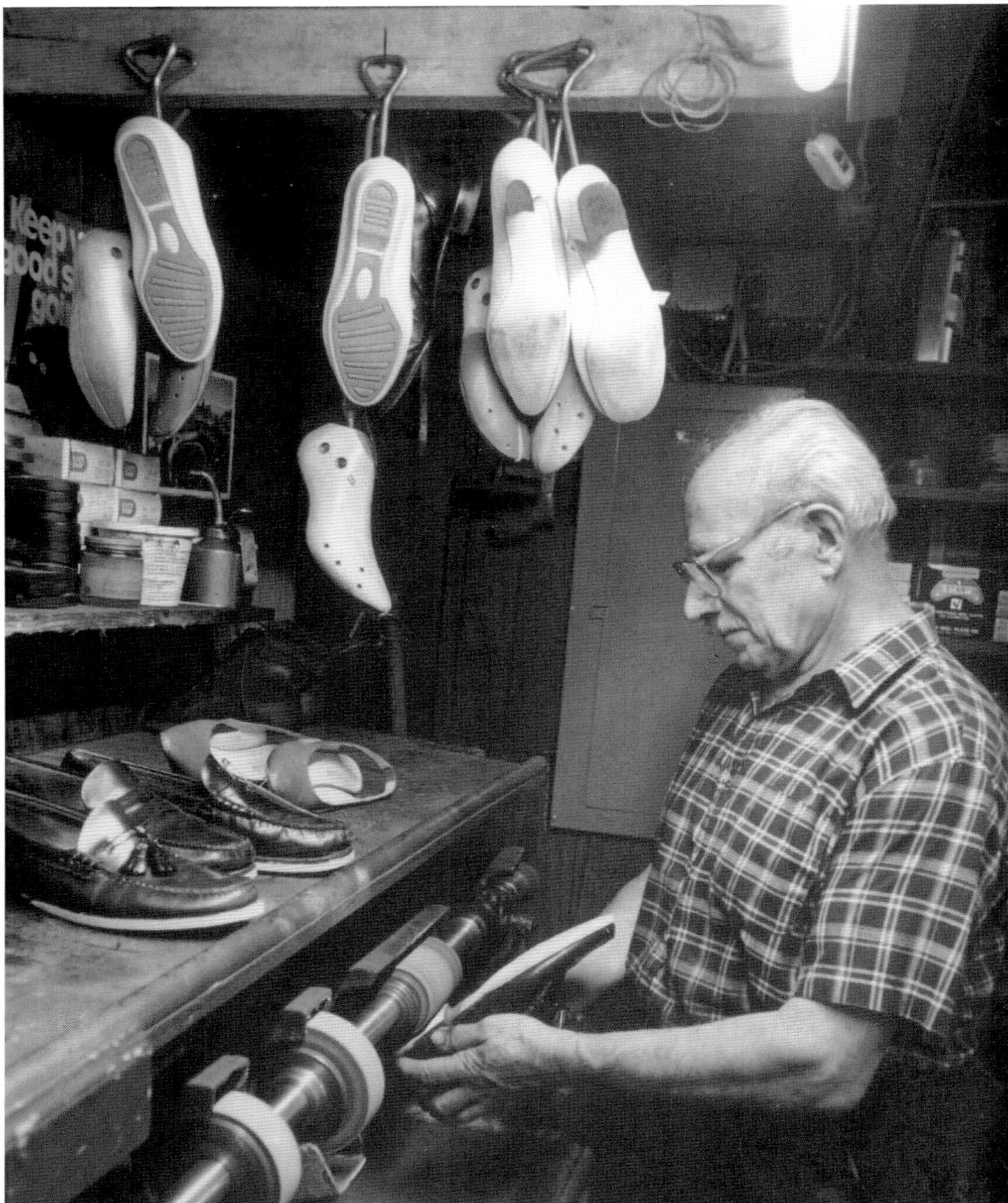

John's Shoe Shop, 18 South Tulane Street

It is sad to contemplate that shoemaking—once an indispensable trade in colonial times, as well as into the 20th century—is as, of this writing, no more in Princeton. Certainly, there remain several popular purveyors of fine footwear in town. But the final shoemaking and repair business was John's Shoe Shop at 18 South Tulane Street. Soulfully fragrant with the healing scent of leather and shoe polish, John's could replace soles or heels, keeping comfortable and still-viable footwear on the move for a modest price. But in the summer of 2007, final owner Jules Persicketti retired and closed the shop. Today, residents must journey to shoemakers in Skillman or other neighboring communities or buy new shoes if they wish to remain shod. (PP/HSP.)

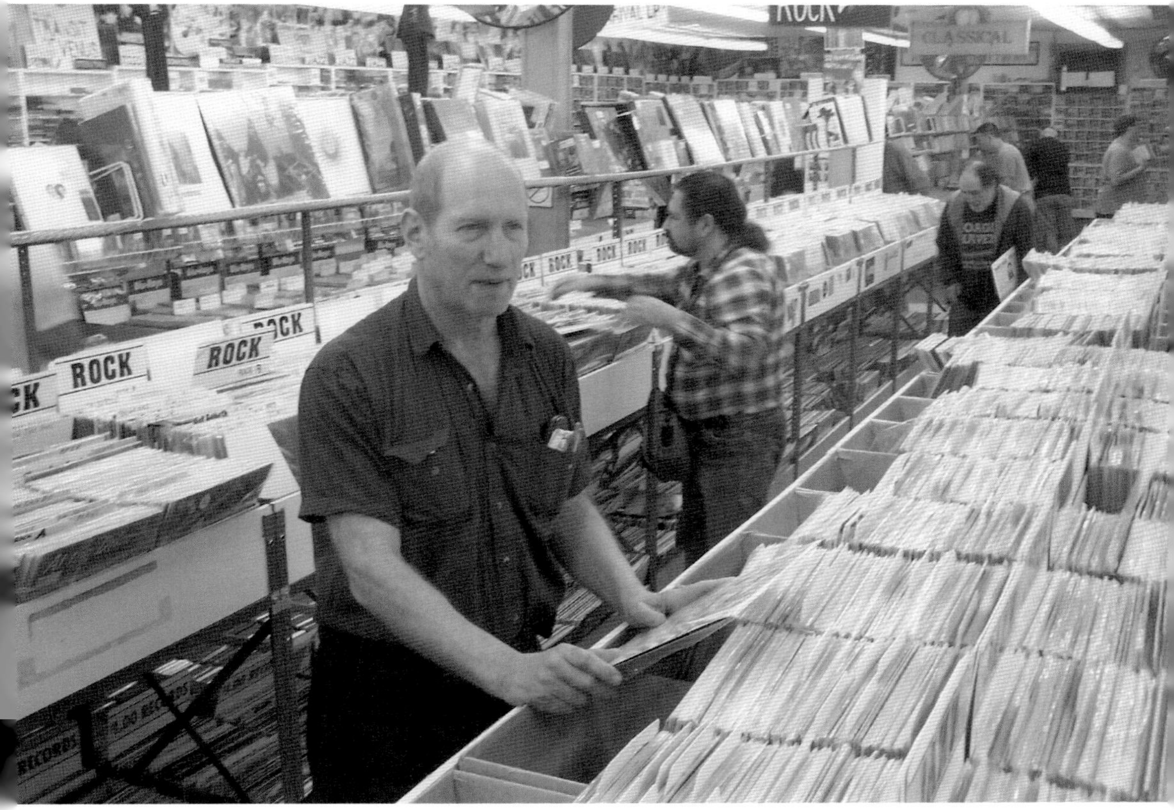

Barry Weisfeld, Princeton Record Exchange

In the brave new world of the Internet and digital downloads, will walk-in bricks-and-mortar record stores go the way of vinyl LPs? Actually, vinyl has resurged, and the Princeton Record Exchange, also known as "PREX," has thrived since its founding, becoming a legend among recording cognoscenti. Founder Barry Weisfeld was literally living out of his van in the 1970s, driving a circuit of 27 college stores with which he had arrangements to display and sell used but high-quality records. "Princeton was one of my best customers," he recalls, and on March 20, 1980, he set up shop and storage at 20 Nassau Street. "We'd outgrown it before we moved in," Weisfeld says. On August 29, 1985, the store moved to its present-day location at 20 South Tulane Street. Young and old, locals and pilgrims, collectors and bargain hunters, and a few famous musicians and movie actors browse its new and used CDs, DVDs, cassettes—and, yes, vinyls—today. Of course, PREX is firmly connected to the Internet. Three decades ago, Weisfeld admits, "I didn't understand our business would be so global. Or, perhaps, so green." Always on the lookout to purchase handfuls or major collections of lightly used products, Weisfeld says, "Our goal is to recycle unwanted CDs, DVDs and vinyls back into the hands of music and movie lovers." (Author.)

Michael Graves

From the large but elegant scale of buildings to the graceful but utilitarian lines of household items, Michael Graves & Associates (specializing in architecture, interior design, and planning) and its sister firm Michael Graves Designs (products and branding) have established themselves in Princeton as well as internationally.

Graves founded his firm in 1964. He has since been awarded an American Institute of Architecture gold medal and the National Medal of the Arts; collectively the Michael Graves companies have won some 200 awards and citations.

After earning his master's in architecture from Harvard and further studies at the American Academy in Rome, Graves obtained a teaching position at Princeton University. He intended to commute from New York, but the university insisted he live locally. He acquiesced. Now, he says, "I won't live anywhere else."

Complications from a 2003 spinal infection have forced Graves to rely on a wheelchair, but he still gets out and about in his cherished town and campus. And he has strongly applied his experience to the future well being of others, recently serving on a presidential advisory committee to improve the accessibility of public spaces and conveyances.

Taking an architect and planner's view of Princeton, Graves observes, "It's not a city with the problems of a city and not a suburb with those problems. It's a town where you can live, work, shop, or go to the theater and not have the challenges of crowds or of travel. I have no problem getting people to come here." (Michael Graves.)

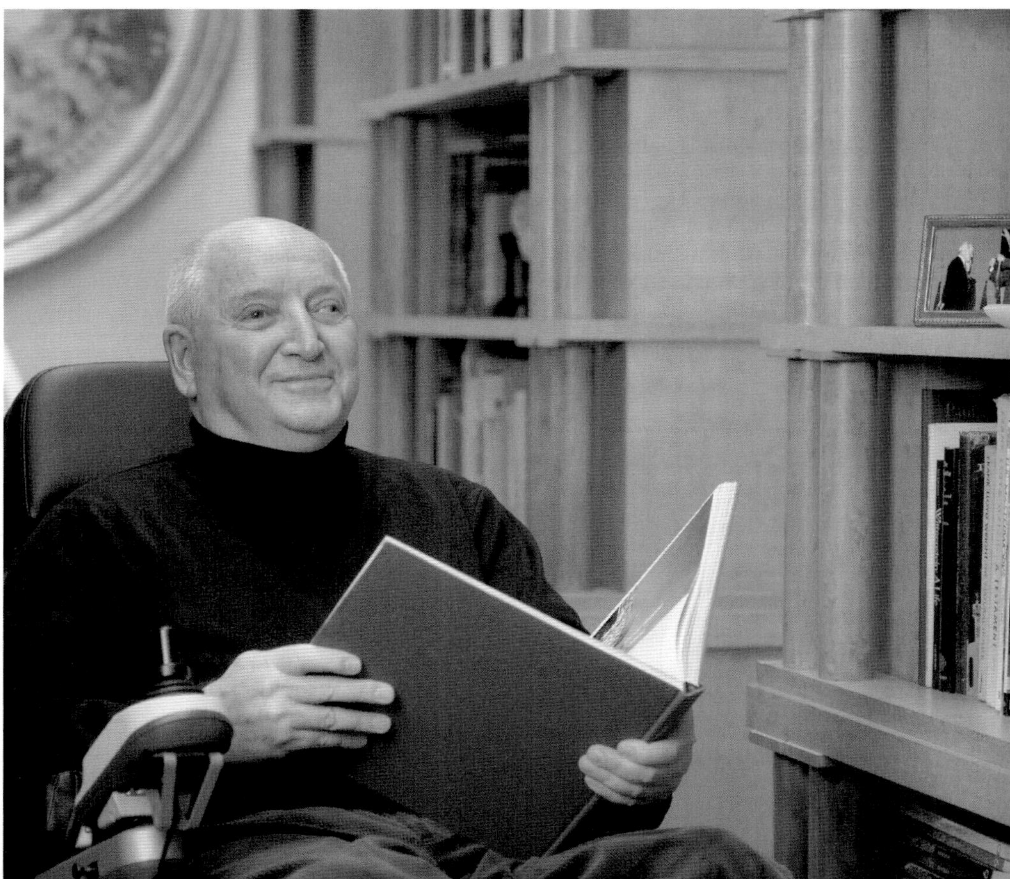

J. Robert "Bob" Hillier

Another world-renowned Princeton architect, J. Robert Hillier, a fellow of the American Institute of Architectures (FAIA), was originally from Canada. But his family moved to Cranbury when he was three; his father took an advanced research position at the RCA Sarnoff Laboratories near Princeton. His mother came to own and operate the Flower Basket and, eventually, two other Princeton flower shops. Bob's earliest work experience was at her shops. He even sold tropical fish at one. En route to lifetime achievement awards from the New Jersey Institute of Technology and the New Jersey Chapter of the American Association of Architects, as well as many other honors, he earned his undergraduate degree at Princeton in 1959 and his master's in architecture in 1961. In 1964, he founded the Hillier group. It became the third largest of its kind in the United States. "The Princeton address was a huge asset, frankly," he says. But so were Hillier's talents, leading to his firm merging with the Scottish RMJM firm in 2007. After observing a two-year noncompetition period, he founded Studio Hillier, headquartered in the former Jefferson Plumbing Company warehouse on Witherspoon Street, beautifully restored and architecturally repurposed, of course. In addition to his national and international commissions, a local project from which Hillier received special satisfaction was the former Witherspoon Street School for Colored Children. The building's exterior was restored close to its original schoolhouse appearance, the interior redesigned as condominiums, and the property renamed the Waxwood in honor of longtime principal Howard B. Waxwood. As a well as a successful business investment, the project also represented an investment in this historic community. "I describe Princeton as the best little city in the world," Hillier reflects. "It has theaters, museums, restaurants and great educational institutions. Yet it's a small town. That's the magic of the place." (Author.)

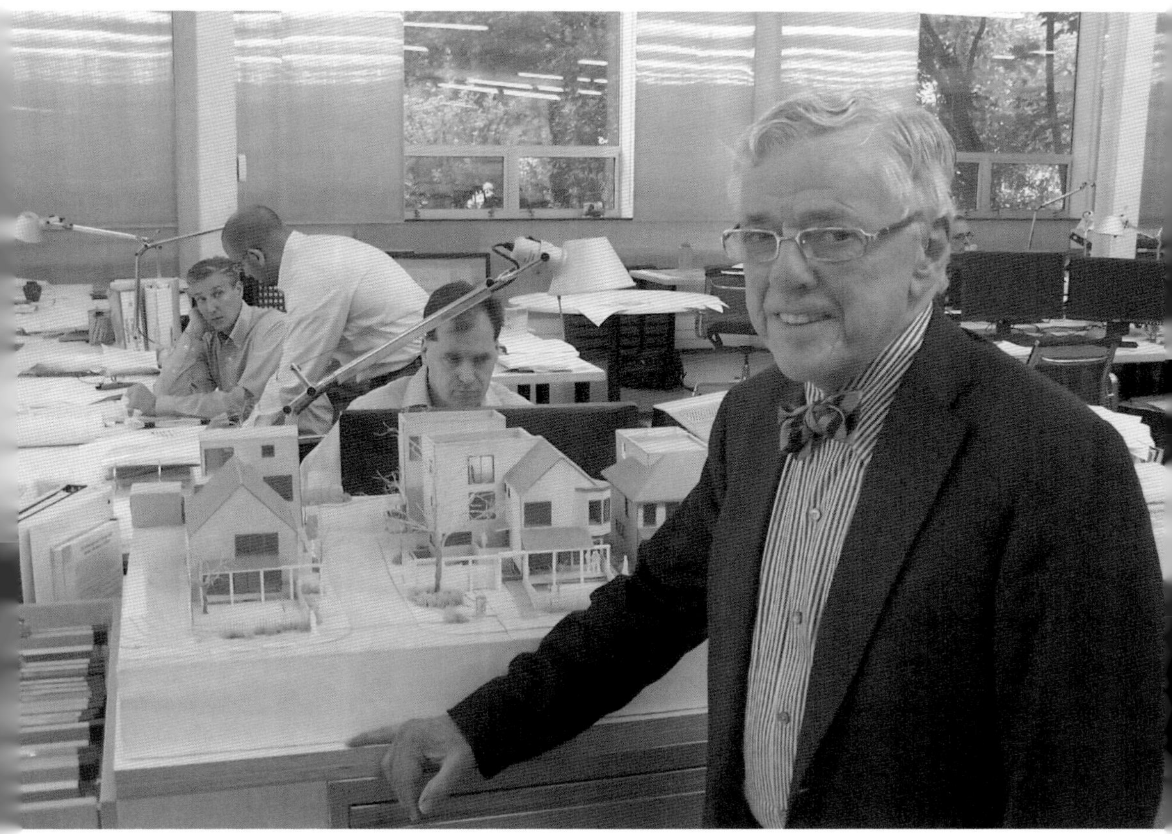

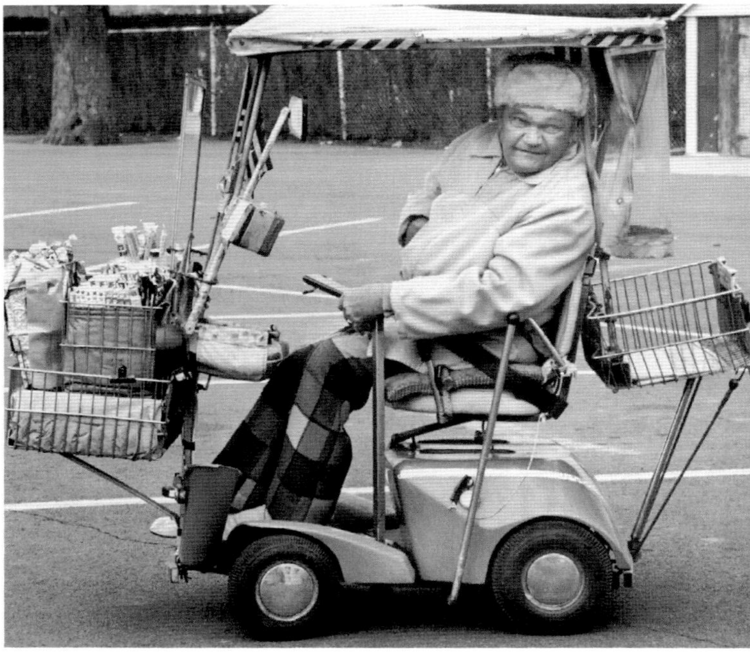

Sonny Perreine

Born with cerebral palsy, Perreine nevertheless determinedly finished his grade and high schooling. He was known to children and adults as he sold candy from his wheel chair in front of the Princeton Playhouse and the Garden movie theaters. When he temporarily moved in with relatives in South Brunswick, Princeton residents anxiously commented on his absence.

Shown below at his Elm Court residence with visitor James Hill, Perreine was able to look on the entire town as his friends. He was especially proud to receive a commendation as a local business entrepreneur from Mayor Barbara Sigmund. When he died in his sleep in August 1991, at age 65, Sonny Perreine's life and passing were front-page news in both the *Princeton Packet* and *Town Topics*. (Above, Robert Landau; below, PP/HSP.)

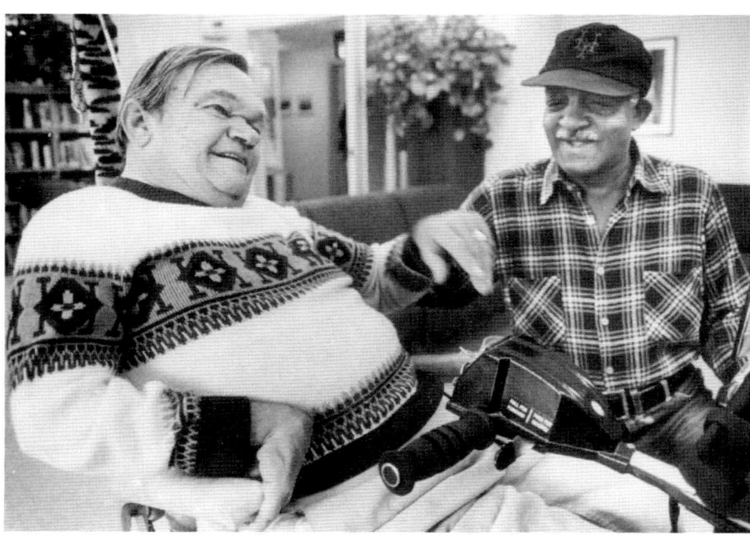

CHAPTER SEVEN

Mystery, Myth, and Controversy

Where there is history, there will be myths. Where there are people, there will be dark passions. Where there is fame and fortune, there will be controversy. Beautiful, bucolic, and seemingly serene Princeton has had its share of all these. And along with many saints, the town and surrounding countryside have had their share of rogues.

Strangely enough, Princeton as a municipality was largely defined by the problem of law enforcement. Not that crime was rampant in its streets, but those streets were originally in different municipalities: Nassau Street lay along the local dividing line between Somerset and Middlesex Counties. So, those accused of breaking the law or disturbing the peace on one side of the thoroughfare could cross over and out of the initial jurisdiction. Such legal issues greatly motivated the 1813 incorporation of Princeton Borough as a single municipality. The 1838 creation of Mercer County from sections of Hunterdon, Middlesex, and Somerset solidified Princeton's statutory status.

Over the years, excellent Princeton police forces and effective local government have kept crime at a minimum. But still, white-collar crimes in business have been discovered and prosecuted, and at least two murders from the 1970s and 1980s remain officially unsolved to this day.

Among local cases of crime and controversy, a few played out in neighboring municipalities but had strong Princeton connections.

Bill MacKay was not a self-effacing man. He was the author of a 1978 autobiography *The Salesman Surgeon*, touting his experiences as a representative for medical implants who sometimes allegedly rushed to hospitals to help a doctor struggling with the products in mid-operation. MacKay purchased a rambling six-bedroom home in Montgomery Township in the 1980s and took the helm of American Biomaterials Corporation, a startup company located in a section of Plainsboro considered part of the greater Princeton–Route One business corridor. MacKay soon added a Jacuzzi and other creature comforts to his property as well as a high-priced boarding kennel. He began driving a huge motor home around the country to transport his own canines to dog shows. Not surprisingly, as American Biomaterials began to founder, its investors took exception to news that the company had shelled out for these perks. MacKay was terminated. He then founded a firm called United Capital but was convicted of financial malfeasance and making false statements to boost its stock. After doing prison time, MacKay seemingly vanished. But the dog boarding business he started in Montgomery continues as of this writing.

Of greater fame—and far greater infamy and sorrow—is the March 1, 1932, kidnapping and death of the infant son of aviator Charles Lindbergh and his wife, author Anne Morrow Lindbergh. The Lindberghs had hosted numerous dignitaries, including many from Princeton, in their home in the Sourlands hill above Hopewell, which they aptly named "Highfields." Lindbergh had selected the site largely as a refuge from the relentless media attention generated by his exploits and popularity. With tragic irony, its isolation proved ideal for the intruder who kidnapped the 20-month-old Charles Jr. from his crib. The child died during the abduction, perhaps accidentally; his remains were discovered more than two months later in the woods a few miles away. And the world news media again descended upon the Lindberghs, who eventually left the Princeton-Hopewell area. Highfields is now a court-operated home for at-risk boys. There have been numerous conspiracy theories about the case, but the evidence against Bruno Richard Hauptmann, an immigrant carpenter living in the Bronx who was convicted of the crime and executed, is substantial; the remaining ransom money was found at Hauptmann's home, a section of wood used to construct the kidnapping ladder came from a roof support in his garage, and the ransom notes (including the first one left at the scene) are demonstrably in Hauptmann's handwriting. Whether the crime merited capital punishment for first-degree murder is still debatable, however.

The town of Princeton provided an unwitting—and unwilling—link to post-9/11 terror. Letters containing deadly anthrax spores, postmarked on September 18 and October 9, 2001, were sent to two US senators and a small group of news media outlets. Five persons died, and at least 22 were sickened. Although marked at the regional postal facility in Trenton, the letters were found to have been dropped in a mailbox at 10 Nassau Street in Princeton. No link to any Princetonians was ever discovered. An FBI investigation eventually centered on a biodefense researcher at a US government laboratory in Maryland, but the subject committed suicide before any charges were lodged against him.

Princeton University has been spared major crimes, but one colorful character deserves mention: Alexi Indris-Santana, a member of the undergraduate class of 1992. Santana's backstory was astonishing. He was orphaned and largely self-raised, self-educated (he had never even taken standard college admission tests), undeniably brilliant, widely read, and an indefatigable distance runner. Recruited for the track team, he was granted admission and given exceedingly generous financial aid. Yes, it was all too good to be true. "Indris-Santana" was in fact James Hogue, an unnaturally boyish-looking 28-year-old originally from Kansas. Hogue's hoax was uncovered 1991 when he was recognized at a track meet as the perpetrator of a similar 1986 scam in California in which he had passed himself off as a high school runner (apparently to avoid superior foreign competitors in his college age group). Hogue was charged with fraud for having accepted $30,000 in student aid, declared persona non grata by Princeton University (subject to arrest if he set foot again on campus), and sentenced to a three-year jail term. After thefts at Harvard and an abortive attempt to insinuate himself back at Princeton University, Hogue pleaded guilty in 2007 in Colorado to stealing from homes in which he had been working as a handyman.

The following stories feature some shady or outright criminal characters directly associated with the town of Princeton. These tales will bring, it is hoped, more diversion than discomfort. And, in the author's view, a few controversial figures have probably been judged inaccurately and unfairly. If so, the record may be set straight here.

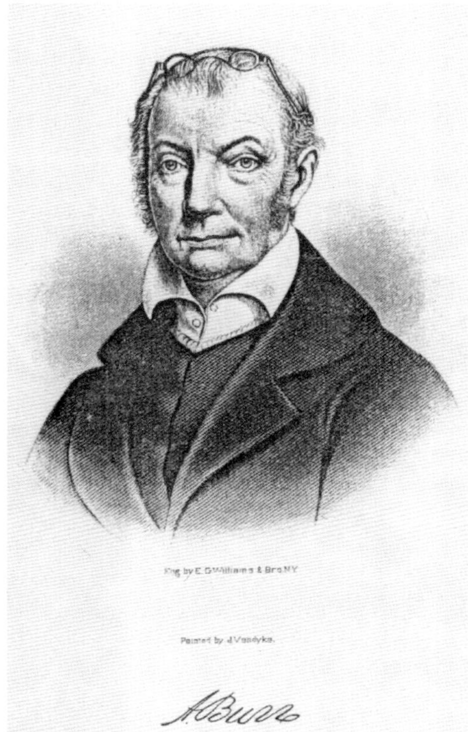

Aaron Burr Jr. (1756–1836)
Burr was a colonel in the Army of the Revolution and the third vice president of the United States from 1801 to 1805. Burr is buried at the foot of his father's grave and near that of his grandfather Jonathan Edwards, both former presidents of the college.

Tragically, his great service to his country—and indeed his entire life—has been overshadowed by the notorious July 11, 1804, duel at Weehawken, New Jersey, in which he shot and killed his bitter political adversary Alexander Hamilton. (Right, HSP; below, Corbis.)

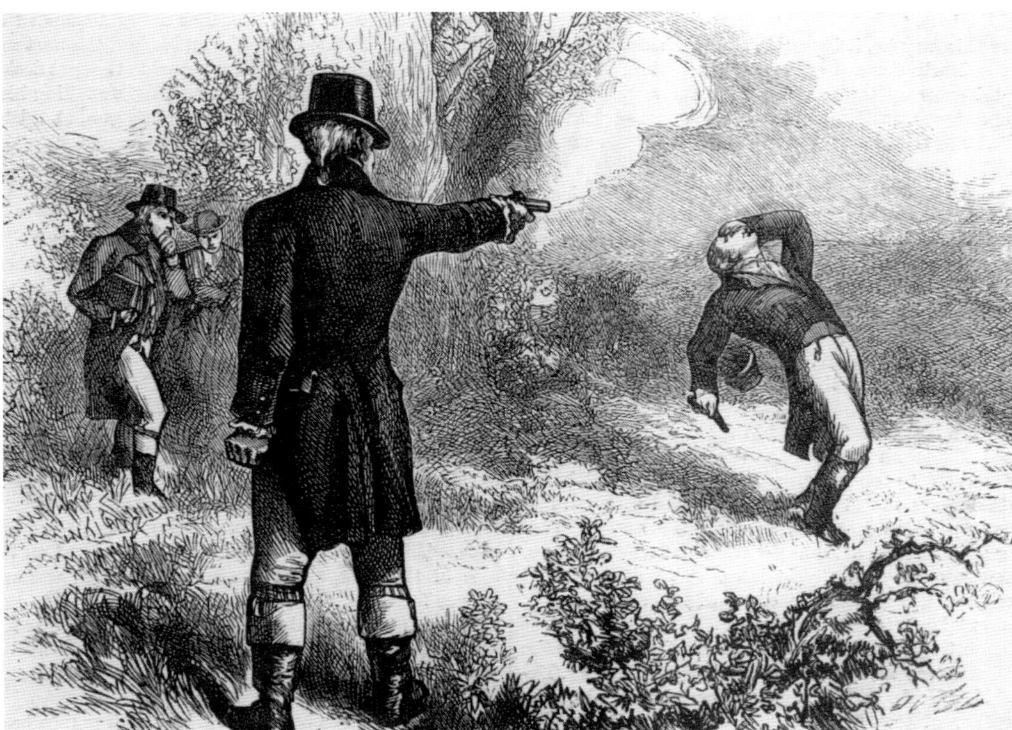

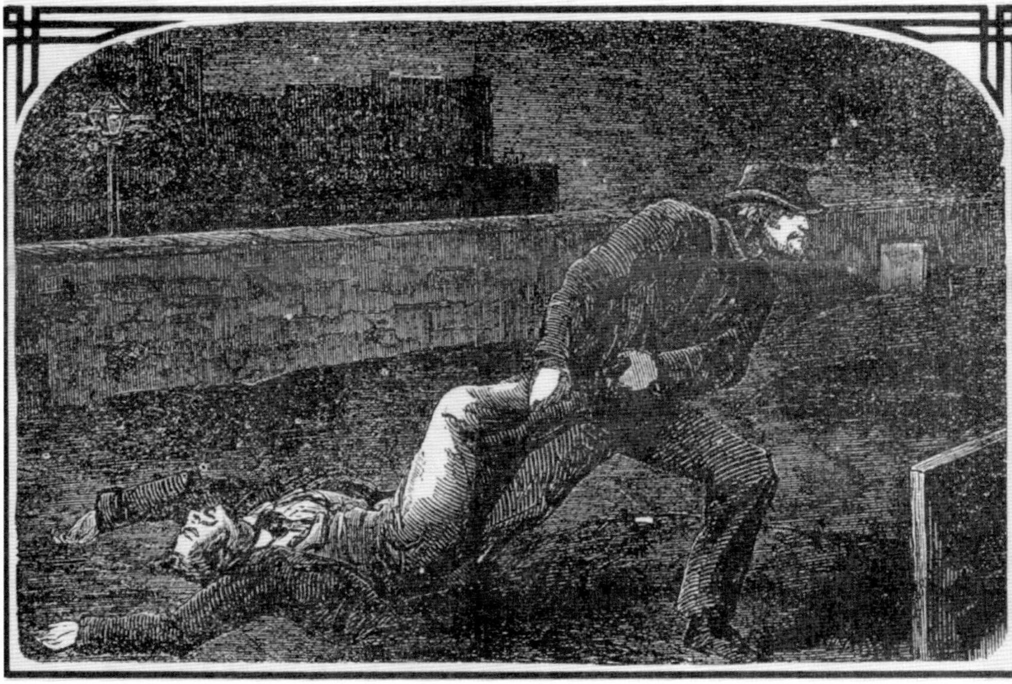

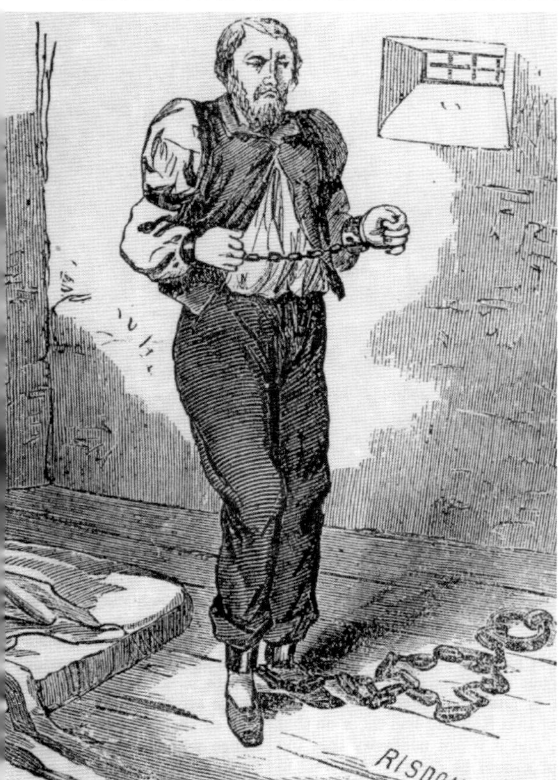

James Rowland and Charles Lewis

The robbery and murder of jeweler James Rowland as he returned to Princeton Junction on the night of November 13, 1862, and the subsequent arrest, conviction, and execution for the crime of Lewis (who went by the alias "Symonds") were such a sensation that the *Princeton Standard* and even the *National Police Gazette*, the sensational and widely devoured 19th-century tabloid, copiously covered the story.

Rowland's wife was Ann R. Berrien, a descendant of one of Princeton's prominent early families.(She died in February 1894, age 84, and was buried beside her murdered husband.) Rowand's mangled body was found in his future resting place of the Princeton Cemetery among the graves. Lewis was found with incriminating money and a watch when located and arrested the next day.

Lewis was hanged at Trenton State Prison on April 3, 1863. When asked what he would like to eat prior to sentence being carried out, he loudly declared, "I'd like to have a piece of pie on my way to Hell!" And he declared he would have no praying said over him at the gallows. (Both, PR.)

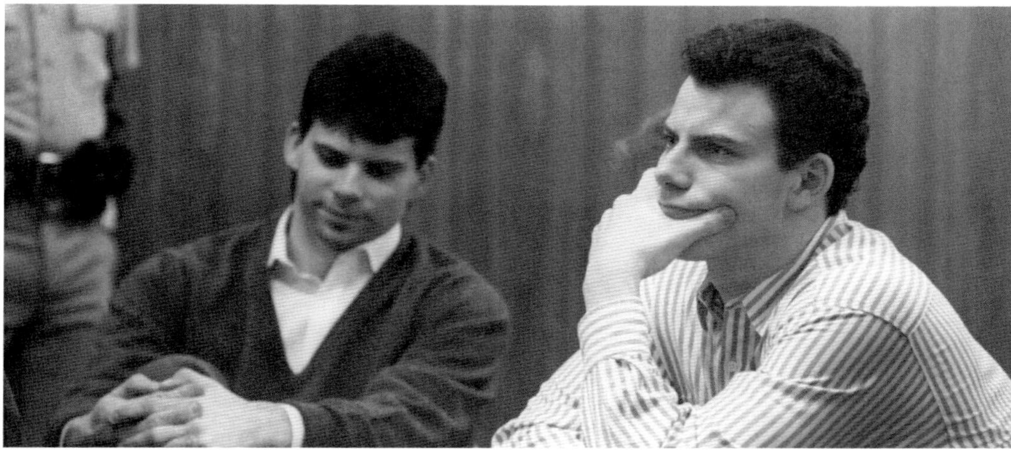

The Menendez Brothers

Lyle Menendez (born 1968) and Erik Menendez (born 1970) were the sons of high-power record company executive Jose Menendez and his wife, Mary "Kitty." The family lived in a country home in wooded acres overlooking a serene lake. The boys had a life of privilege, attending local prep schools, with Lyle later enrolling at Princeton University. They were formidable youth tennis competitors. When Jose left his New York job to take a position in Los Angeles, the family relocated to Beverley Hills. On the night of August 20, 1989, Jose and Kitty were brutally gunned down at home in what seemed to be a mob hit. Inheriting their sizeable estate, the sons purchased a plot for their parents in Princeton Cemetery. Lyle soon began spending extravagantly, putting money down on popular Princeton buffalo wings restaurant Chuck's Spring Street Café, with plans to create a franchise. But the boys were linked to the purchase of shotguns, and a confession made to their psychotherapist was deemed admissible evidence. They are seen here during in an early hearing on murder charges; Lyle is on the left, and Erik is on the right. Their first trial, a nationally televised sensation, ended in a hung jury. But a retrial saw a unanimous rejection of the boys' claim that they had killed their parents out of fear that they themselves were about to be murdered. Lyle and Erik are expected to spend the rest of their lives in prison.

The former Menendez country estate is now the Mountain Lakes Preserve, administered by a nonprofit organization. Its trails are open for hiking. The house with its sloping back lawn is a lovely and popular setting for weddings. The empty flower urn before Jose and Kitty's headstone testifies to the loneliness of their grave. (Above, Corbis; below, author's.)

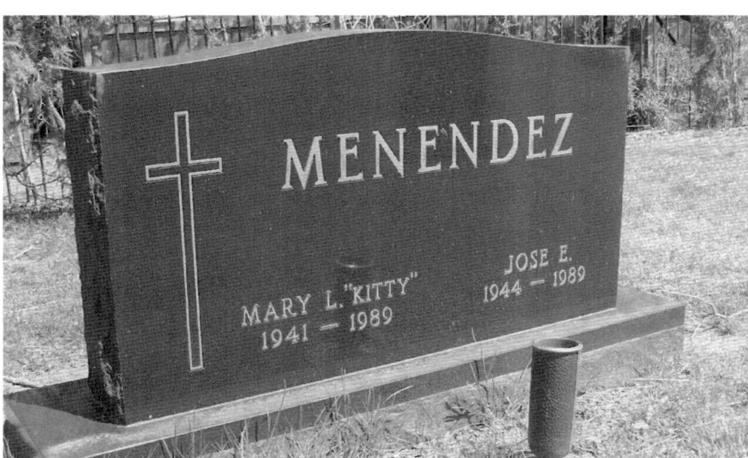

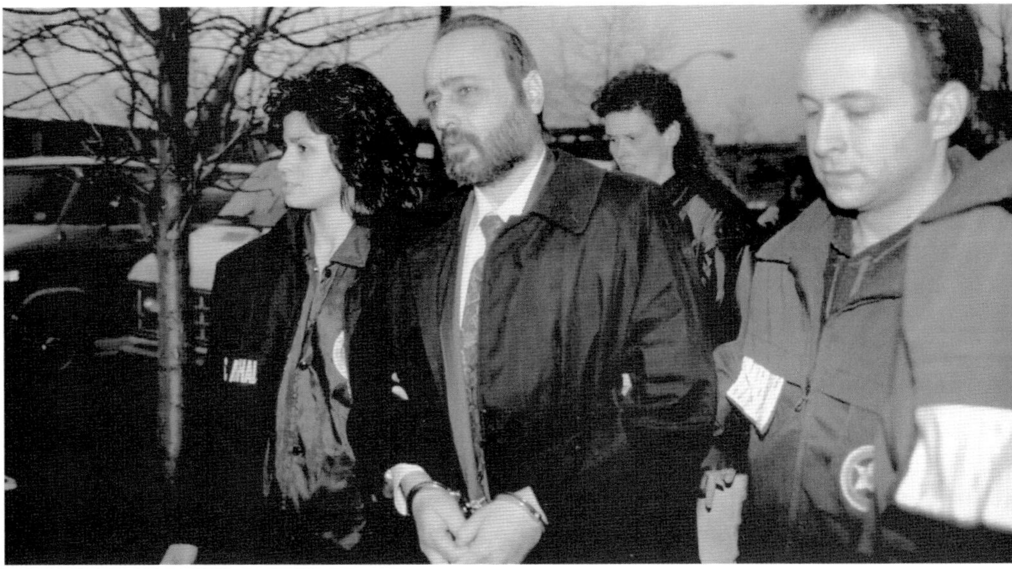

Eddie "Crazy Eddie" Antar

The television commercials for Crazy Eddie, an ultra-discount consumer electronics store chain, might as well have been in 3-D. Pitchman Jerry Carroll was not Crazy Eddie himself but became firmly associated as such in the public mind thanks to his manic, high-frequency style, culminating with the declaration "His prices are INSANE!" and a wide-handed climatic gesture that practically reached out of the tube into the viewer's living room. Eddie Antar with his brother Sam M. Antar founded the appliances store chain. The company eventually went bankrupt, and Eddie (center) was convicted of financial crimes. (Corbis.)

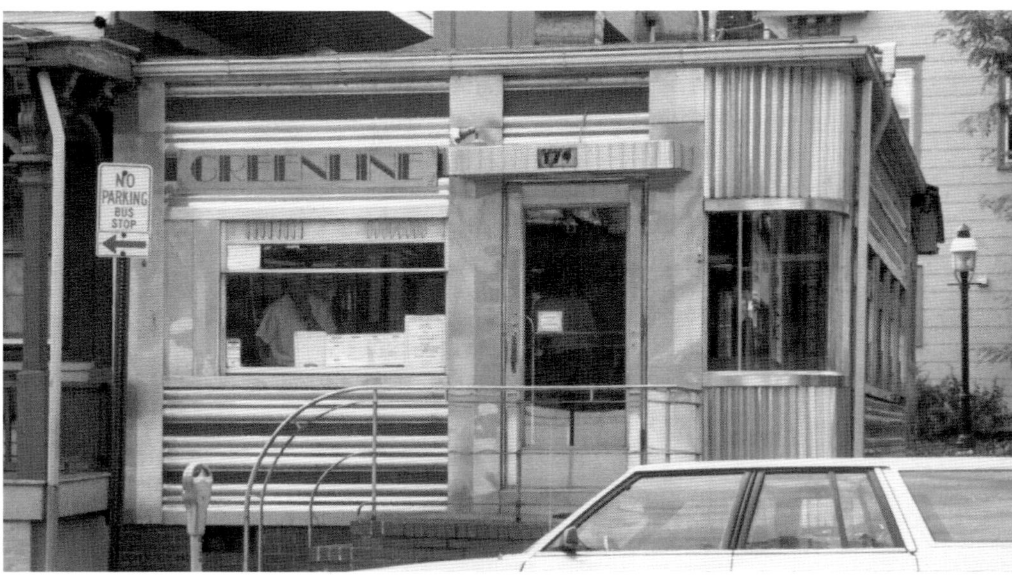

Greenline Diner

Eddie Antar lived for a time in the Princeton area and owned the Green Line Diner at 173 Nassau Street. It featured a natural foods menu and became a trendy alternative-dining destination for college students and town youths. The diner burned down in April 1990, but the disaster was ruled an accident. (PHP.)

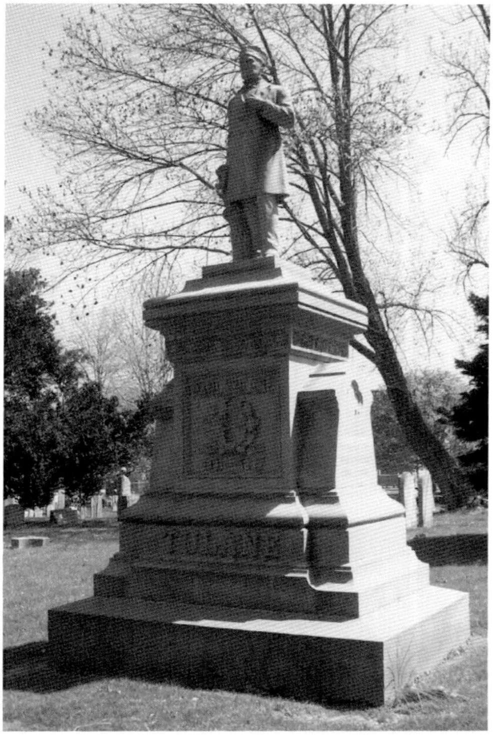

Paul Tulane

One of the most pervasive of Princeton myths has unfortunately cast a generous man as being ego-driven in life and vindictive in death. Paul Tulane (1801–1887) was born to French parents just north of Princeton, in the Rose Valley section. After working as a clerk in a Princeton store, he traveled to New Orleans, where he founded a successful dry-goods business in 1882. He shrewdly invested in real estate there and in Princeton. He retired here in 1857 and purchased Morven, the historic Stockton estate. He became justly known for his philanthropy, with the greatest beneficiary of his largess being the Medical College of Louisiana, later renamed Tulane University. And there lies the rub; according to local legend, Tulane had first offered aid to Princeton University if it would bear his name; however, the university declined. Many believe his magnificent likeness in Princeton Cemetery faces away from campus so that Tulane would forever have his back to the university that had spurned him. But in fact, his statue was placed in a positive pose—facing north toward Rose Valley, his beloved birthplace. (Author.)

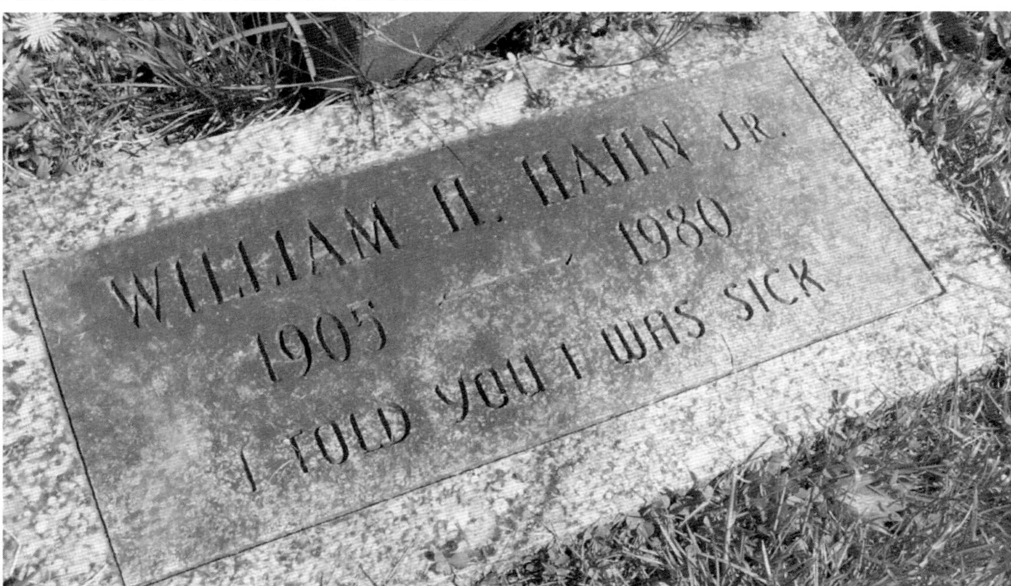

William H. Hahn Jr.

And, ironically, what seems an utterly apocryphal story is actually true. So true that it is literally carved in stone. Just days before his passing, William H. Hahn Jr., instructed that his headstone in Princeton Cemetery be inscribed with "I Told You I Was Sick." There is no evidence that his family or physicians doubted his illness, but Hahn made sure that he had a good last laugh. (Author.)

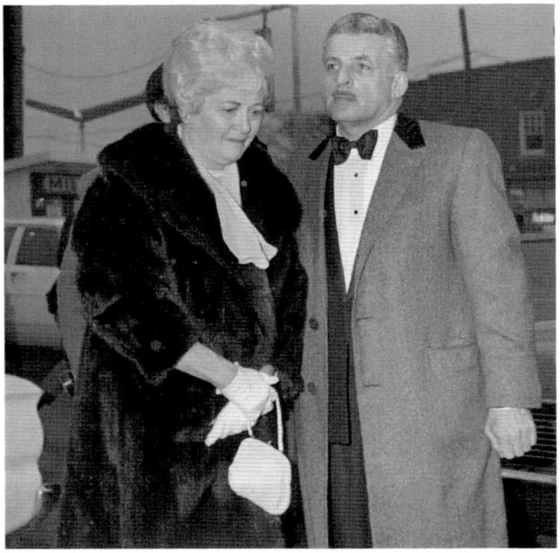

Simone Rizzo DeCavalcante ("Sam the Plumber") (1912–1997)

Arriving with his wife for their son's wedding in Trenton, Simone DeCavalcante looks every bit the successful businessman, and in a sense, he was. But he was also a Mafia don of south-central New Jersey who maintained a home and a low profile in Princeton Township. It is said that instead of the moniker "Sam the Plumber," a nod to his legitimate plumbing business in Kenilworth, New Jersey, he requested in vain that his mob colleagues call him "Princeton Sam." Smooth and rarely violent, he was nevertheless eventually convicted of racketeering and briefly imprisoned. After retirement in Florida, he was buried in Trenton's Greenwood Cemetery. (Corbis.)

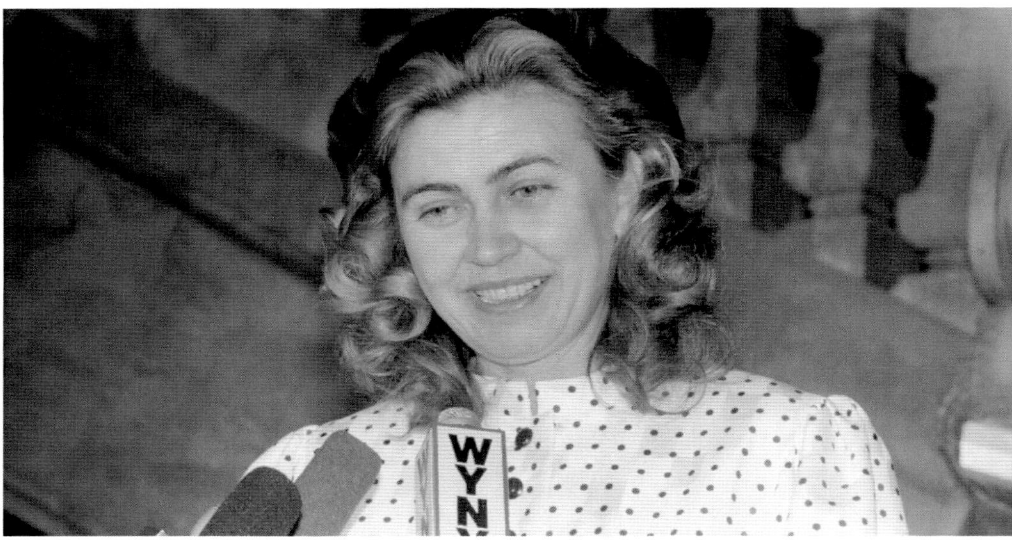

Basia "Barbara" Piasecka Johnson

By contrast, Basia Piasecka was a law-abiding citizen. But she became caught up in one of the most contentious legal battles in recent memory. After earning a master's degree in art history in her native Poland, Basia Piasecka immigrated to America. She found employment in the household of Johnson & Johnson heir Seward Johnson Jr. Captivated by her, he divorced his second wife, and Basia became the third Mrs. Johnson in 1971. He was 76; she was 32. They purchased a large Princeton Township property, which they named "Jasna Polana," Polish for "beautiful meadow," which it certainly was. The mansion they constructed was reckoned the most expensive American private home to date. Seward died in 1983, and Basia inherited most of his $400 million estate. Having received much less than expected, his children and foundations sued. Their attorneys portrayed Basia as a viciously tempered wife who had exercised undue influence over her ailing husband. Her attorneys argued that Seward had remained of discerning mind, and she had cared for him tenderly. A settlement finally was reached. Jasna Polana was later converted in a Tournaments Players Club golf course, a project thoroughly scrutinized by Princeton Regional Planning Board for potential impacts on neighbors and the environment. Mrs. Johnson spent most of her remaining years in Poland and funded charities and programs for her countrypersons before passing away in April 2013. (Corbis.)

CHAPTER EIGHT

Community Mainstays

Princeton is so blessed by public-spirited individuals that this concluding chapter could potentially be many times its allotted length—perhaps even the size of the entire book.

"Why Princeton?" must be asked. The answer is a tautology as twisted as a Möebius strip. Princeton has been home to so many wonderful people because it is a genuinely special place, and it is a genuinely special place because it has been home to so many wonderful people.

Many residents, from many walks of life, express this feeling. Community mainstays include businesspeople, who have literally rebuilt sections of Princeton for the common good; possessors of old money or newly acquired wealth, who are moved to generosity toward good deeds or those in need; "elders of the tribe," who have inspired generations; public servants, who truly deserve that often clichéd designation; and unelected persons, who simply elect to be helpful. It is hoped that each of their stories have a special, even inspirational tale to tell.

And there are groups. The number of legendary local charities and nonprofit organizations, serving both Princeton and the nation in general, is profound. Some 130 such concerns are based in Princeton, many making the town their headquarters, a profoundly impressive count by anyone's measure. It is worth noting that a Princeton address might add a certain cache to fundraising but confers no special tax or other considerations. Clearly, Princeton is associated as much with good works as with good learning.

One Princeton-based nonprofit that has served over a long time and changed with the times is Learning Ally at 20 Roszel Road. Founded in 1948 as Recording for the Blind, it later took the name Recording for the Blind & Dyslexic as the organization began serving students and others with learning as well as visual challenges. It now serves more than 300,000 young people and lifetime learners.

Other efforts are less structured, incorporated only in faith, vision, and a sense of duty.

Again, the honor roll of legendary community mainstays is long, and space to honor all is short (or regrettably, suitable images could not be located). Among those deserving at least a brief mention are Lillian Schafer, who was a leading citizen of the "Jugtown" district near the intersection of Nassau and Harrison Streets, which was known as "Queen's Town" in colonial times. During World War II, Schafer and her neighbors yearned for news about their young men gone off to service. In February 1944, she founded the *Jugtown News* to print accounts of and letters from community servicemen. Schafer typifies the thoughtfulness and initiative typical of service-oriented Princeton residents. And it is worth noting that she was a mainstay of a community within a community: in those days, Jugtown, named for the ceramics manufacturing that flourished there in the late 1800s and early 1900s, had a distinctive identity within Princeton at large.

Community mainstays often become well known, such high-profile recognition often being crucial to their ability to attract funding and helpers to worthy causes. But many labor humbly and almost anonymously, coming to the recognition they richly deserve only through the subsequent praise of others.

It is tremendously important to note that Princeton's—and America's—evolution through the historical process of immigration will have major and happy implications for new generations of community mainstays. Just as Dutch, Scottish, African American, Jewish and Italian families established themselves in business and also in public service—lifting themselves and their people—it is increasingly clear that relatively new Princetonians of Asian, Latino, Middle Eastern, and South Asian heritage are poised to become leading citizens in the 21st century. Surely a future book will tell the stories of the next generation of legendary locals of Princeton.

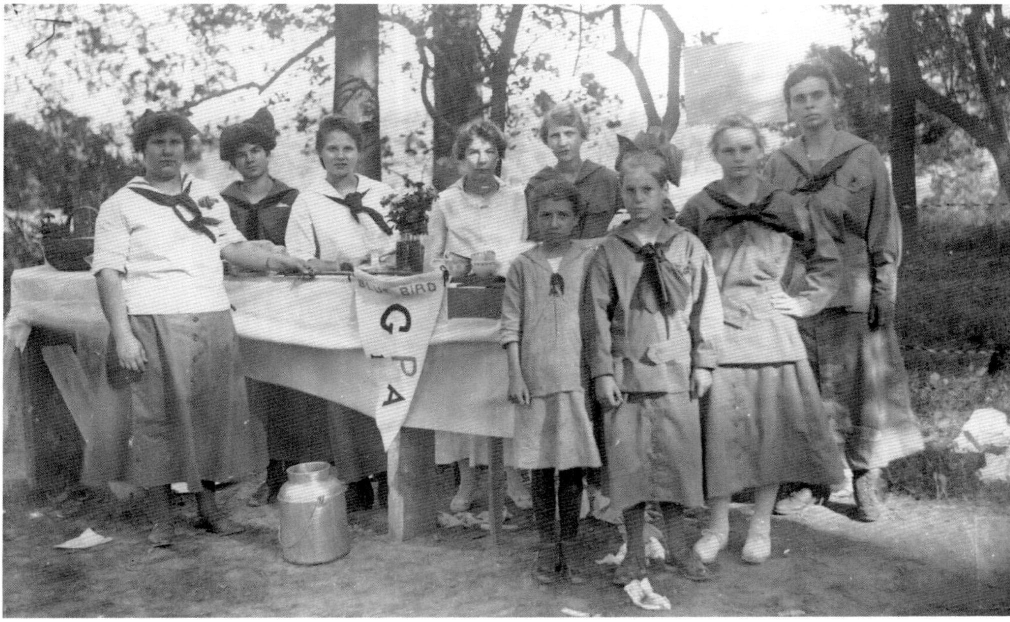

The Bluebird Patrol

This early forerunner of the Girl Scouts taught young local women the basics of camping and crafts. Though little recalled today, its organizers helped pioneer today's numerous Princeton youth organizations. (HSP.)

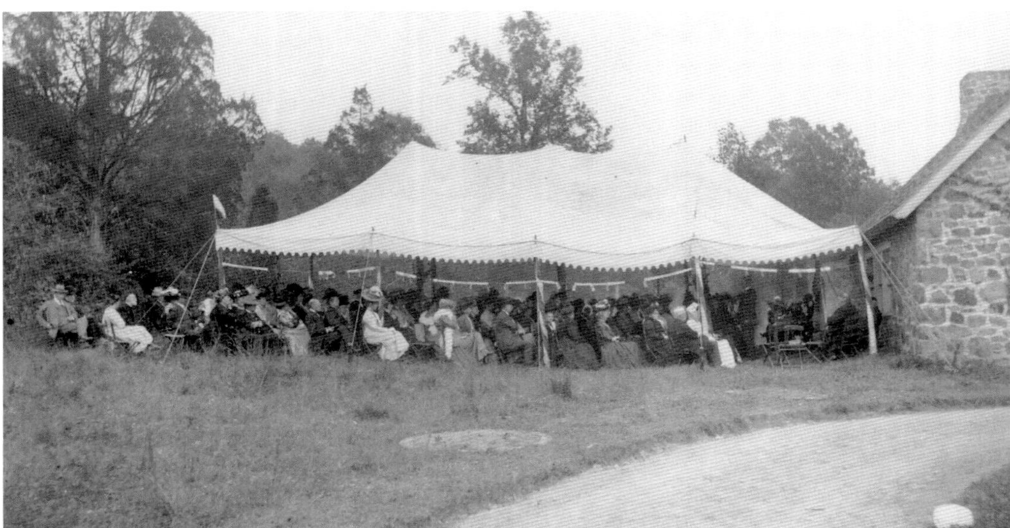

Alfred Britten Baker (1836–1928)

Alfred Britten Baker graduated from Princeton University in 1861 and received a degree from the Princeton Theological Seminary the following year. In 1866, he was called to be rector of Trinity Church in Princeton in 1866, a position he held until 1914. But Dr. Baker was also a local booster of the Boy Scouts movement. He presided over this 1908 tent meeting of Princeton Scouts and their parents, its size showing the popularity of the troop. (HSP.)

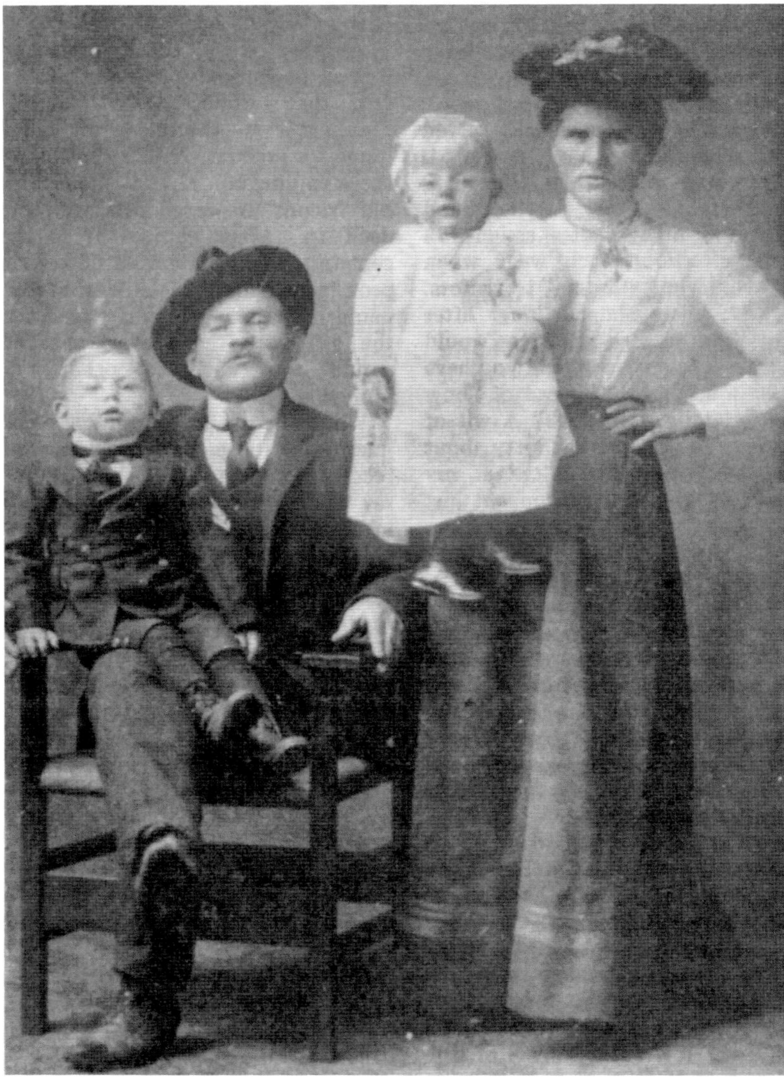

Achille Carnevale

Head of one of Princeton's longest established Italian American families, a native of Pettoranello, Italy, he came to these shores in 1884, a 14 year old who found work as a gardener and laborer. Shown here c. 1908 with his wife and two of their children, Carnevale was a true American success story; he eventually founded his own general contracting company and employed as many as 20 men. He is credited with bringing many of his countrymen to America to start new lives, often, at first, through hard work in the local quarries and on campus buildings. Among those helped were skilled Italian stonemason William Fiabane, the Procaccino family from the Abruzzi region of Italy, and the Pietrinferno family as well as others. Additional "Pettoranesi" families in the area include Nini, Pinelli, Pironem, and Rossi. Pettoranello Gardens in Community Park North was established and is maintained through their efforts. In addition to helping to establish the gardens, descendant Nicholas Carnevale has organized delegations from Princeton and Pettoranello to make exchange visits of delegates every several years. The American citizens thrilled at visiting the small town of their roots, and the Italians are equally moved at seeing the impressive buildings and businesses grown by their relatives in the New World. (PR.)

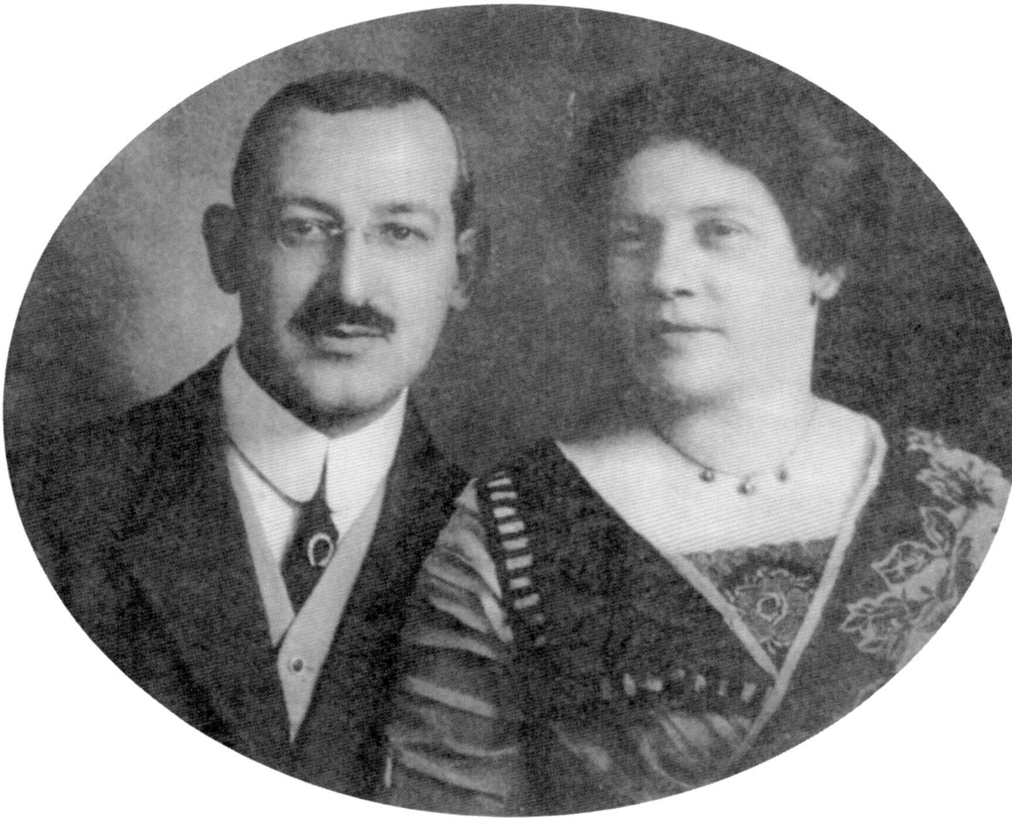

Isadore P. and Sarah Hurvitz Braveman

Seen here in their engagement photograph, these early leaders of the Princeton Jewish community helped organize the first synagogue in town in the early part of the 20th century. There was already a small but successful Jewish enclave in town when the Bravemans arrived in 1926. In addition to the Marks family, other members of the Jewish community in the 19th and early 20th centuries included Harris Rubin, operator of a boarding establishment; Harry Haveson and Louis Kaplan, owners of clothing businesses; and Louis Vogel, founder of a popular meat business, which was later run by his brothers Issac and William after Louis became a partner and proprietor at the Nassau Inn. Sarah Braveman's sister Fannie had already come to Princeton with her husband, Nathan Wolman, from Pennsylvania. But it was the Bravemans whose home and jewelry and watch repair store became focal points for the growing Jewish community, which had about two dozen families by then. And for visitors, the Bravemans befriended many lonely "Hebrew" students and instructors at the university and local boarding schools. Isadore Braveman collected the first locally raised monies for the United Jewish Appeal; he raised a very successful $100. He also oversaw the establishment of Princeton's first Jewish Congregation, which initially met in a building on Spring Street. The new congregation allowed local Jews to worship in town instead of taking the trolley to Trenton to seek a minyan for services. In 1941, Isadore Braveman completed Rosh Hashanah Eve services and then passed away. (PR.)

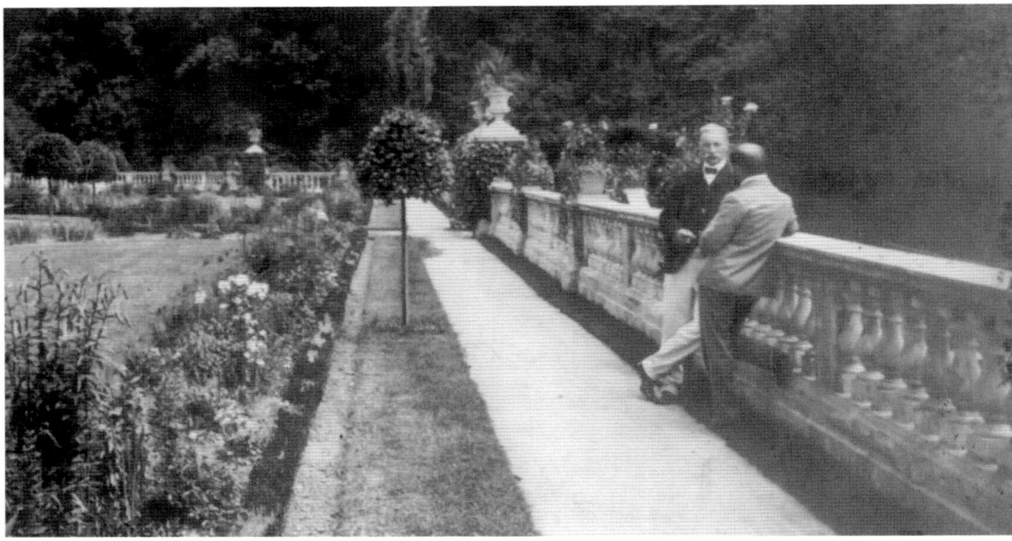

Moses Taylor Pyne (1855–1921)

A financier and philanthropist, Pyne is perhaps the most lauded and beloved Princeton alumnus of all time. The son of Percy Rivington Pyne and Albertina Shelton Taylor, he inherited the resources to express his generous instincts from his maternal grandfather and namesake, Moses Taylor, a New York banker and one of the richest men in 19th-century America. Mose Taylor Pyne was a director at numerous banks and insurance companies, industries and utilities, and railroads and was also a supporter of schools, public libraries, and the Episcopal Church. Moses Taylor Pyne (facing the camera) is seen in 1893 conversing with a visitor in the gardens of Drumthwacket, the Princeton estate he purchased and, with the help of prominent architect Raleigh Gildersleeve, greatly expanded and renovated. Drumthwacket's central grounds and mansion house are now the official New Jersey governor's residence. (HSP.)

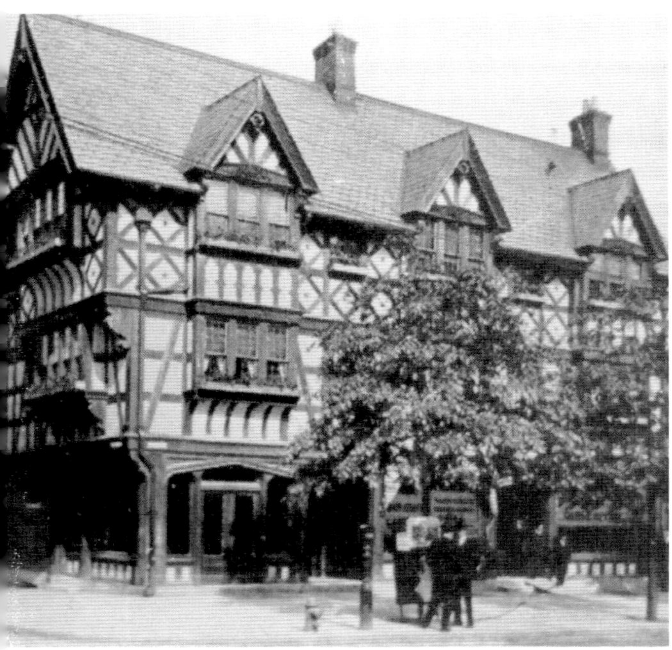

Dedication to School and Town

Pyne devoted much of his considerable monies and energy to the university, and it has been said that he did more for his alma mater "than any other man has done for any college." He was also committed to the town, constructing several memorable buildings in the Tudor Revival style that he cherished. Notable examples include Lower Pyne at the corner of Nassau and Witherspoon Streets, shown here soon after its 1896 opening and still standing today; its sister, Upper Pyne, which was demolished in 1963 for the ultimate construction stage of Palmer Square; and "White City," a neighborhood at Prospect Street and FitzRandolph Road. Named for the bright paint highlighting its timbers, it was erected in 1908 to provide elegant but affordable dwellings for the university's junior faculty. (HSP.)

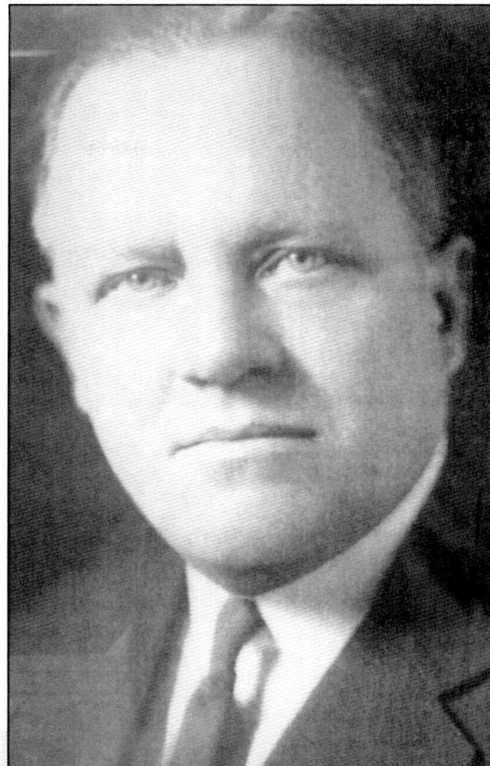

Edgar Palmer (1880–1943)

Palmer had numerous business interests and was chairman of the board of the New Jersey Zinc Company. He was a generous benefactor of Princeton University from which he graduated in 1903. Palmer Stadium, given in his father's memory, opened in 1914 as a marvel of reinforced-concrete technology and stood until 1997. His most prominent legacy in the town was Palmer Square, a project proposed in 1929 and realized in its first stage from 1936 to 1939.

The development was controversial as minority residents were displaced when the "eyesore" of Bakers Alley was razed, although many residents and even their houses were relocated. But it has been rightly said that Palmer Square finally "broke the back of the Depression in Princeton." The construction of this mix of retail spaces, apartments, a new Nassau Inn hotel, and new post office not only provided badly needed jobs but set a foundation for future economic activity and prosperity. The building activity on the square's western side is shown in this March 1939 image. (Right, Palmer Square; below, HSP.)

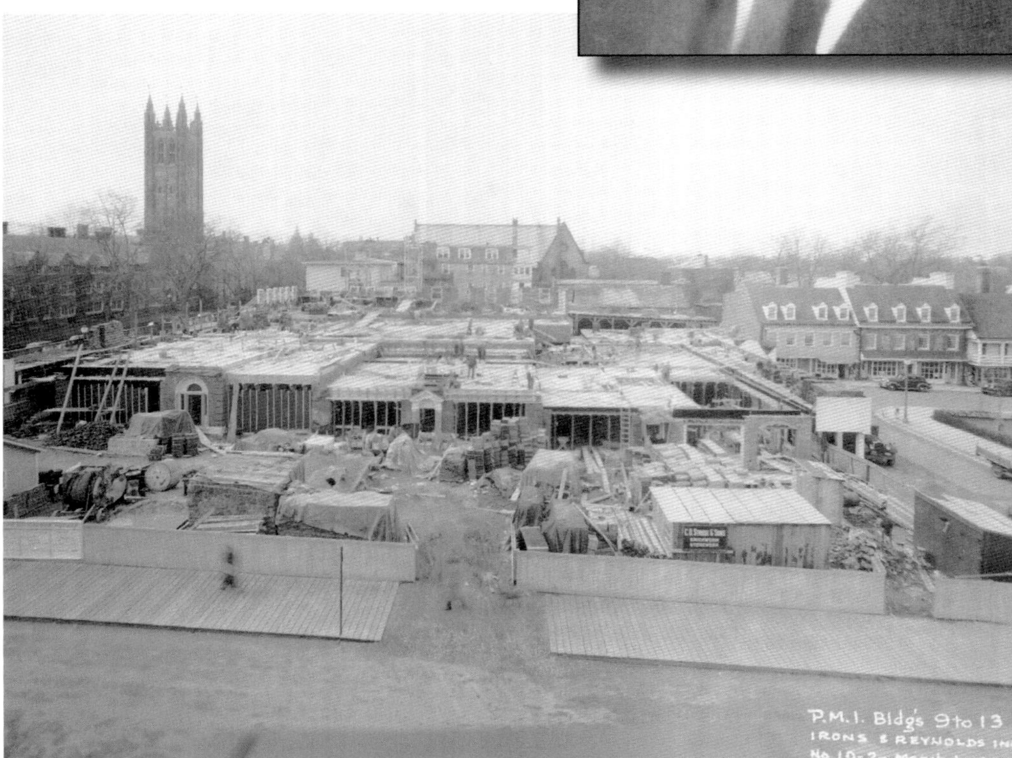

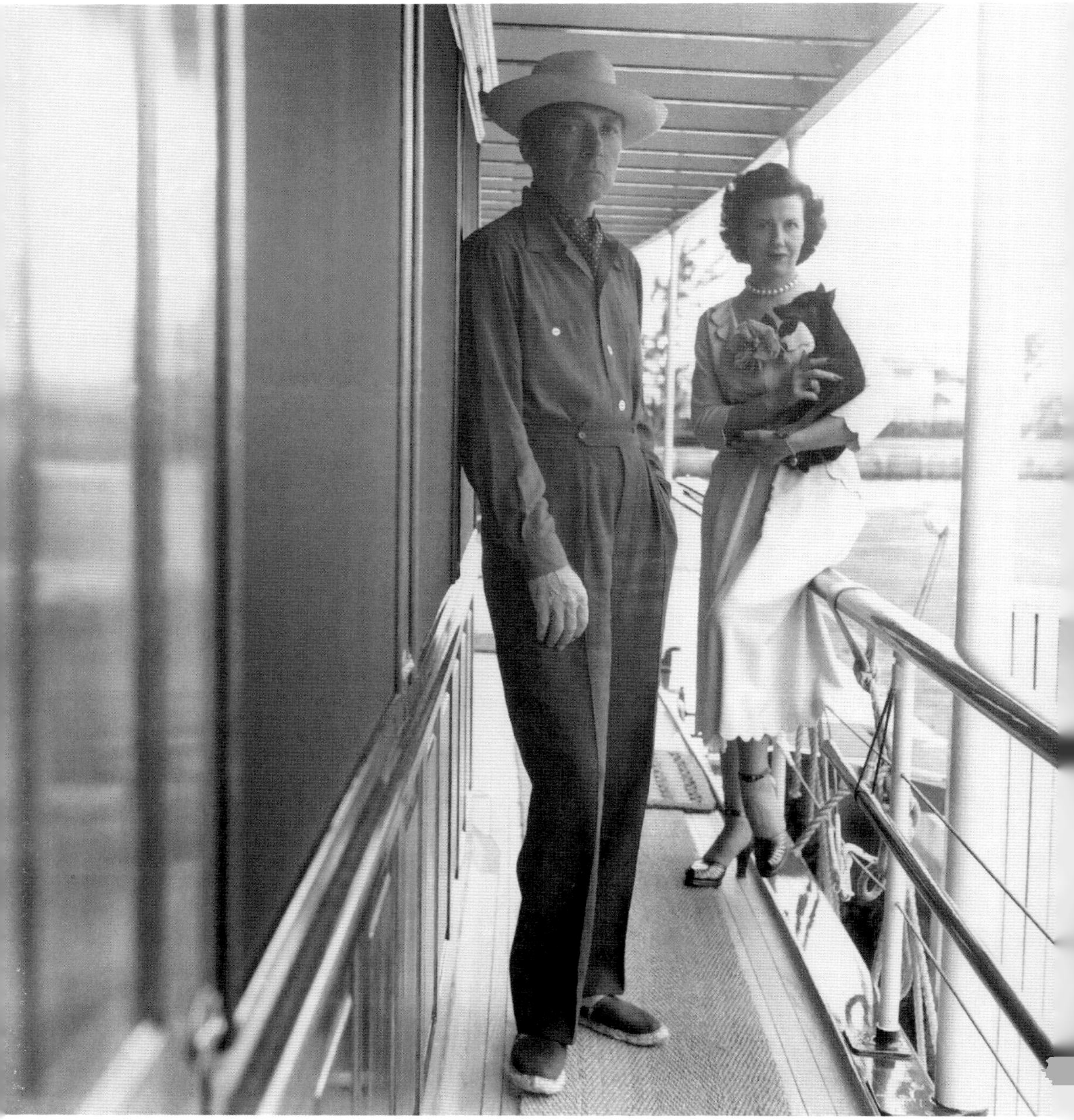

Gen. and Mrs. Robert Wood Johnson Jr.

Although an heir to the New Brunswick-based Johnson & Johnson fortune, Johnson, shown here with his first wife, was a generous benefactor to his residential town of Princeton. Born in 1893, he moved to Princeton in 1928 and acquired Morven, the former Stockton mansion. Upon his death in 1968, it became the official governor's mansion, which is a distinction now held by Drumthwacket, just a short distance down Stockton Street (Route 206). General Johnson was given his title during his active World War II logistical service. His second wife, Margaret Shea Johnson, was especially valued for her community service and generosity. Johnson's fortune of $400 million endowed the Robert Wood Johnson Foundation, still active in Central New Jersey and nationally. (Corbis.)

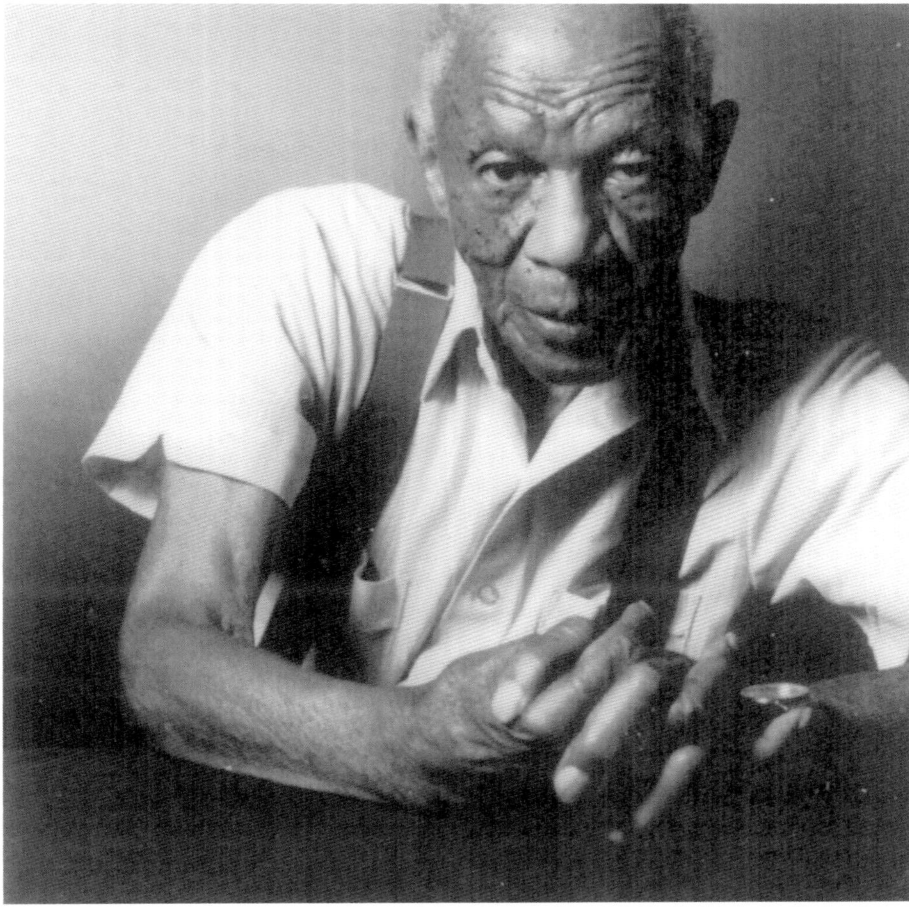

Albert E. Hinds (1902–2006)
A genuine patriarch of the African American community, Hinds was an active figure in town history at large. As a child, he delivered milk from a farm on Witherspoon Street and Franklin Avenue; the property was later the site of the Medical Center of Princeton. As a teenager, he worked on the initial paving of Nassau Street. His industry was boundless: shining shoes, driving a horse-drawn "hack" conveyance, and tending to the furnace in Bainbridge House, then the town's public library. In the mid-1930s, a shipment of wood for the construction of Palmer Square arrived in town that was infested with carpenter ants; Hinds helped to treat the wood, saving this crucial economic project. His community service was profound. In the mid-1920s, after graduating from Princeton High School, he attended college in Louisiana and helped reopen New Orleans's languishing colored YMCA, serving as its athletic director. Returning to Princeton, he directed an early community playground where the Stanworth Homes are today. "The church has been a big part of my life," Hinds recalled in June 2002, on the occasion of his 100th birthday. "I used to walk up the back stairs at the back of the Mount Pisgah AME Church to pump the organ." He was later a church deacon and trustee and served on the zoning board and the Historical Society of Princeton Board. He lived to the age of 104, leaving a treasure trove of memories for local oral historians and a sterling example of work and service. The powerful studio portrait reproduced here captures Albert Hinds's strength, sincerity, and directness. Fittingly, the public space on Witherspoon Street, next to the Princeton Public Library and adjacent to the town's historically black neighborhood, has been memorialized as Hinds Plaza. (Photograph by Peter C. Cook.)

Ann Reeves

Of course, Ann Reeves could have been considered among the legendary figures in Princeton's art scene. But her work with the Arts Council of Princeton, which has proven to be one of the most enduring and influential of local organizations, also merits the consideration of Reeves and the council among the true mainstays of the community. The Arts Council of Princeton was founded in 1967 by author, historian, and Princeton alumnus William H. Selden with a committee of art-loving citizens. It moved from location to location, just managing to survive while organizing shows, classes, and concerts. Then in 1983, Ann Reeves became its executive director and oversaw its renaissance. Born in Maine and raised in Cleveland, Reeves developed a love for the arts and social justice. She had moved to Princeton with her husband in the mid-1960s. In 1970, prominent local architect and supporter of the arts Jerry Ford persuaded her to join the Arts Council of Princeton Board. Under her highly effective leadership, the organization settled in at the former colored YMCA at 102 Witherspoon Street, and it flourished. The group eventually completed a beautiful renovation and expansion of the 1939 structure. But the new Arts Council of Princeton—overlooking what is now known as Paul Robeson Place—is only part of the legacy of the woman hailed as "the Talented Town Muse." In 1980, together with Princeton University undergraduate Douglas Platte, she initiated "Communiversity," an annual April downtown and campus one-day festival. From its inception, Communiversity helped dissolve calcified misunderstandings between town and gown, and it remains one of Princeton's truly legendary celebrations. (PP/HSP.)

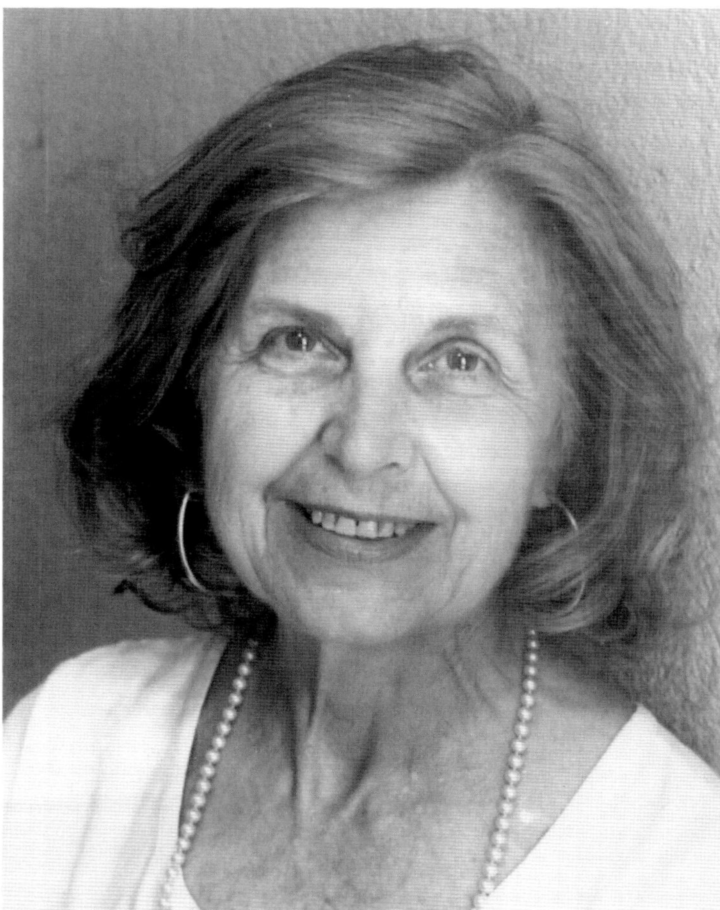

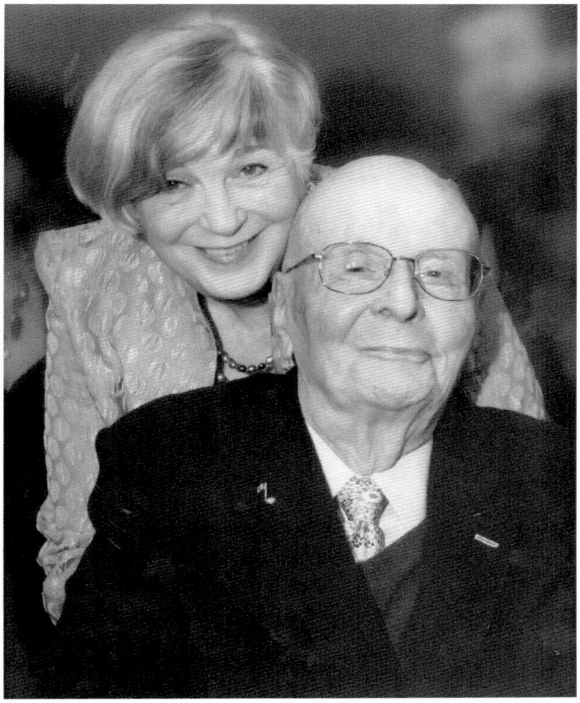

William H. Scheide and Judith McCartin Scheide

Musician, scholar, and philanthropist William Scheide (born 1914) is matched by few in the range of his generosity to Princeton causes. Although the orchestral and keyboard music of Johann Sebastian Bach had undergone a revival in the 19th century, his music composed for voice had fallen in estimation. Scheide's founding of the Bach Aria Group in New York City in 1946 was the powerful, pioneering boost of its return to critical and audience acclaim. Indeed, it was his involvement with the ensemble that led him to return to Princeton, not only for its ambiance but also to be close to New York. Scheide's paternal grandfather, William T. Scheide, was a "wildcatter" in the early days of Pennsylvania oil exploration. The elder Scheide's expertise led to his hiring by John D. Rockefeller as vice president of pipelines at Standard Oil, thus founding the family fortune and beginning the collection of early printed works and rare musical manuscripts. These works have formed the foundation of the world-famous Scheide Library (housed at Princeton University but officially still owned by the family). William H. Scheide's official retirement from the Bach Aria Group in 1980 was not an end but a new beginning; he said, "Then I got to work on the Library!" Although the Scheides lived for many years in Titusville, New Jersey, the family had close ties both to Princeton University (from which both William and his father, John H. Scheide, graduated) and the town. Says wife, Judith, "He knew Princeton and he was crazy about football. He never missed a football game." Young William H. Scheide, Princeton class of 1936, majored in history because there was not yet a music department. Scheide received a master's of art degree from Columbia in 1940; his thesis topic was Johann Sebastian Bach. The names of the beneficiaries of the Scheides' generosity might themselves fill a magnificent library or certainly many shelves. Numerous regional nonprofits thank the Scheides for wise and generous patronage in the promotion of symphony, opera, and other music; general education; history; health; community gardening; and, notably, civil rights, free speech, and justice. In 1953, William Scheide staunchly supported the NAACP Legal Defense Fund during the landmark *Brown v. Board of Education* desegregation case successfully argued before the US Supreme Court. Judith Scheide relishes her behind the scenes, but widely admired, role as husband Bill's supporter. By helping groups in good works that also unite Princeton's diverse peoples, William and Judith are truly legendary linchpins of the community. (William and Judith Scheide.)

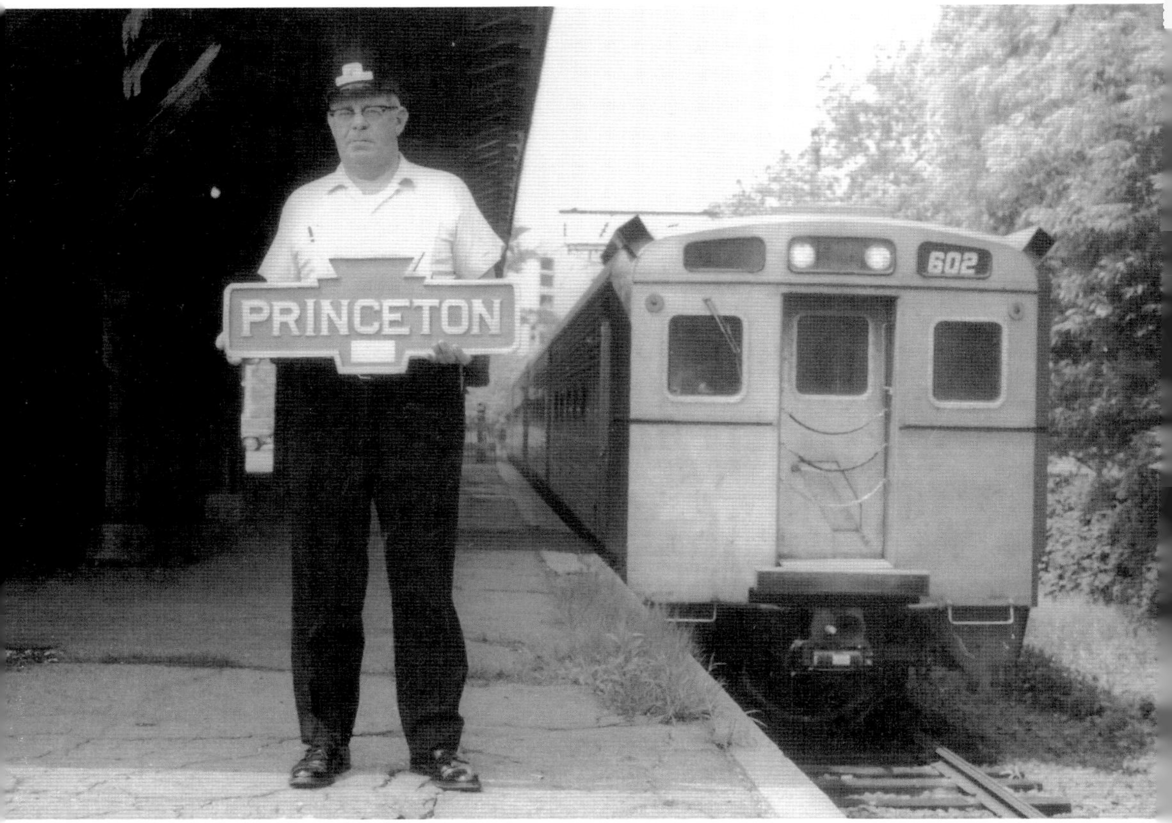

John Bancroft

Bancroft was one of the best-loved and longest-working conductors on the branch line train, the Dinky. It shuttled passengers between the town of Princeton and the main railroad station at Princeton Junction, and Bancroft was a true fixture on that two-mile route. Fittingly, his charges and fellow conductors feted him when he retired in July 1978, when he received the transit sign he holds as a memento of his valued service. In 2013, the Dinky station, seen here behind Bancroft, began to undergo a major renovation and commercial repurposing as part of Princeton University's creation of its new Arts Neighborhood. The cherished little train seems destined to survive, although it will operate from a new station a few hundred feet south of this location. (PR, Jeff Macechak.)

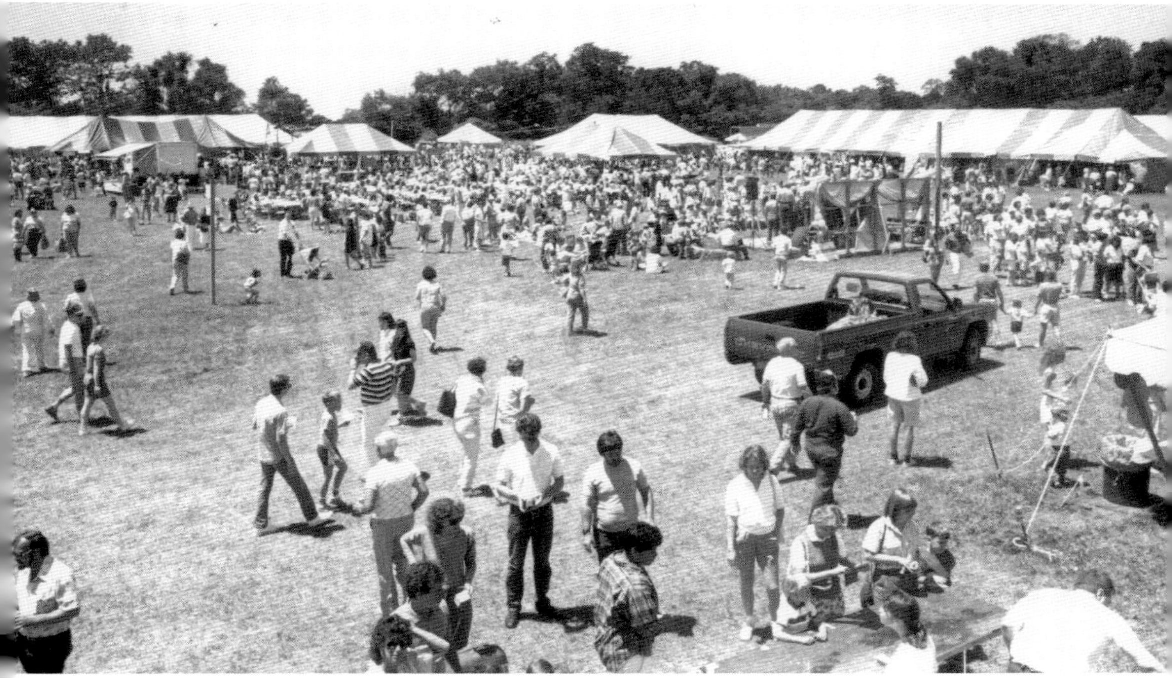

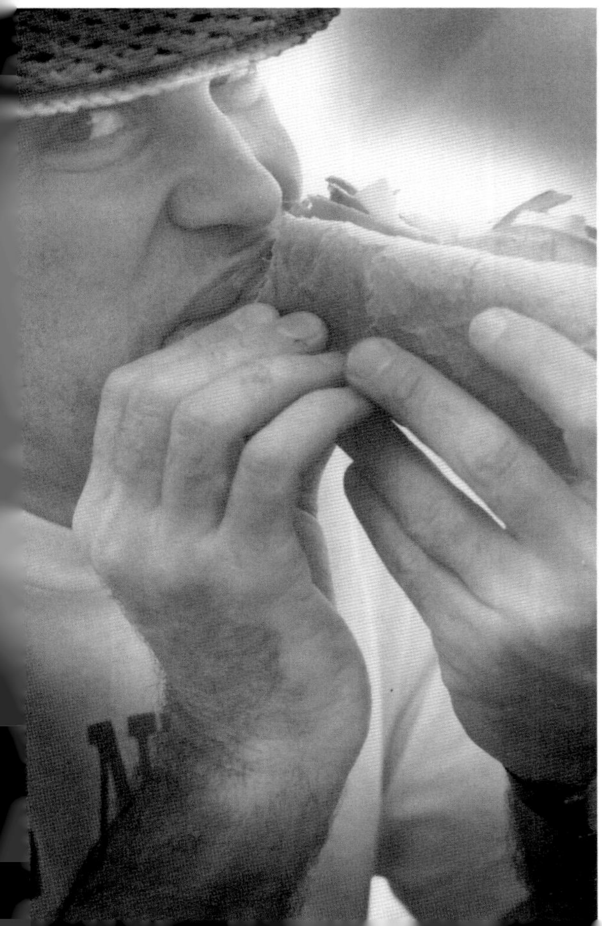

Hospital Fete

For 53 summers, starting in 1953, the Ladies Auxiliary of Princeton Hospital, later known as the Auxiliary of University Medical Center at Princeton, presented on the second Saturday of June—rain or shine—a Princeton fundraiser unequaled in its size, variety, and vitality, before or since. The Hospital Fete was truly legendary in the festive scope of its entertainment and food. Here, David Quinlan happily address an all-American culinary treat at the 1988 edition. Its memory remains a tribute to the volunteers and the attendees who made it work. Each fete had its own name and special theme; the final edition, for example, was the "Greetings from the Beach Fete" of 2005, with a seashore ambiance in its decorations and entertainment. Space concerns grew as fields and other available space shrank in increasingly developed Princeton, but the university did end up providing its stadium as the venue; however, the rising liability insurance premiums and general expenses made the beloved event less cost-effective than other fundraising efforts. Perhaps people can look forward one day to a revival. (Both, PP/HSP)

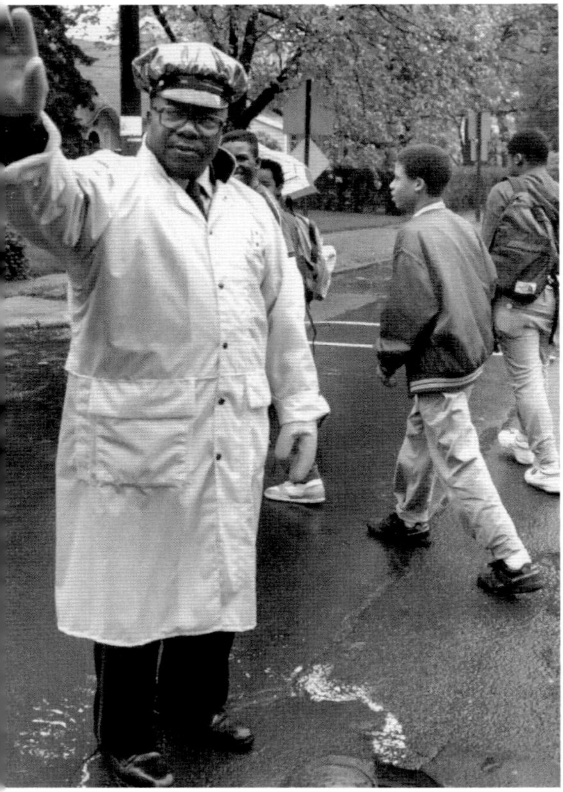

Crossing Guard and Night Nurse

The support system of caring, well-trained professionals has almost been a given in Princeton, but their dedication does not go unnoticed. Here, Oscar Rhodes of the borough police guards students crossing busy byways en route to school, and night nurse Anne Marie Sagarese catches up on paperwork at the Medical Center of Princeton, founded as Princeton Hospital in 1919 at 253 Witherspoon Street. In 2012, the hospital relocated to a larger facility at Route 1 and Plainsboro Road and is now known as the University Medical Center of Princeton at Plainsboro. (Both, PP/HSP.)

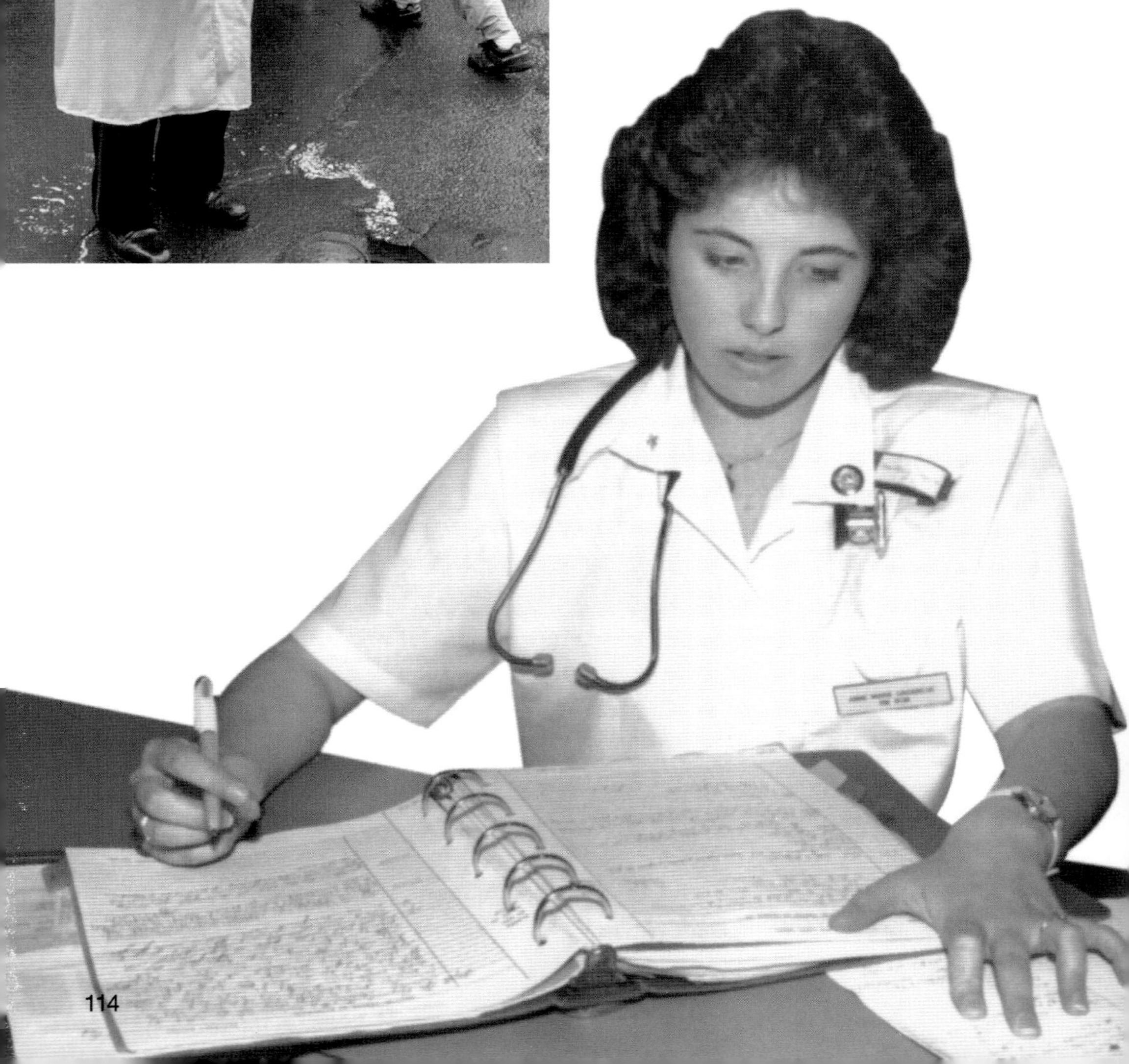

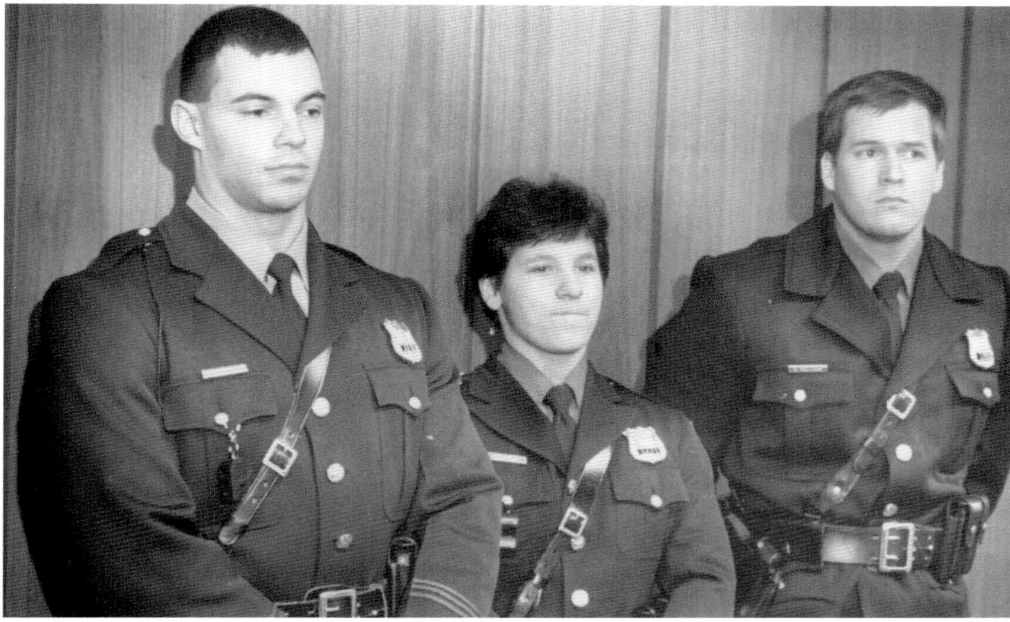

Police and Rescue and Fire Squads

The effectiveness of Princeton's police departments and rescue and fire squads has been yet another factor in the area's high quality of living. It will continue as the organizations merge during the consolidation of the borough and the township. New police officers—from left to right, William E. Iron, Lori A. Sanella, and Edward T. Sullivan—are poised in January 1988, ready to undertake their duties. Their dedication surely matched that of firefighter Kevin McCloskey of Princeton Hook & Ladder (below, far right), giving his all at the scene of a July 1988 accident on Route 206. (Both, PP/HSP.)

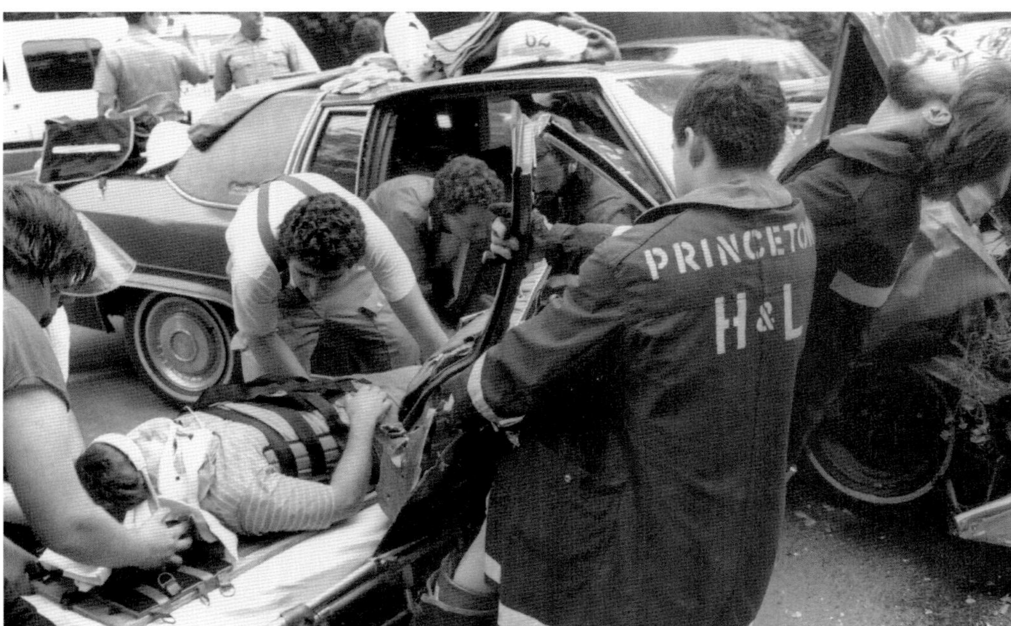

Shirley A. Satterfield

Shirley A. Satterfield's mother, Alice May Satterfield, worked at the Institute for Advanced Study at a time when day care was simply not affordable or even available for most African Americans. So, four-year-old Shirley often came to work with her mother. There, an IAS faculty member named Albert Einstein thoughtfully took the child on little walks. "He was a very kind man, and we used to walk quietly," Shirley A. Satterfield recalls today. Like the Moores, the Satterfields, transplants from North Carolina, were one of the leading families in what was once Princeton's "colored" community. And like many other African Americans, Shirley Satterfield's sixth-generation local heritage is intertwined with that of Central New Jersey, with the Dutch farming family of Van Zant in nearby Montgomery Township being among her forbearers. She has also experienced firsthand Princeton's transition from a largely segregated, if genteel, town of the past to the multicultural community of today. Education is part of her family heritage. Her grandmother taught little Paul Robeson in the local school for colored children; Shirley Satterfield herself taught in grade and high schools in Nevada, New York, and New Jersey. She earned a master's in guidance counseling at Trenton State (now the College of New Jersey) in 1979 and did counseling at Princeton High School before finally retiring in 2006. Her urge to educate others and her personal connection to the history of Princeton's black enclave—along with her frustration and concern that it was being ignored and lost—has led her to preserve irreplaceable artifacts, photographs, printed material, and all-important memories of her neighbors. Today, she is a pillar of the Historical Society of Princeton and leads popular walking tours of the Witherspoon Street neighborhood, named in honor of the late Albert Hinds (page 109), whom she affectionately recalls as "my history partner." (Shirley A. Satterfield.)

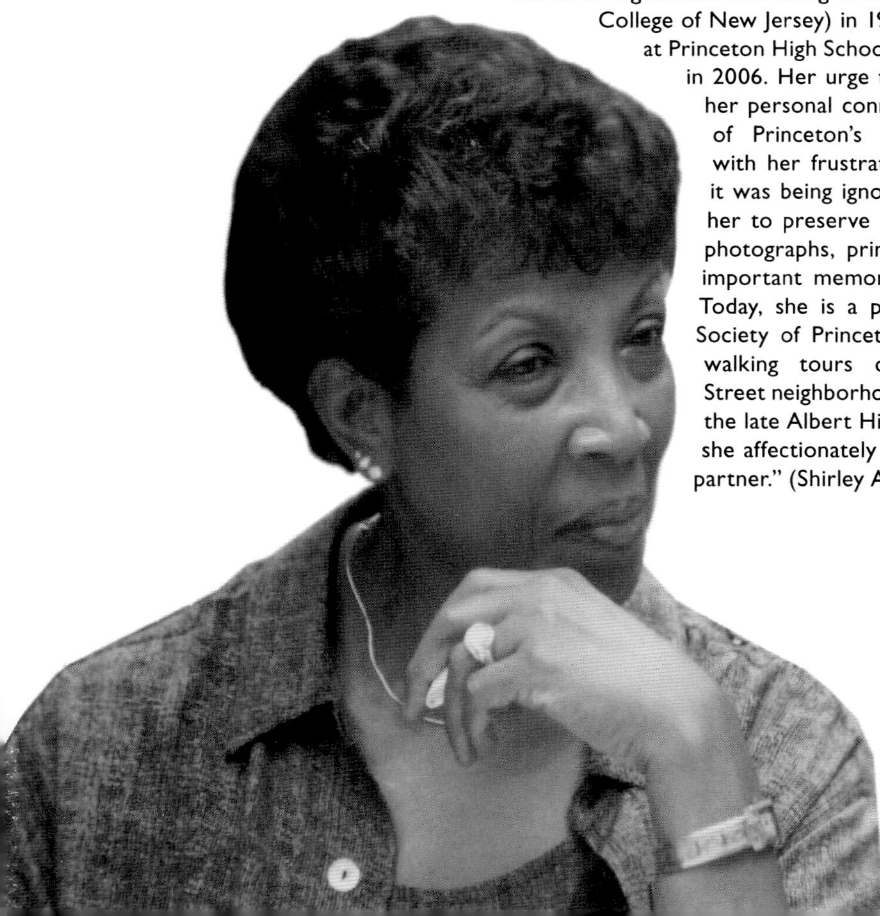

Karl Light (1925–2012)

An accomplished and sought-after actor in his free time, performing at McCarter Theatre and having recurring roles on television's *The Guiding Light*, Karl had additional success with his day job as a realtor, cofounding K.M. Light with his wife, Lucy. Light often exhibited his public spirit and ideals in his business, as exemplified by his firm becoming managers for Princeton Community Village (PCV), a successful affordable housing complex, established in 1967. His role in its success was immortalized when the complex's central street was named Karl Light Boulevard. Light was encouraged to undertake the affordable housing project by Light Realty staffer Marcy Crimmins, who became PCV's first managing agent. This was an early challenge that speaks to the local need for affordable housing, and Crimmins had to evaluate thousands of applications for the 238 available units. Another effective champion of Princeton affordable housing was Harriet Bryan, who had previously been involved with civil rights issues and served with the League of Women Voters before joining the board of Princeton Community Housing, helping shepherd other local affordable housing projects, such as Griggs Farm and Elm Court. Quite fittingly, one of the main apartment buildings at PCV has been named Harriet Bryan House. (Right, Lucy James; below, Jean Stratton.)

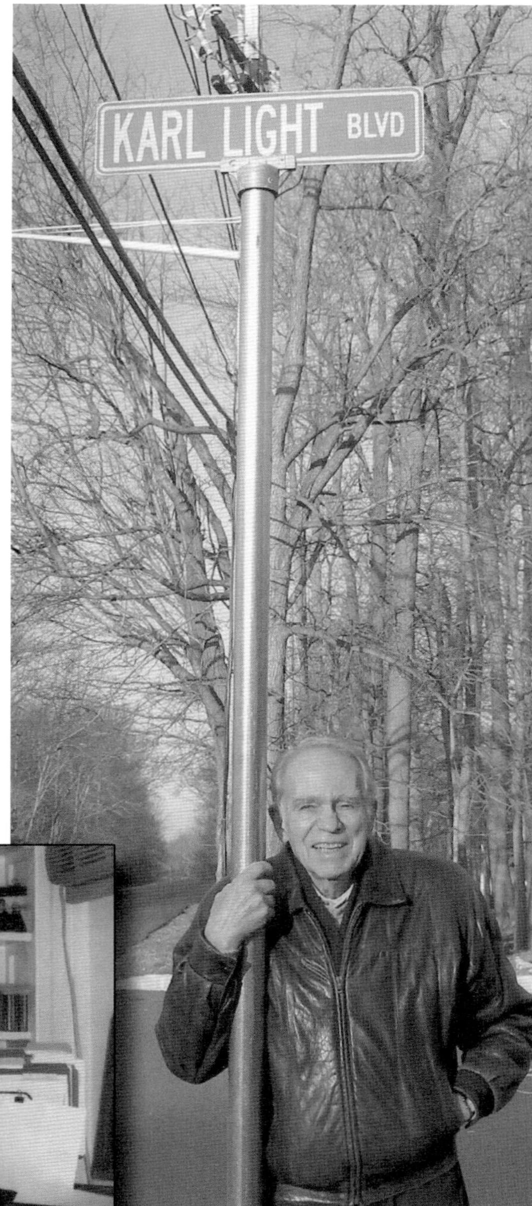

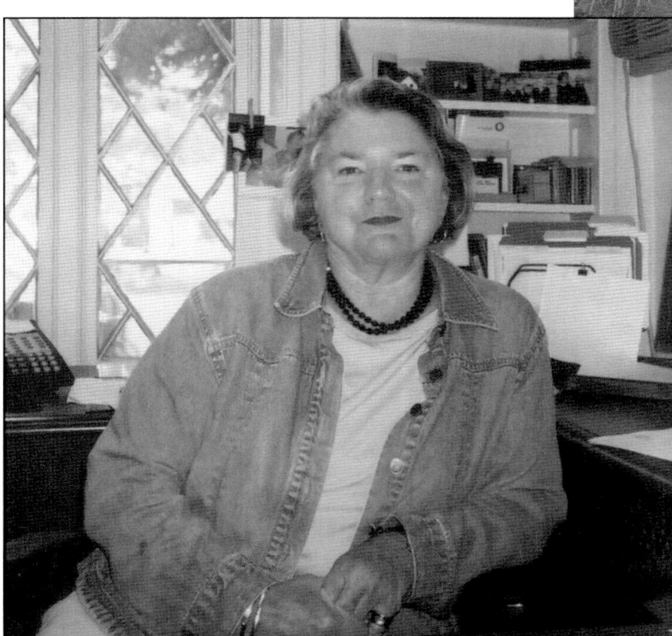

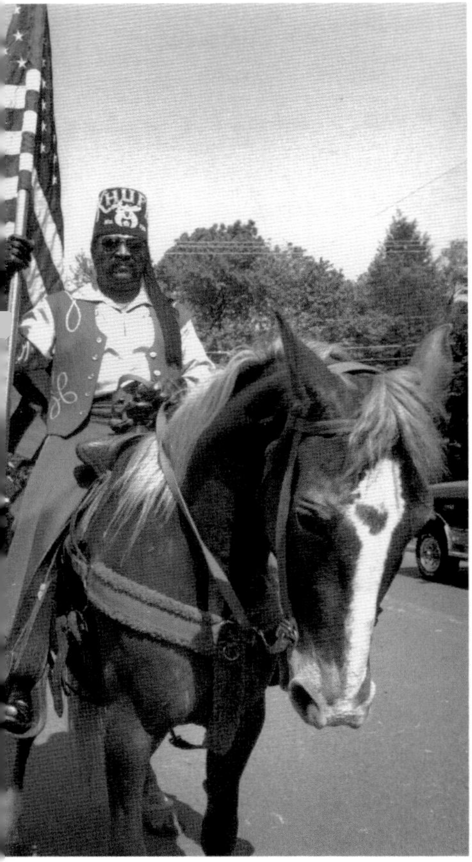

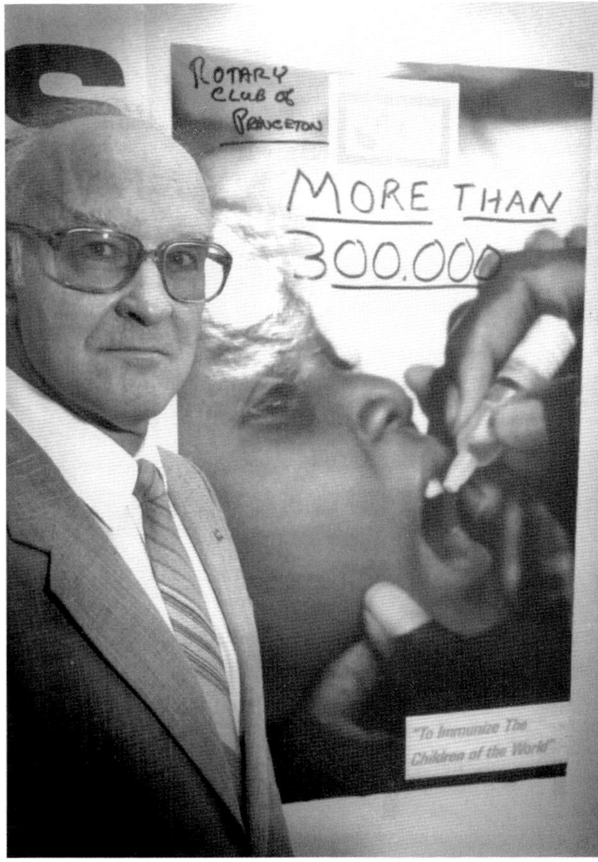

Rotary Club and Shriners

In 1836, Alexis de Tocqueville, French chronicler of American culture, observed approvingly in *Democracy in America* that the United States was "a nation of joiners," with many associations serving the greater good. These have included national fraternal and business organizations, which are well represented in Princeton. John Ford (top left) is mounted to carry the flag for the Princeton Shriner Khufu Temple No. 120 at the May 31, 1988, Memorial Day Parade in Lawrence; he is clearly proud of the Shriners' administration of children's hospitals. Rotary International has similarly focused on children's health and sanitation issues. The Rotary Club of Princeton was established in 1942. In June 1988, officer Donald Dickson (top right) poses by a poster celebrating the success of a fundraising drive for international childhood immunization. (Both, PR/HSP.)

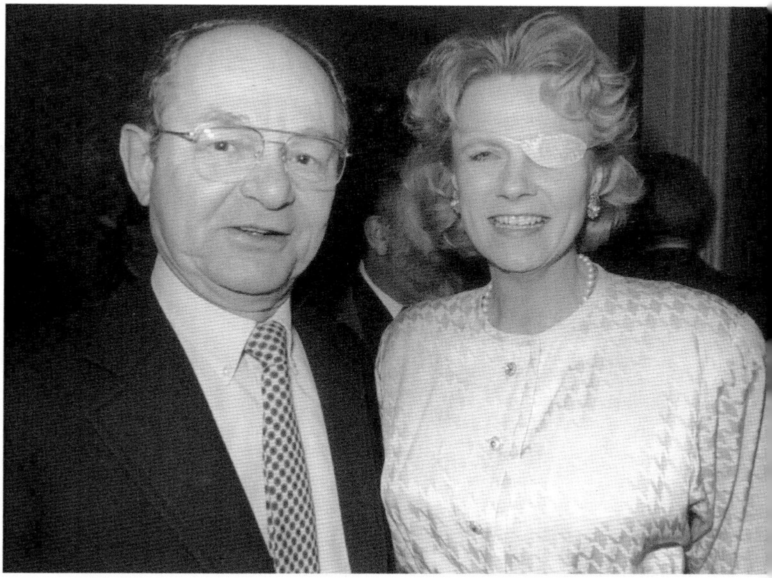

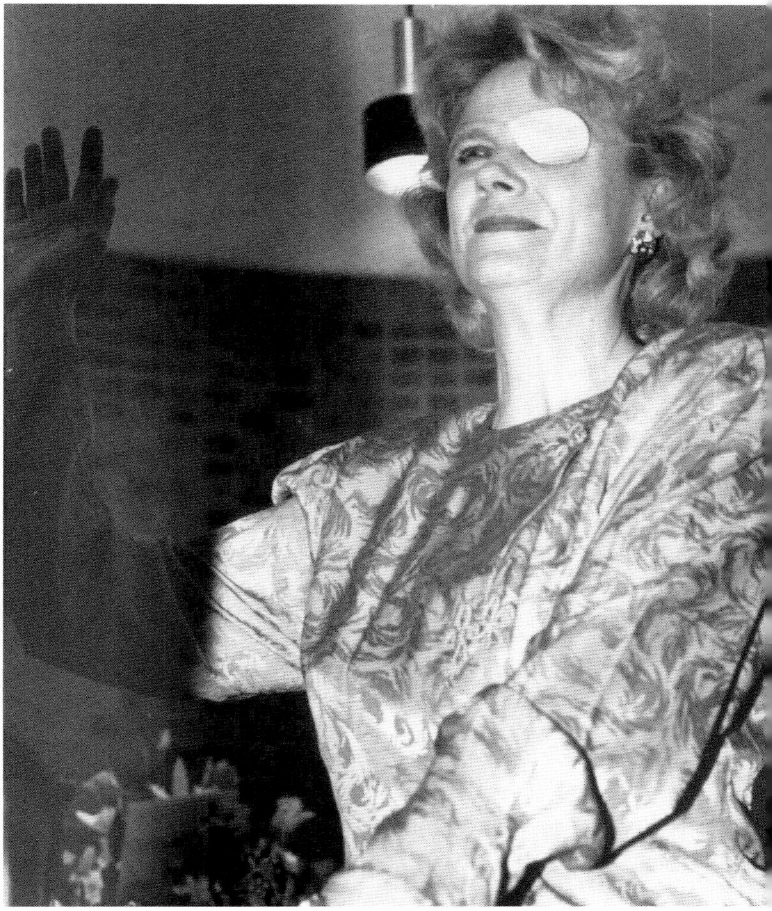

Barbara Boggs Sigmund (1939–1990)
Sigmund, acclaimed for her "passion for beauty and justice," was a highly respected mayor of Princeton Borough from 1984 until her untimely death from cancer in 1990. She was a daughter of the politically prominent Louisianan parents, former US House of Representatives majority leader Hale Boggs and his wife, Congresswoman Lindy. Her sibling Cokie Boggs Roberts is a popular National Public Broadcasting journalist. Moving to Princeton in 1963, Sigmund, shown above with borough council member Thomas Poole, distinguished herself as a borough councilperson (1972–1975) and Mercer County freeholder (1975–1982) before her mayoral success. She was also a cofounder of Womanspace of Mercer County, a shelter and resource center for abused women.

When Sigmund lost an eye to cancer, she opted not to be fitted with a discreet prosthetic eye. Instead, she wore a series of eye patches as cheerfully as if they were fashion accessories. But her cancer came out of remission. Shortly before her death, she published *An Unfinished Life*, a poetry collection. (PP/HSP.)

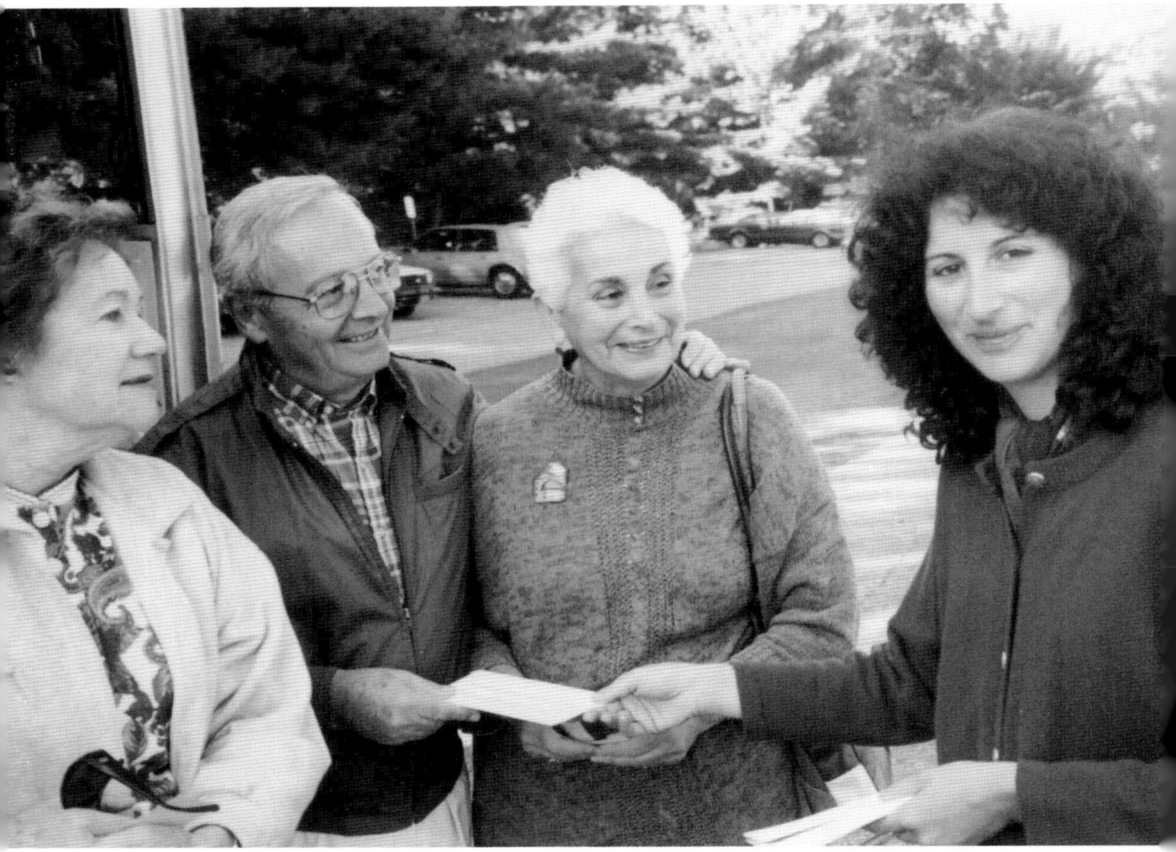

Sandra Starr

Sandra Starr was decades ahead of her time on public health issues. As vice chairwoman of the Princeton Regional Health Commission and president of the Princeton Borough Board of Health, she campaigned successfully for removal of cigarette vending machines from Princeton restaurants, convincingly arguing that these establishments could not control access by minors. Her positions were both impassioned and scientific. She had received degrees in epidemiology and public health from Berkeley in 1976, and from 1980 to 1982, she taught these subjects at Yale Medical School. Shown here during her victorious 1995 campaign for borough council, she also lobbied on behalf of increased recreational space, emergency heart defibrillators in police cars, and other health/quality-of-life initiatives. Her husband, Princeton University professor Paul Starr, recalls that when she awakened from major cancer surgery in April 1998, her first request was for him to relay to the mayor some concerns she had just heard from municipal employees. She passed away peacefully at home that October, at age 44. (Paul Starr.)

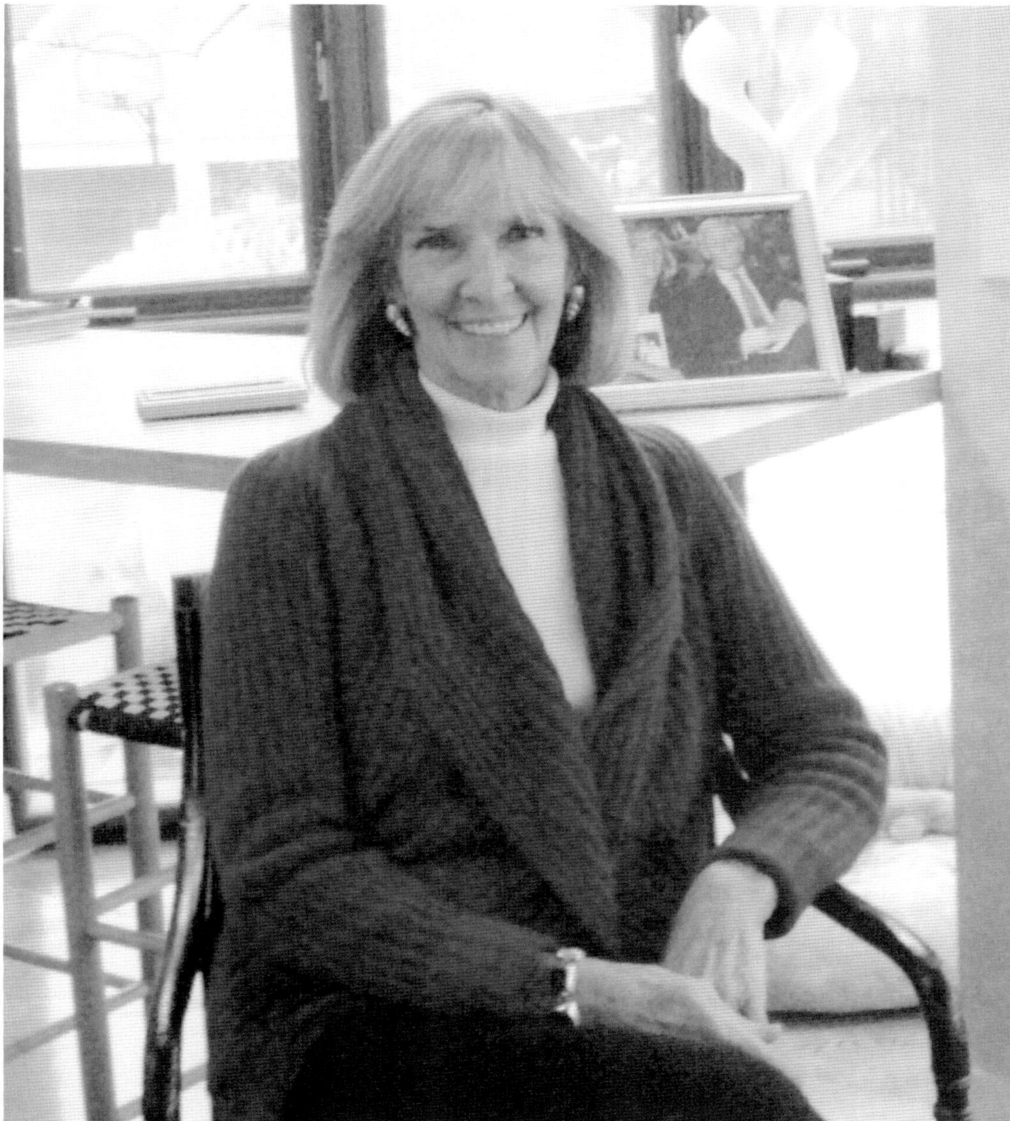

Wendy Benchley

The wife of late author Peter Benchley (page 54), Wendy Benchley has had her own significant achievements. She cofounded the New Jersey Environmental Fund in the 1970s and still serves on the boards of major environmental organizations. She helps oversee the Peter Benchley Ocean Awards for outstanding contributions to marine conservation. Locally, she served three terms on Princeton Borough Council and was also elected to the Board of Mercer County Chosen Freeholders. Looking back on "thirty superb years" of residency, she praises Princeton for "creating open spaces, supportive social services, affordable housing and the downtown development with its centerpiece, the Albert E. Hind Plaza" (page 109), which celebrates "the importance of Princeton's African Americans in the life of the town." (Jean Stratton.)

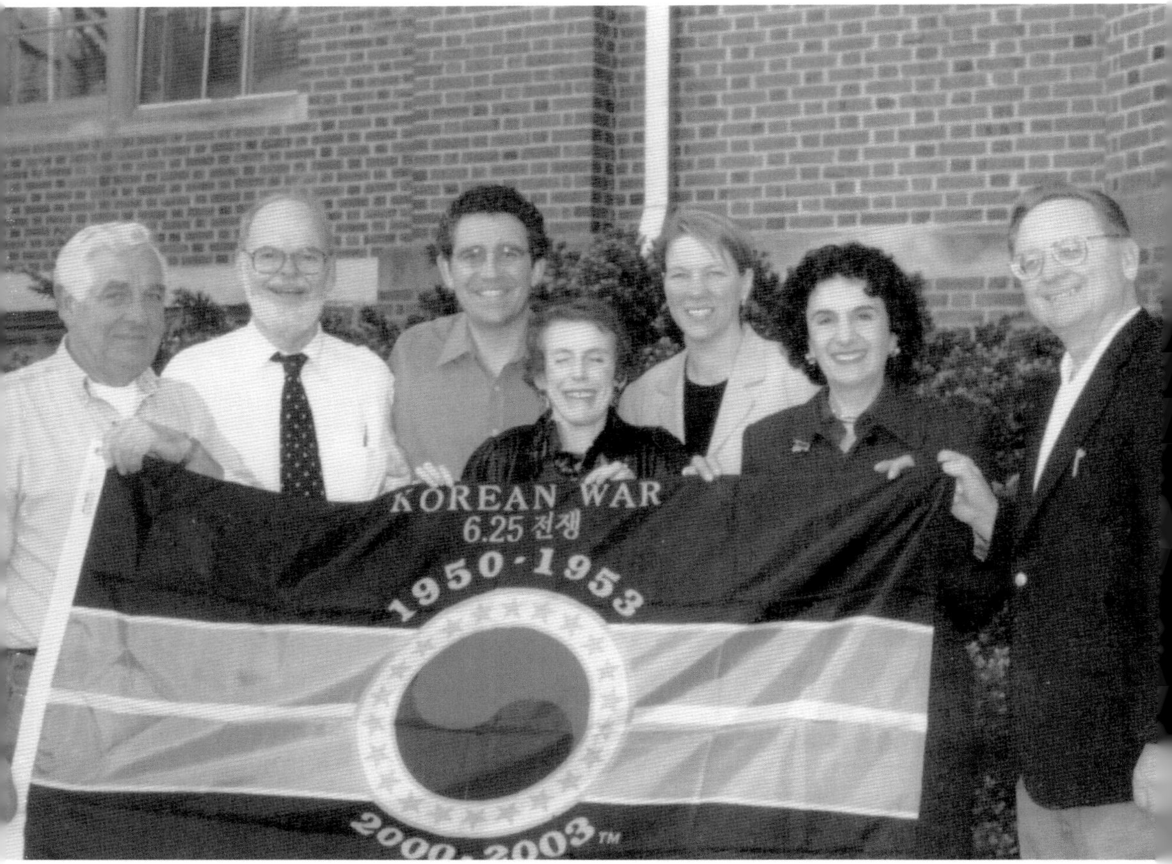

Spirit of Princeton (ABOVE AND OPPOSITE)
Organized by Ray Wadsworth in 1996 to facilitate and fund-raise for the local Memorial Day parade, Fourth of July fireworks, and other patriotic celebrations, the Spirit of Princeton Committee succeeded with, well, flying colors. With initial funding of $200,000 handled by the Princeton Area Community Foundation, the committee raised an additional $175,000 through its "20th Century Recognition Brick Walk." As the name suggests, the project involved the purchase of engraved bricks commemorating persons—living or deceased, related or simply admired—who had lived, worked, or studied in Princeton some time in the 20th century. The bricks were laid in a path leading to and surrounding the landmark bronze tiger statue in the central plaza of Palmer Square. For 87 consecutive weeks, publisher Jeb Stuart ran a high-profile "Brick Watch" feature in his *Town Topics* newspaper to encourage donations. Some 2,500 bricks were eventually bought (with Bonnie Chiravalle, assistant to committee member Herb Hobler, somehow managing to keep track of their installations and locations). After expenses, nearly the entire amount of a desired $300,000 permanent endowment was realized. The committee gathered before the 2001 Memorial Day parade, and smiled for the camera with well-earned satisfaction. From left to right are Ray Wadsworth, Herbert W. Hobler, Mark Freda, Pam Hersh, Teri McIntire, Phyllis Marchand, and Frank Tylus. (Above, courtesy of *Bricks and Mortals: The Story of Princeton's 20th Century Recognition Walk*, Herb Hobler; opposite, author's.)

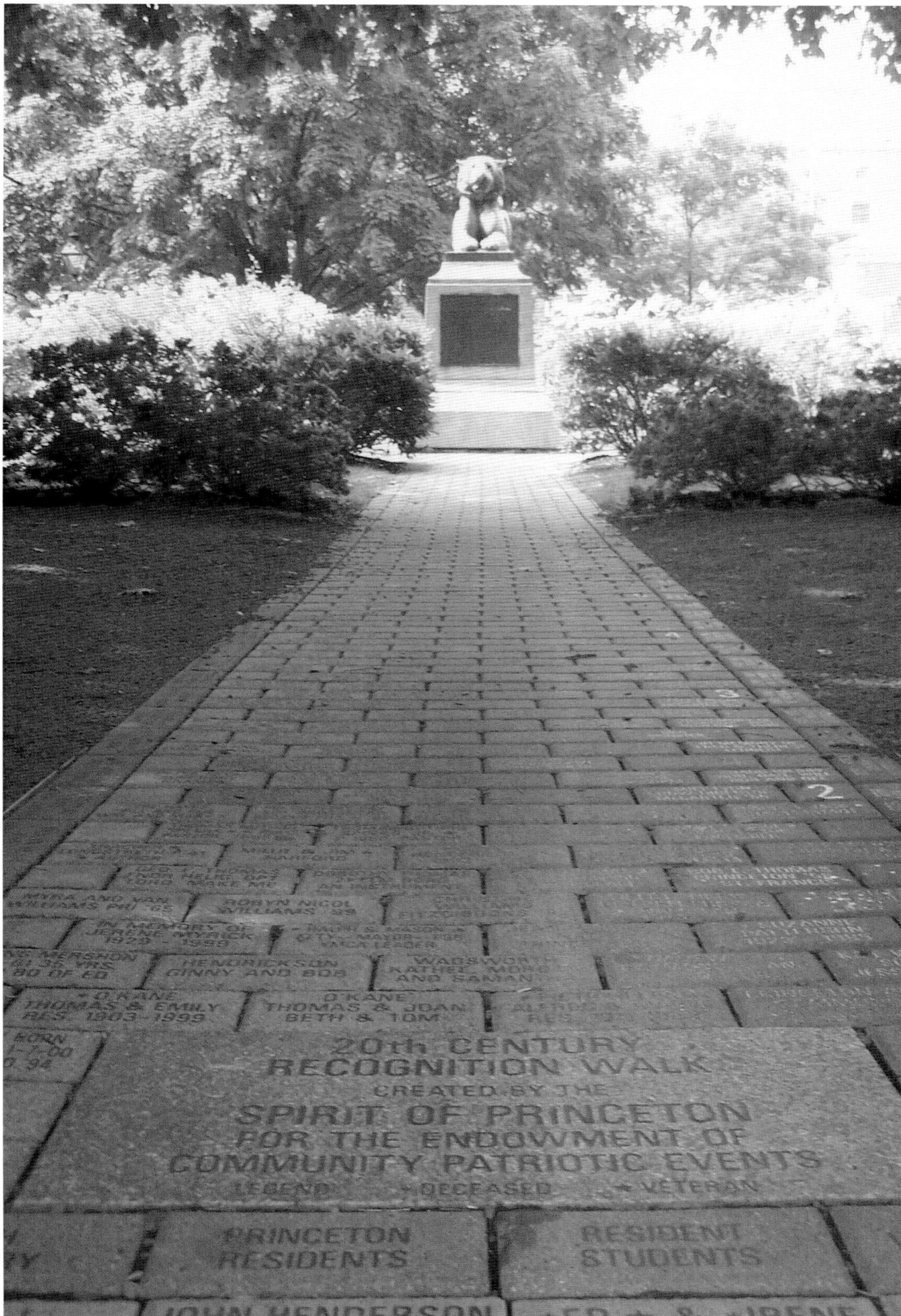
HENDRICKSON
GINNY AND BOB
O'KANE
THOMAS & JOAN
BETH & TOM
20th CENTURY
RECOGNITION WALK
CREATED BY THE
SPIRIT OF PRINCETON
FOR THE ENDOWMENT OF
COMMUNITY PATRIOTIC EVENTS
PRINCETON
RESIDENTS
RESIDENT
STUDENTS
JOHN HENDERSON
*ED ★ & *IRENE

William Rieszer

His life might have been defined by tragedy but William Rieszer persevered to win the town's admiration and respect. Born in Trenton in 1947, he was a four year old living on Cherry Valley Road when a car hit him; he suffered crippling injuries. But in 1968, Rieszer earned his degree at Hopewell Central High School and, for years, has lived a largely independent life. A thoughtful and dignified man, he is a familiar figure, sometimes seen sweeping up on Nassau Street or wearing his safety helmet with headlamp, piloting to the Princeton Shopping Center in his motorized transport. His mode of transportation is a Pride Pursuit vehicle modified with an extra-powerful batteries; "It can do fifteen miles per hour, it really takes off," Rieszer says with satisfaction. Rieszer performs his largely pro bono Nassau Street sweeping service, he says, because he loves Princeton, and "I can't stand filth." (Author.)

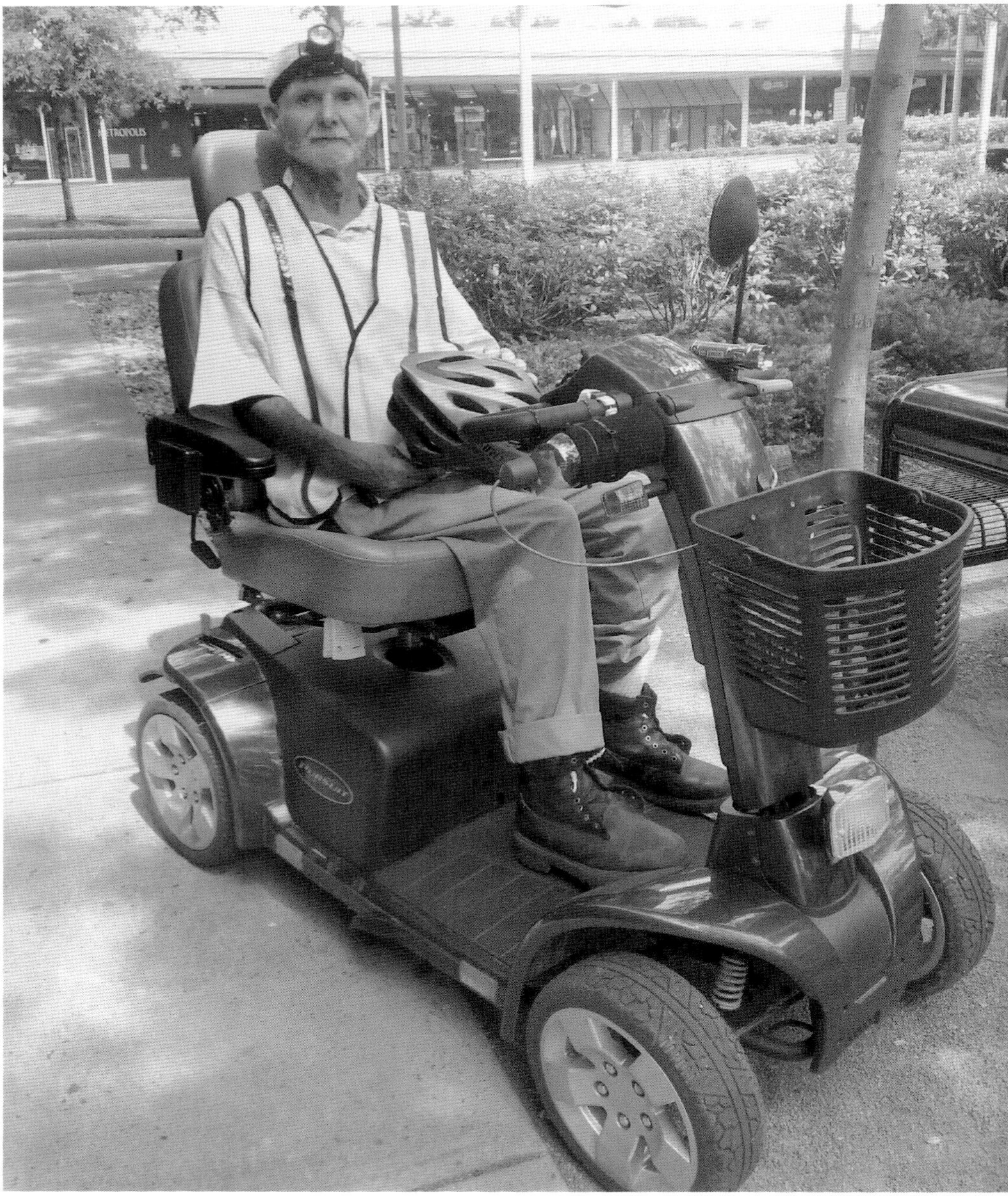

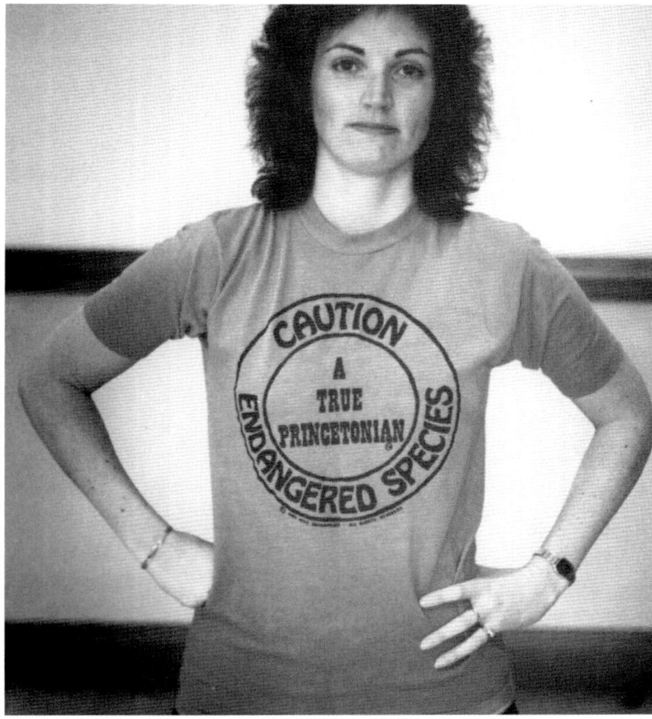

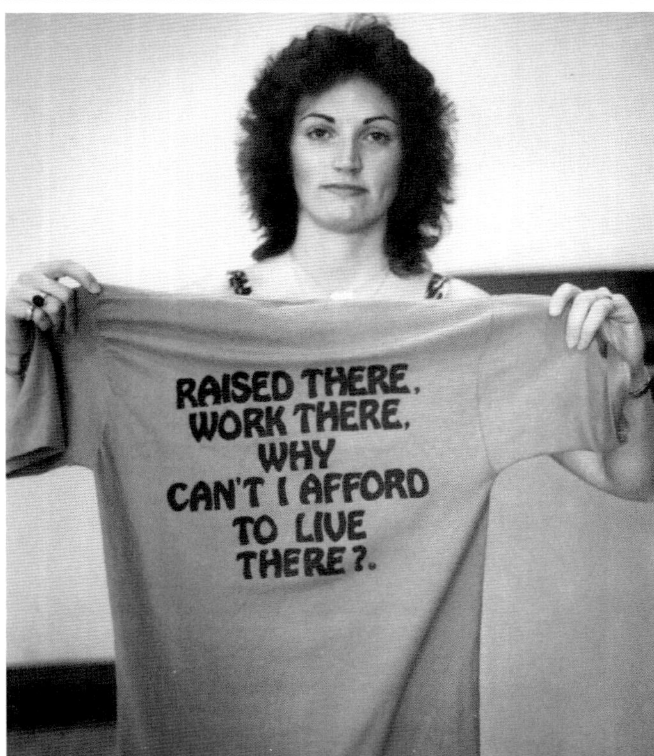

T-Shirts

Finally, the true legendary locals are the natives of Princeton, who have cast a wry eye on the blossoming property values and leaping cost of living—consequences of the town's popularity and success—that forced many to be commuters and visitors to the place of their birth. As a popular T-shirt from 1988 (designed by Willie D. Shields and modeled here by Blair Turner) put it: "Caution: Endangered Species, A True Princetonian; Raised There, Work There, Why Can't I Afford to Live There?" But with affordable housing subsequently constructed in the area and with the ongoing motivation to live in Greater Princeton, the answer is "You can." (Both, PP/HSP.)

INDEX